Ultimate Guide
to
Job Interview
Questions
and
Answers

Ultimate Guide
to
Job Interview Questions
and Answers

How to Answer Interview Questions

How to Answer Interview Questions II

Asking Questions in the Job Interview

How to Ace Your Phone Interview

By Peggy McKee

2

About the Author

Peggy McKee is an expert resource and a dedicated advocate for job seekers, with a unique perspective that gets job seekers hired fast.

Peggy's years of experience as a nationally-known recruiter for sales and marketing jobs give her an advantage in developing the tools and strategies that help job seekers stand head and shoulders above the competition. She was named #1 on the list of the Top 25 Most Influential Online Recruiters by HR Examiner, and has been quoted in articles from CNN, CAP TODAY, Yahoo!HotJobs, and the Denver Examiner.

Originally from Oklahoma, Peggy grew up on a 1000-acre ranch (and still loves horses and ranch life). She earned a B.S. in Chemistry and an M.B.A. in Marketing from the University of Oklahoma, and quickly rose to success with internationally-known companies in the medical sales arena. In 1999 Peggy founded PHC Consulting, a medical sales recruiting firm. When she consistently found herself offering advice to jobseekers who weren't even her own candidates, she developed a new business model in order to offer personalized career coaching as well as the tools jobseekers need to thrive and succeed in the job search...and Career Confidential was born.

Today, Career Confidential offers job-winning products, tools, and webinars for job seekers, along with Peggy's 1:1 coaching and group coaching courses. Peggy is also the author of several popular job search and interview books available on Amazon.

Peggy receives positive responses every day from candidates who have used them to land the job of their dreams, and she loves that she has been able to contribute to their success.

Table of Contents

11

17

How to Answer Interview Questions

101 Tough Questions That Could Kill Your Interview Chances—Answered!

By Peggy McKee

Job Interview Question 1:

Are you overqualified for this job?

If you get asked this question, you may jump straight to frustrated—especially if you're an older worker and assume they're telling you you're just too old. But companies facing hiring issues really don't want to make a mistake. They don't want to go to the time and expense of hiring someone who will just move on to something that pays more as soon as they find it. And most people want to climb the ladder and make more money, so why wouldn't you?

So when they ask you if you have too much experience, think about the question behind the question. What they're really asking is, are you going to be bored? Is this really the right position for you? Are you really going to be satisfied here? Drill down a little more and it's: Are you a good fit for this job?

Answer **that** question. They're looking for you to help them feel better about hiring you. You can do that with the answer you give and believe me, they're listening. They know they can learn a lot about you from what you choose to say.

Here are some suggestions:

"I might be overqualified, but wouldn't that be wonderful for you? Because then you'd have someone who was more than ready to do well in this…someone who's done this before, who understands what it takes to be successful at it and can do it again." Remember, they always need to know the answer to those 4 unasked job interview questions: Do you understand the job? Can you do the job? Will you do the job? Do you pose a risk to their own continued employment?

Or you can say, "The truth is that I am overqualified for the job. But it looks wonderful to me because of X, Y, and Z." X, Y, and Z are your own reasons why this job fits you (other than money or responsibilities or possibility for advancement).

And it could be anything. I remember speaking to one gentleman who was clearly overqualified for the job he was applying for, but who wanted it because the commute was significantly shorter. The company was freaking out because they didn't understand, but he said, "Hey, my house is paid off so I don't need the money, and I like where I live. I'm not interested in moving. I just want to live my life. And right now, my job requires a 2-hour round-trip ordeal every day. I don't want that anymore. This place is 5 minutes from my house. That extra time in my day would be worth a lot to me."

Once he communicated that to them, they understood and were excited about hiring him.

You have to tell them why they're perfect for you. They may not always understand it on their own.

And they will make assumptions about you. You can't just think that they will take you at face value. This is a big risk for them and they want to not make a mistake. So help them see why you're a great fit.

Job Interview Question 2:

Are you willing to relocate?

Are you willing to move for a new job? In many companies, this is a typical question. Sometimes it's a deal-breaker, sometimes it isn't. Even if this particular job doesn't require it, many companies want that flexibility in their employees for long-term growth potential.

The knee-jerk answer that most people give ("I'd consider it for the right opportunity.") is not your best answer, even if it is the truth. Because it puts your motivation for wanting the job more into the 'money' category rather than the 'fulfilling work / great fit' category. It's a subtle but important distinction, and it will take the shine off your candidacy if you say it.

Here's how to handle the relocation question for several different life circumstances you might be in:

If you're a 'No'

If your answer is unequivocally 'no', you have to say so. It's only going to cause you problems if they do end up offering you the job and you won't move. (Although, let me just say that if it's "absolutely not", remember that life can turn on a dime. What looks like "never" right now might not look like that in a few months or a year.) If you really want this job, and you can't move immediately, say so. But consider saying something like, "I'd rather not move right now, but you never know what tomorrow will bring. And I'm very interested in this position and this company."

If you're a 'Maybe'

But maybe you feel like there's some wiggle room. You'd rather not commit to packing up your entire life just yet, but you don't want this job to slip through your fingers because of it. It may be that you really don't want to move...the kids are settled, your family is here, and so on...but for the right offer you'd consider it. You know you can't say that, so try something like, "I'm interested in growing my career, and if relocating for the job is a necessary part of that, of course I'd consider it." That doesn't commit you to moving. It just confirms that your career (and this job) is important—and it's tactful.

Or, you could toss it back to them: "Where I live is not the most important issue for me. Utilizing my skills, developing new ones, and advancing my career are really my driving interests, and I've become more and more convinced that this company and this job is a really great fit because of my skills in X, Y, and Z. Do you agree?"

You've stayed on track, selling yourself for the job, and redirected the conversation (hopefully). If they keep pushing, you can fall back to the "of course I'd consider it" statement.

None of these answers commit you to anything. But all of them help you appear to be more sincere, flexible, tactful, and reasonable than "I'd consider it for the right opportunity." They keep the conversation going in a positive direction, which is a big plus for any job interview.

Job Interview Question 3:

Describe a time when your work was criticized and how you handled it.

Have you ever been asked this question? I know...to you, it feels like oral surgery without the Novocain...but interviewers love behavioral interviews because they tell them so much about you—in the story you choose to tell, how you tell it, with what kind of attitude, and the results you're capable of producing under pressure. They just can't get as good a picture of what life would be like with you on the job from only asking about your skills and qualifications.

The criticism question is one of those **adversity pieces** that you've always got to have a story or two about in your back pocket for interviews.

The truth is, to be a good employee (or an overall successful person), you've always got to be open to criticism. If you're not open to criticism, then you're not coachable. If you're not coachable, then you're less valuable than you could be.

Are you coachable? Coachability is huge. Taking criticism is important. If, when you get criticism, you have a problem with always wanting to be defensive and not simply soaking up how you could have done it differently, then you'll find that people will give you less and less criticism. That might sound like a good thing, but it isn't.

If they can't communicate with you and help you be better (which helps them to be better), they'll eventually just fire you. Does that seem extreme? It's because your boss (or anyone you need to learn something from) can't teach you anything new without correcting you once in a while. Since no one's perfect, everyone needs to be corrected or coached to a new place or behavior in order to keep being successful.

So what they're really looking for is, **are you coachable?** Tell me about a time when someone told you how you could do something different or better, how you did do it different or better, and then what the results were.

This is the **STAR technique** that all job seekers should be familiar with for behavioral interviews. STAR stands for Situation or Task, Action, and Result. Stories put into that structure are particularly effective in job interview situations. You talk about the situation you were in and the task in front of you, the action you choose to take and the results you got from it (what happened). Choose an incident or experience from your work history, put it into that structure, and you've got yourself a story that illustrates why you're such a great pick for the job.

Job Interview Question 4:

Describe a time when your workload was heavy and how you handled it.

Asking you to describe difficult situations (and your reactions to them) is a favorite tactic of interviewers. It's called behavioral interviewing. Behavioral interview questions get way past your basic skills and qualifications and get to the heart of "how will you act once you're hired?" Past behavior predicts future behavior better than anything else.

The reason you have to be able to speak to this issue in an interview is that they want to know if you're going to freak out when they have a rough time. And everyone eventually has a rough time. Accountants tend to get swamped in March, and retailers at Christmas. But even jobs without a seasonal aspect like those can have times when the workload is particularly stressful.

Describing a time when your workload was particularly heavy and how you handled it is a great view into how you approach day-to-day problems.

They want to know that you can handle your workload changing. Can you adapt? Basically, they want you to show them the tools or the process you'd use to handle that situation. So, you walk them through it.

You should say something like, "We all have times when our workloads become heavier than they normally are. I've found that the best thing to do is to take a look at what I have to do and prioritize tasks. What I've found is that not everything has to be done immediately. Some things are more mission-critical than others, and in times of stress you have to be able to prioritize."

And then you tell a short story that reflects your experience in prioritizing tasks in high-stress situations. (Use the STAR technique.)

Or you'd say something like, "In those situations, I take a look at what the workload is and prioritize critical tasks. I speak with my supervisor to see if there's a need for help in prioritizing from his point of view and execute. Just taking that look at it helps me feel less stressed and more in control."

And then you can tell a story about providing assistance to your boss on a critical task.

Either one of those is a much better answer than, "I stayed until the work was done." Many people give an answer that focuses on the long hours they worked on a project because they want that employer to know they work hard, but I think it's even more important for that employer to know that you can work smart.

I'm not saying don't talk about getting things done. Of course, talk about your follow-through and your dedication. But take them through your **thought process** of **how you approach a problem and think critically about it** and make great decisions that will benefit the company. It will make you stand out from other candidates and be very impressive to your future boss.

Job Interview Question 5:

Describe how you would handle a situation if you were required to finish multiple tasks by the end of the day, and there was no conceivable way that you could finish them.

Job interviews are like very intense speed dating—they need to get to know you well in a very short time. For many companies, talking about your resume and what you've done is just not enough. They need to know how you'll behave on the job, how you'll react to situations. To get to the meat of those issues, they use behavioral interviewing. You must know how to answer behavioral interview questions before you go into your next job interview.

This question, asking you to describe how you'd handle a "too much to do and not enough time to do it" situation on the job is a classic. Who HASN'T had to deal with a day like that on the job?

You don't have to get into specifics here… what they want to know is how you THINK. How do you approach problems? What tools or strategies do you use to approach and solve challenges in your daily life on the job?

With this question, it all comes down to prioritization: How do you prioritize tasks? CAN you prioritize tasks? They don't want someone who's going to collapse into a "get me to therapy" heap or explode in anger over the issue. And they'll know by your answer.

A bad answer would sound like, "I expect my boss to give me a reasonable workload and recognize that not everything can get done."

Another bad answer is "I would just until I completed everything, as late as that needed to be." On the surface that sounds good, but in reality, it says nothing about your ability to think on your feet, analyze the situation, and implement a reasonable solution. **That's** what they want to know.

So walk them through your thought process when you prioritize: Does everything truly have to be done today? Even though you may have 25 tasks, maybe the truth is that the person who wants those done can't really do anything with all of them immediately anyway. Maybe they can only deal with 5 or 10 of them in the next couple of days, so those are the ones you concentrate on first.

Or maybe in your position, you would have people that you could delegate work to. When you talk about how you'd do that, they get a peek into your management style, too.

A lot of people take on tasks and never really take a look at "When does this have to be done?" They just look at the list and pull it onto their plate. That's not strategic thinking.

Show them your strategic thinking abilities and you'll be very impressive in the interview.

Job Interview Question 6:

Describe your work style.

Do you know what your work style is? This is a popular interview question, but a lot of people go wrong in their answers because they don't understand what that employer really wants to know. They're not interested in your personality or your likes and dislikes. (They're not interested in how you dress for work, either.) They want to know how you work.

So some people really shoot themselves in the foot because they say things like, "I'm really laid back." First, that's a personality trait. Second, no one wants to hear that. No one wants to pay for your moseying along through your day. They want to get their money's worth out of your salary.

It's not about your personal preferences, either. For instance, some people will say things like, "I'm not a fan of conflict." What's that got to do with your work style? Nothing. Work style has to do with the work.

First, you want your answer to mesh nicely with the job itself. How does your style fit with that job?

If it's a data-driven role, you don't want to talk about how you like to come up with creative solutions for problems. That's not needed so much in that job.

What they really want to know are things like: Do you like to work alone, or as part of a team? You may actually prefer one or the other, but you should know what the job requires. Most companies appreciate someone who can do both. Teamwork is important, but sometimes you've got to just saddle up and go it alone. Talk about how you are comfortable with both.

Are you comfortable with minimal direction, or do you need lots of details before you complete a task? I think it's important to be upfront with this one if you really can only function one way. If you hate being micromanaged and your future boss believes in it wholeheartedly, then you are not going to want that job and it won't be a highlight on your resume.

You always want to pick out a few of your best qualities (again, that fit especially well with the job you want) and talk about those:

- Are you organized?
- Do you work quickly?
- Are you a good multi-tasker?
- Do you enjoy taking on extra projects?
- Are you a great planner?
- Are you consistently a top performer?

You can't be all things, but you can successfully approach this question like you do all interview questions: with a strategic answer that thoughtfully addresses the question and provides an answer that meshes your best qualities with the needs of the job.

Job Interview Question 7:

Describe yourself to me in one word.

Sometimes job interviewers try to get inside your head. Why? Hiring you feels like a gamble to them. The person who hires you has a big stake in you doing well on the job.

Remember the 4 basic questions of every interviewer:

- Do you understand the job?
- Can you do the job?
- Will you do the job?
- Do you pose a risk to their own continued employment if you don't do well? (This is a prime reason why 30-60-90-day plans are such great interview tools—they answer all those questions VERY well.)

The end result of all this is that they sometimes ask you weird interview questions like, "Describe yourself to me in one word."

This is a tough one. My personal answer would be "dynamic," because I change, I adapt, and I do whatever I need to do to succeed. That's a good, all-purpose word that could apply to many different jobs.

But don't think only about a word that describes you. That could lead you down the path to picking something like "happy" or "resilient" that might describe you very well but doesn't speak to the job at all.

As in all things in the job search and interview process, be **strategic**.

Every part of the process is a step that needs to lead you to your ultimate goal—the job offer. Be mindful of that.

Think about answering this question not just by thinking about what you are, but by thinking about **what you are in relation to the job**...what the job requires, what would make someone a standout employee in this position, what you're going to do for them.

So "bright," might accurately describe you because you're smart, but "successful" might mean more to them. (If you're successful in other areas, you'll probably be successful for them.)

Responsible, motivated, dedicated, those are all good words. So are: strategic, flexible, creative, dependable, reliable, helpful, fair, honest, focused, steady, organized, enthusiastic, or maybe even valuable.

Bottom line: Think about the job itself and what a fantastic characteristic would be for someone in that role, and tell them the one that applies to you.

But here's an extra hint: They might not let it go with just your one-word explanation. The follow up might very well be "Really? Can you give me an example?" So have a story that tells about how you embodied that trait at least once in your work life.

Job Interview Question 8:

Do you prefer working in a team or alone?

Even though asking if you prefer working independently or as part of a team is a standard job interview question, it's also a bit of a tricky one. I can't think of any job that doesn't at some point require both work styles. So even though you probably do prefer working one way or the other, you will shoot yourself in the foot if you say so. It's better if you are comfortable with both, and very important that you indicate that. But there are subtle distinctions in the wording you use that can make the difference between an adequate answer and a standout answer.

The standard answer that most people give: 'I work well either way—I'm great as part of a team, and I'm comfortable working alone" is an OK answer, but you can do better.

The way to be strategic about this question is to really know the typical working conditions of the job you're going for and how much of your time will be spent on a team or by yourself. That requires some research on your part—but that kind of job interview prep is an essential part of creating your 30-60-90-day plan, which you should be doing anyway.

If the majority of the time you'll be **working alone**, you can say, "I prefer to work alone, but I find that occasionally working with a team feels creative because we can bounce ideas off each other. I like to learn from other's experiences."

If the majority of the time you'll be **working on a team**, you can say, "I like the dynamics of working in a group, but appreciate sometimes having a part of the project that's my own personal responsibility."

The general idea is to say what you prefer without being negative about the thing you don't.

Maintaining a **positive attitude** is important, and it will make the hiring manager feel good about hiring you. Everyone wants to work with people who are flexible rather than rigid.

But here's **one neat trick:** Instead of just offering an answer, add a question to toss the conversational ball back to them. Say something like, "About how much time do you think will be spent working on my own vs. working with a team in this position?" Or, "Does the corporate culture encourage one style over another?"

Asking questions of your own like this during the course of the interview gains you more information while keeping the tone conversational and helpful.

Job Interview Question 9:

Give me a specific example of a time when you had to conform to a policy with which you did not agree.

Even though a good STAR story is the backbone of answering Behavioral Interview questions, here's one where it's actually a good thing NOT to have a great story for. Asking you for an example of a time when you folded under pressure is a situational interview question that's even worse than "Describe a difficult situation and how you handled it." At least in that one you can come out looking like you've overcome something. In this one, there's not any way to make yourself look good.

Think about your choices with this question:

Did you not want to conform to the policy because it was unethical—but then you did? You may think of yourself as the martyr in that situation, but you'll just come across as someone who is OK with being unethical. That's not the image you want to project.

Did you not want to conform because you knew best? Saying that you knew more than your previous boss is a bad tactical error in an interview because then you're badmouthing them—and that's always a no-no. That answer sets you up as an adversary for your future boss even before she hires you—and she won't. Not with that attitude.

The truth is that the vast majority of directives, instructions, etc. at work you just won't be able to have any influence on. The few things that you can influence are still limited. You can try to communicate, grab more information, educate, and so on. But in the end, you're going to have to execute or you might lose your job.

But this question does get asked in interviews, so how do you answer it?

The interview wants to know how you would really react in a difficult situation. What's your communication style? Did you confront your boss? Did you avoid the whole discussion?

Your best answer probably sounds something like, "Sorry, I can't think of a time when that happened." If they press, you might give a general, hypothetical answer like, "I might ask questions or express concerns over a policy because I believe it's part of my job to support the team and that includes spotting potential issues before they become actual problems…but in the end the decision belongs to my supervisor and I always respect that."

With that answer, you've shown you're a critical thinker, a team player, and respect the chain of command. What potential boss wouldn't be comfortable with that?

Job Interview Question 10:

Give me an example of a time that you felt you went above and beyond the call of duty at work.

If you get asked to describe a time you went above and beyond the call of duty on the job, be thrilled because this is a great behavioral interview question that has the potential to make you look like an amazing candidate.

You should ALWAYS have one of these stories because it's a great thing to talk about how you not only met, but exceeded the expectations of your employer. That's value.

Before you go into the interview, think about what story you'd tell in this situation. Choose one that not only describes a past success but also speaks to your potential success on this job. Good choices would be ones that highlight skills you need on this job or tasks you'll need to accomplish, although stories that highlight good character traits are also helpful. Relate your story to the job you're trying to get in some way.

Your answer or your story should talk about a difficult situation that you overcame. Conflict and resolution always makes for a good story. Always tell it along the lines of "Here was the situation….we needed X done, these were the tasks that needed to be done, these were the actions I took, and these were the results."

That's the STAR method. STAR stands for the Situation or Task you faced, the Action you took, and the Results you received. It's just a process to follow to make sure you get all the necessary elements in your answer. I've also seen it called CAR: Circumstance, Action, Result. Same thing.

Do not be afraid to brag. This is your shot. In fact, this is also an excellent time to pop open your brag book and do a little show and tell. Show them the note you got from a customer or your supervisor that congratulated you on a job well done. Show them the graph of the stats that improved dramatically after you took action.

Brag books are excellent communication aids for job interviews. They're visual, which gives you another interesting element in the interview. Not everyone takes the time to put them together and bring them, so they'll help you stand out. And they provide powerful evidence that backs up your story: I can do what I say I can do, and here's proof."

Combine a great story with the brag book, and you've got a solid point in your favor in the interview.

Job Interview Question 11:

Have you ever been on a team where someone was not pulling their own weight? How did you handle it?

Asking about any difficulties with team projects in the past is a great behavioral interview question, and interviewers love to ask it. Everybody's been on a team where someone didn't pull their own weight. Remember group projects in school? And at some point in this job you're applying for, you'll almost certainly be asked to participate in another one. So it's a fair question to ask.

Be very careful about what you say in responding to this question or you'll sound whiny. It never worked to whine to your teacher, and it's not going to work to whine to your interviewer, either.

When you face this situation at work (or in school), your best bet is to focus on what YOU are supposed to be working on, not what someone else isn't working on. Try to do your job as best you can and support the supervisor in getting the whole job done. Maybe once you get your job done you could help the slacker, but that's a case-by-case decision.

Hopefully, you can truthfully say that you did just that: "I concentrated on getting my own work done and then went to ask my supervisor what I could do to help him finish the task."

You never want to say, "I reported that person to my supervisor" or "I told that person they better step up and get with the rest of the team." Neither is a great response.

It might be OK to say, "I got my task done and saw that person struggling, and I knew that the team success depended on all of us cooperating and succeeding, so I offered my assistance. John was grateful to get some help, and we've had a great relationship ever since, working together on several projects."

Of course, that's a very general response. It might be more appropriate for you to be more specific in your story, or it might not.

The bigger thing I want you to see is that you never ever badmouth your former supervisor or your former co-worker. That always makes you look unprofessional. And it gives them the (generally accurate) idea that if you'll say things like that about those people, you'll say things about them, too when you leave. None of those things are going to earn you points with the interviewer.

Try to always keep your responses positive and focused on how you got the job done. That's great job interview strategy.

Job Interview Question 12:

Have you ever had difficulty working with a supervisor or manager?

When your interviewer asks, "Have you ever had difficulty working with a supervisor or manager?" they're not really asking about your past supervisors. They're asking about **you.** They want to know how YOU are to work with. The answer you choose will tell them more about you than about your previous boss.

So if you launch into a story about how your old boss yelled at everyone or was unreasonable in his or her demands or was a bad manager, the only message they'll get is that you badmouth people.

If you talk about how your boss accused you of not working hard enough when you clearly did, they'll assume that you are someone who doesn't work hard.

If you mention a boss who played favorites, they'll think you're a difficult person to work with.

So be very careful about answering this question. Even if you had legitimate complaints about your old boss (and lots of bosses earn every one of those complaints), you can't say so. It's never a good idea to badmouth your former boss, for any reason.

If possible, avoid it: "I can't say that I've ever had much trouble working with anyone. I actually appreciate the personality differences I've seen in my various supervisors and found that I could learn something from working with each of those styles. It hasn't been hard for me to adapt to working with anyone."

If you can't avoid it, tell them the story along with your thought process. But keep in mind that any story you tell should be the Disney version: positive, and with a happy ending. For example, you could say something like, "I did get off to a bad start with my manager in my very first job because we had different expectations and at the time, I didn't know enough to ask about those before I started work. But I got some very good advice to go talk with him about it, and we cleared the air. It turned out to be a great experience for me, and it was a good lesson to take forward in my career. Good communication is essential to a productive working relationship."

See? You haven't said anything negative about yourself or about your manager. It was the situation that was difficult. You took proactive steps to resolve it in a mature fashion, and the end result was a productive relationship. (By the way, that's a STAR structure: Situation or Task, Action, and Result. It's a great way to tell a story.

Keep your answer positive, show them how you think, and add one more point to the plus column for hiring you.

Job Interview Question 13:

How can you apply your specific skills to help the organization achieve sustainable growth and generate revenue?

To answer this question, it's very important that you understand the role you're applying to fill.

If they ask you in the interview how you can apply your skills in "X, Y, and Z" to help the organization achieve growth and generate revenue, you're probably interviewing for a higher-level position. At that level, you should be very clear and very specific on how you can help. What benefits do you bring to the table? Why should they hire you over someone else? If you can name 3-4 ways in which you would benefit the company in achieving those twin goals of growth and revenue, you're in good shape.

That means that you better have expended considerable effort to think about the company and the position before your interview. And you've moved into bonus territory if you've put that into a 30-60-90-day plan to show them how you plan to get started achieving success for them. There are lots of reasons why 30/60/90-day plans help you stand out, and this is a big one.

But the truth is, this question about growth and revenue is important to answer for every position. Every position has financial value for the company, or it wouldn't exist. There's really only one purpose or mission for every job, and that's to make the company money—either directly or as a supportive role. Every role contributes to the bottom line.

Even the janitor does his part by keeping the place spic-and-span so that customers enjoy and feel comfortable in that space (increasing revenue) and so that workplace accidents are kept to a minimum (reducing costs).

A waitress does not just serve food. She's the face of the company that owns the restaurant. She directly affects the customer's image and opinion of the business, and whether or not they come back.

I was once asked by someone trying to stump me, "What about the person who puts the screws into the plane?" To them, that person was the lowest on the totem pole. In reality, that person is crucial to the success of the business. No one wants a plane falling apart in the sky, do they? That would definitely be bad for business.

So what does the role you're applying for do for that business? How will your skills contribute to the growth of the business and generate more revenue?

If you understand how your job fits into the bigger picture goals and can show the interviewer how your skills contribute to those goals, you're going to do very well.

Job Interview Question 14:

How did you deal with the situation the last time your boss chastised you or strongly disagreed with a statement, a plan or a decision you made?

There are a lot of potential landmines lurking in this behavioral interview question.

Maybe your knee-jerk reaction would be to say, "Why, I don't recall that ever happening and I can't imagine that it would." Why is that? Are you a yes-man? That's not a good thing. It could say that you can't contribute in a way that means anything.

Maybe it did happen and you're still angry about it because it was unfair and your boss obviously missed his medication that day. Be careful what you say or you'll end up badmouthing your ex-boss…a big interview no-no.

Maybe it happened and you're not upset because it happens all the time. To you, you're a strong, independent go-getter. To them, you're a loose cannon who can't be trusted to make decisions. So what do you do?

First of all, if that ever happens to you at work, you want to make sure that whatever they're chastising you about or disagreeing with you over isn't a simple communication issue.

A lot of times, that's all it is…a communication issue.

Then you want to seek to understand their position. What's their point of view? How are they coming at this and why? Is there something you could have done differently? If so, own it: "I should have done this differently." And in the future, you won't make that mistake again. Seek to understand, see it from the other person's perspective and 'fess up when you make a mistake.

If your answer is in fact, "I don't really have a good example of a time that my boss strongly disagreed with something I did," say so. Maybe you haven't worked that long, or in more than one or two jobs. But that answer doesn't tell them much about you, and they do want to know how you handle conflict. So follow up that answer with a bit of your philosophy on communication: "I try to keep the lines of communication open so that doesn't happen. But misunderstandings happen, so I would try to see if that was the case first. If I make a mistake, I correct it and take steps to not make the same mistake twice." Or whatever. Now they know that you have a reasonable response to difficult situations.

If you did have a conflict, don't lie and say you didn't. Very few people can lie without triggering a "hmm..." response in the other person's brain. They might not even know why they don't trust you, they'll only know that they don't.

Address the past conflict by walking them through your process: you hit it head on. You spoke directly to your boss about the issue, tried to see where he was coming from, and learned X lesson. Keep the end result positive. And if you do tell a story about making a mistake, make sure it's clearly a one-time mistake.

"I realized I'd made a mistake because I didn't have all the information. Now I ask a lot more questions before I start a project to make sure that doesn't happen again. I'm a much better communicator now."

Job Interview Question 15:

How do I know you still have the 'fire in the belly' to do this job?

If you're of a 'certain age' in the job search, you already know that age is a big issue. It's a very real obstacle to getting a job. Older workers have a reputation of not being up on the latest technology, not being willing to adapt, not being willing to take orders from younger bosses, and not having the energy or motivation to keep up with a heavy work schedule. That's what this 'fire in the belly' question is really asking: Are you still motivated to work hard?

There are several ways you can answer it.

(1) You can say, "I understand that hiring is risky, but one of the ways I can help make you feel better about hiring me and knowing that I am going to come in and do what I say I will do is to have you talk to my references. They'll tell you that I am what I say I am and I am someone who will exceed your expectations."

I personally really like this response. Your references are always going to be strong evidence for you and I would use them to bolster my candidacy. Everyone likes a recommendation. Choose the best references you can (past supervisors, if possible) and prep your references before the interview and before they're called. (All that means is to give them a heads up that a call is coming and tell them what's going to be the most helpful to talk about.)

(2) You can lean on your past experience. "You know, it's only been 6 months since I won X award for performance." Or, "...since I accomplished Z for my company."

Your brag book would be helpful here, if you've got recent accomplishments to point to.

(3) You can turn it around on them. If that person is the same age as you or older, you can say, "Well, have you lost the fire in your belly? Because I haven't."

This might seem flip at first, but anytime you can point out a way that you're similar to them, that's a good thing.

(4) You can be straightforward and say, "I absolutely do. It's a new challenge for me that I can't wait to tackle. In fact, I've even put together this 30-60-90-day plan to show you how I intend to be successful as soon as possible. Can we go over it to make sure I've got the details right?"

I'm not sure there is a more definitive answer to the motivation question than a 30-60-90-day plan. Just putting one together takes a lot of work and says very clearly that you care about getting this job and doing it well. Once you start discussing your plan, they will see very clearly that hiring you would be a very smart decision.

Job Interview Question 16:

How do you deal with difficult customers?

Dealing with difficult customers is a fact of life for a TON of jobs: sales reps, customer service reps, retail store clerks, receptionists, restaurant wait staff, and hundreds of other service-industry jobs.

The people in those roles are in the front lines. They are the face of their respective companies, and have a tremendous impact on the company's image, which directly affects growth and revenue. Your answer should make it very clear that you understand how important your role is and take it very seriously.

You can absolutely tell a story about dealing with a particular difficult customer (what the situation was, how you handled it, what the results were) and if you happen to have a note from that customer or your supervisor in your brag book about your positive outcome from the situation, that's even better. There's nothing more powerful than evidence that you can do what you say you can do.

But overall, you need to make sure that your customer service philosophy is clear, so your answer should sound like this:

"I deal with difficult customers the same way I deal with easy customers. I want to make sure they have an exceptional experience with my company. I won't let a customer say bad things about us, or things that aren't accurate, but if we haven't met their expectations, I want to take responsibility for that and see if I can fix it. If I can't fix it, I still want to make the experience as positive as I can by doing something that would make up for the problem—maybe give them their money back, or provide some other benefit so that they exit that situation as happily as possible. I want to treat every customer as well as I'd treat my grandmother. "

Do you see what this answer does? It lets them know that you take personal responsibility for your customers and their experience with the company. The reputation of the company will not suffer under your watch, because you will do what you need to do to. They can trust you, they can depend on you. It's another selling point in your favor. And it's exponentially a stronger answer than: "I hand them off to my supervisor. "

Personal responsibility is a character trait in short supply these days, it seems. If your answer to this interview question highlights that quality in you, you will absolutely stand out from the crowd.

Want other ways to show the hiring manager what you'd be like on the job and convince them to hire you? Bring a 30-60-90-day plan to your interview.

Job Interview Question 17:

How do you deal with stressful situations?

If I got asked about how I deal with stressful situations, the first thing that would pop into my head is, "You mean like this one?"

As if you didn't know, job interviews are very, very stressful. The way you calm your nerves is by recognizing that it's going to be stressful, preparing for the interview as much as possible, and taking a few deep relaxing breaths before you start.

But now is not the time to make that joke. My philosophy is 'never let them see you sweat.'

This 'stressful situations' question is a legitimate job interview question. Who doesn't have stress? Every job is going to have some time when you're going to feel overwhelmed and stressed out. They'd like to know that you'll react in a calm, rational fashion instead of erupting into a temper tantrum, screaming, hiding, or something else that would either alienate your co-workers or be otherwise unproductive. Stress management is a valuable skill.

'How do you deal with stressful situations' is a more generalized version of 'Tell me about a time you found yourself in a stressful situation and how you resolved it.' Both are behavioral interview questions. If you get the 'Tell me about a time..." version, you absolutely should have a story to tell. I always recommend using the

STAR method (Situation or Task, Action, Result) to answer it—it keeps you from rambling off topic and makes sure you hit the most critical aspects of the story.

If you get the more generalized question about dealing with stressful situations, you have a little more leeway to talk about your overall approach to handling stress, but always keep in mind that you're talking about work. Keep it professional and always bring it back to an accomplishment:

"If a situation seems overwhelming, I mentally break it up into smaller steps, or doable goals, and just focus on reaching each one on the way to accomplishing the larger task. In fact, that's what I did with XYZ project. We had a major issue with X problem, but I broke it down into 'what needs to happen first,' and concentrated on one step at a time. I was able to see more solutions to the larger problem, and in fact, we got the entire project done in record time."

Or, "I find it best do concentrate on remaining calm, maybe taking a few deep breaths. When I run into a customer who's upset, it helps them to calm down if I'm calm and we can work together to resolve the situation."

Above all, choose an answer that shows that you can meet a stressful situation head-on in a productive, positive manner and let nothing stop you from accomplishing your goals.

Job Interview Question 18:

How do you evaluate success?

I think the answer to this has to be related directly to your work. Don't wax philosophical about what success really is, or what a successful life is all about—you'll just knock yourself out of a job. They don't care that you'll consider yourself truly successful if you have great relationships, or if you are able to retire to the beach at 60, or anything else relating to your personal life.

Always remember your agenda in a job interview situation: to sell yourself for the job. That hiring manager is your customer, essentially, and you're the product. You need to know what that customer's problems and needs are (that's why you do your interview prep ahead of time and ask questions in the interview) and your entire conversation needs to be about how you (as the product) meet those needs better than any other product out there…and in some ways, exceed them. (It's like the 'bells and whistles' on a product. What are the extras that you bring to the table that make you unique or even more valuable to the company?)

For this situation, success is based on the goals you've set for yourself, the progress you make in achieving those goals, and how happy you make those who you work for with you. It's based on achieving objectives and satisfying the people who are paying you for work.

So a general answer might sound like: "I evaluate success based on meeting the goals set by my supervisors, how quickly I accomplish those goals, and the feedback I get based on my performance."

Or, "Success means finishing a project on time, under budget, and to the complete satisfaction of the 'customer' of that project." (This could be your supervisor, the person you built a house for / made a part for / created a marketing campaign for / organized a wedding for, etc.)

If you're in a management role, you might say, "I evaluate success based on meeting my professional goals while ensuring that everyone on my team is working both individually and together, smoothly and in peak form."

You can talk about customer satisfaction, increasing revenue, gaining more customers, improving accuracy, or any other business-growth or revenue related goal.

And you can certainly mention a few things, and then toss it back to the interviewer: "How is performance evaluated here?" Getting some details about how THEY evaluate success (their performance methods) will help you hone your answers for the rest of the conversation.

Job Interview Question 19:

How do you handle stress and pressure on the job?

Hmmm....how DO you handle on-the-job pressure?

(a) I cry, yell, or complain.
(b) I hide in the bathroom.
(c) I love stress! It's so motivating!
(d) I don't get stressed.

Obviously, the right answer is (c) or (d)...either one works. Either you get some kind of adrenaline high off of the pressure and perform better, or you maintain a Zen-like calm and don't ever get stressed out.

And of course, everyone knows that those are the preferred answers to this particular question, so if you say one of them without really meaning it, you run the risk of sounding fake. (It's a little like saying "I'm such a perfectionist" in answer to the 'what's your greatest weakness' question.)

If you really can honestly say that deadlines motivate you to work harder, then go for it...especially if deadlines are a big part of your job. That's a great thing, and some people really do work well under pressure.

If you've learned to take a deep breath and focus on the task at hand, then talk about that. (Although that may apply only to surgeons and bomb squad personnel.)

What you can do to answer this in an honest, authentic way while still making them feel great about what you say is to talk about how you have learned to deal with the stress of the job.

Maybe when the job becomes extra stressful, you prioritize tasks so that it's manageable.

Maybe you can say that you've learned how to harness the energy from the pressure and make it work for you.

However you answer, follow it up with an example of how you've dealt with a stressful or pressure-filled situation in a previous jobs or other situation (certain volunteer experiences can be pressurized, too).

All jobs can, at one point or another, be stressful. Retailers get stressed out during the holiday season, accountants get buried during tax season, project managers run into people who aren't cooperating with their timelines, plans get sidetracked, customers get cranky, and shipments don't arrive on time.

Because stress is everywhere, you always want to have an answer to this question in your back pocket. You always want to answer the question positively, one way or another. Think about what desirable qualities are for top performers in your area and consider how you exemplify those qualities. And tell a quick story that provides evidence of what you say to hammer the point home. It's all part of your job interview strategy.

Job Interview Question 20:

How do you rate yourself as a professional?

There are people who will tell you that your automatic response to rating yourself (on a scale of 1 to 10) should be "11". They say that anything less would be admitting a weakness. I don't agree. An over-the-top answer like that is bragging, which is a lot different than selling yourself for the job.

I think that if you answer "11," you're running a strong risk of coming off as arrogant in the interview, and I don't know too many hiring managers who relish the thought of hiring someone who thinks they're more than perfect. It makes for a strained working relationship.

I think that on a scale of 1 to 10 (10 being the highest), that an answer of 6, 7, or 8 is a reasonable, positive, sincere-sounding answer. It means that you recognize that you have room to grow and develop and become more and better than you are today.

If you're a young rookie, straight out of school or with only one job under your belt, you should answer 6 or 7.

If you're anything else, answer 7 or 8.

Only a true Subject Matter Expert with a lot of experience should put themselves at a 9 or a 10.

But once you give your answer (and pay attention to the surprise on their faces when you don't give the automatic, knee-jerk, follow-the-crowd response of '11'), offer an explanation of why you rate yourself that way.

Say, "On a scale of 1 to 10, I see 5 as a true average, and a 10 as perfect. I believe I'm better than average, and I don't know that anyone could be a 10, because no one's perfect."

Talk about how you rate yourself based on how others perform in the same roles that you have had.

In every arena, there are 4 or 5 (at least) things that set people apart...what are they in yours? How do you rate in each of those areas?

You really have to know yourself and your 'market' in order to answer this question. If you're in the job search, you better know these things anyway. You can't sell yourself for the job otherwise. And it makes it pretty hard to negotiate salary unless you know what you're worth.

If you can answer this question with a sincere, honest, reasoned response, you're going to stand out from the other candidates and earn big points with the interviewer.

Job Interview Question 21:

How does this position fit in with the career path you envision for yourself?

I think a lot of people hurt themselves with their answer to this career question.

To be fair, it's hard to answer, just like "Where do you see yourself in 5 years?" or "What are your long-term goals?" Unless you're a person who has their life planned out, it's hard to predict what you'll want to be doing that far down the road. Especially if you're just starting out and still learning what jobs you love and what jobs you could do without.

But.

Employers like to see people who don't just float along with the tide. What's going to motivate you to do a great job for them (besides the paycheck)? What's going to make you want to do more, be better, take on new tasks, achieve? Do you have vision? Can you plan?

And, your answer tells the interviewer whether you want just any job or whether you're interested in THIS job.

That's a big part of what they're asking here: "Why THIS job?"

My general response to this question would concentrate on what I'm going to learn from this job:

"I would say that my career path is such that my career serves me, and I serve my career. I'm looking to grow and become more and contribute more and be more than I am today in my next role. And I know that if I do that I'll be rewarded professionally, personally, and financially. This position fits that for me because it's a growth role that will benefit me professionally because I'm going to be able to learn and develop more skills. As I do well, I'm going to be paid financially and personally in terms of personal satisfaction. It's a stepping stone to the next role. It's an opportunity to hone my skill set. It's an opportunity to learn this particular skill."

If you have a general end destination in mind, that's great. Talk about how this job is going to help you meet that goal. But only in the most general terms: "I plan to add value in this position, develop my skills to help grow the company, and eventually move into roles of greater responsibility." An answer along these lines tells them you're ambitious without any negative side effects, like being a threat to the interviewer's job.

Bottom line: You don't have to have a written-in-stone life plan done to answer this question. You just have to know what you're getting out of this job besides the paycheck.

Job Interview Question 22:

How have you responded to a colleague who is putting you down at work?

This is a pretty specific question, but it's basically just another version of "How do you react in difficult situations?" This type of question is often asked in one version or another in behavioral interview situations. Employers want to get a sense of your judgment and decision-making abilities. Your answer here gives them a good idea of how you react to stress.

However, this really is a very specific question, and you have to answer it as it's asked. In this case, it's very possible that you just haven't had that happen. So if it's true, it's OK to say, "I'm glad to say that I haven't had that happen."

I've never had someone put me down. I've had someone criticize me to my boss, and he was in a larger role than me, so that was bad. But my boss saw his criticism as a weakness on his part because she saw that I was a threat to him. Even though she told me about the criticism and suggested ways I could be less threatening to him, I didn't do anything different except try not to step on his toes. I certainly didn't call him on the carpet. It wouldn't have been productive.

In some cases, maybe it would be productive to speak directly to that person and help them see how it's not only damaging to you, it's damaging to them (as it was to the person who criticized me).

You could also talk to your superior, but when you do that you're admitting that you can't handle a difficult situation on your own.

In some companies, people file complaints with Human Resources, but I don't think it's a good career move. Again, it's saying that you can't handle things on your own.

If you haven't had this happen, just say so and don't spend time talking about what you might do in that situation. You always have to think strategically in an interview situation, and wandering down paths of "what if" is not going to be a benefit to you.

If you have had this happen, it's important that you frame your answer in a positive fashion. Don't tell the story about how you went to HR. Don't tell the story about how you reported them to your boss. Don't talk about what a jerk that person was and how glad you are that in this job, you won't have to deal with them anymore. You don't ever want to concentrate on the negative in your interview answers, because it just reflects badly on you.

Tell a story that says, "I'm a capable professional with good judgment and the ability to handle difficult situations on my own and get to a positive outcome."

Job Interview Question 23:

How long will it take for you to make a significant contribution?

I love, love, love this question. This is a 'roll out the red carpet, here's your golden ticket' opening to introducing your 30-60-90-day plan.

If you've never heard of a 30 60 90 day plan, it's very simple: it's a strategic plan for what actions you will take in your first 3 months on the job to ensure a successful transition from brand-new employee to fully-functioning, productive leader or member of the team. The first month usually requires some training, some getting to know the company's procedures and systems, and by the third month you should be at the point where you're initiating at least a few projects, sales, policies, improvements, etc. on your own. The more specific it is in the details to the company you're interviewing with, the better.

Why are these so great?

First, the research required to create a good plan automatically makes you a very well-prepared, knowledgeable candidate. That's impressive. It's very obvious that you know what you're doing—even if you've never done that job before.

Second, they demonstrate all those character traits that hiring managers look for but that are very hard to pin down: enthusiasm, drive, initiative, personal responsibility, goal-setting, and much more.

Third, as you go through the plan with your future supervisor, he or she begins to visualize you in the job. Once they can "see" it, they're much more likely to offer you the job.

I've seen these plans get offers for people on the spot, I've seen them get offers for people that were for positions at higher levels than what they interviewed for in the first place, and I've seen them get offers for candidates who were less qualified than their competitors. If there ever were a job interview miracle tool, this would be it.

So...create your own 30/60/90-day plan for your next interview. I have tons of information about these plans on my blog at Career Confidential.

And when the interviewer says, "How long will it take for you to make a significant contribution?" you're not stuck with responding, "I don't know...6 months to a year?" or, "Well, I'd really have to get settled in to see, but I would hope to start making real progress soon."

Instead, you could say, "I'm so glad you asked. I've thought about that quite a bit, and I've put together a preliminary plan for what I could do to get rolling as fast as possible. Can I get your input on it?"

When they say "yes," you walk them through your very detailed plan for success and get their feedback. Even if you don't have all the details right, the conversation you'll have will, without a doubt, be the best interview you've ever had.

Job Interview Question 24:

How long would you plan to stay with us?

Asking about your future plans in this way is really not asking you about your future plans. You don't have to go into your 5-year plan or your career goals. It's a brief question that requires only a brief answer.

Personally, my response to that question would be to smile and say, "How long would you like me to stay?" (But then, I often go for the humor.)

Another great response might sound something like this: "I plan to stay as long as I can. I don't want to change jobs if I can avoid it. I understand that there are learning curves to deal with, and that the grass isn't always greener and all that, but there's also something to be said for history and being able to rely on people."

For some people, this question is a beautiful thing. If you've worked somewhere for a long time, then you can say, "I stayed at my last job for 14 years. Do you think I'll be able to stay that long here?"

But if you have "short-gevity" rather than longevity, you might have to help them understand why you haven't stayed long at the other jobs, IF it puts you in a positive light.

Maybe there was a layoff situation or a reduction-in-force that was just a matter of "first in, first out" and had nothing to do with you or your performance. You can say that you would never have left that job.

Maybe you just outgrew your job. It was a small company, or there was just no place for you to go with your new skill set so you had to look outside the company. Everyone understands the desire to improve and grow and accomplish.

Either of those explanations is really something that's out of your control, so they don't reflect negatively on you.

But what if you don't have a nice convenient excuse? Maybe you have to do a little confessing: "I made a mistake. I left too soon and I will never make that mistake again. I understand now that just because the grass looks greener, doesn't mean that it is." It's OK to admit that you made a mistake and that you learned your lesson.

Hiring you is an investment for the company. They end up spending a lot of time and money in the hiring process, training you, getting you settled in. It takes time to get someone up to full-capacity. They'd rather you not work for a few months and then take off for greener pastures. Eliminate that doubt with your answer and call it good.

Job Interview Question 25:

How much money did / do you make?

Here's a question guaranteed to make you uncomfortable in the job interview process. It's one of the big hot-potato questions. No one wants to say a number first. But you don't have to feel pressured or stressed. There are some great ways to handle this question.

In general, for all salary issues that crop up before you have an offer in your hand, your first goal should be to deflect. Try to avoid talking about money for as long as you possibly can. (That's why you never, ever bring up money questions yourself.) You want them to fall in love with you before you start talking about commitment. Your bargaining position will be much stronger when they decide they want you to work for them. It will be easier to negotiate salary and ask for what you want.

If you can't deflect, there are a couple of ways you can go:

(1) You can go ahead and tell them how much you make because it's not relevant to this job.

(2) You can refuse to tell them how much you make because it's not relevant to this job.

In both cases, the reason it's not relevant is that it's probably a pretty good bet that this job has different (probably greater) responsibilities than your last one. So it's easy to make the case that what you made in your last job doesn't matter so much, because this job is different.

In my personal opinion, it's not a big deal to tell them how much you made in your last job. In my experience as a recruiter, most companies have a salary range for the position and they won't make an offer outside of that range. They're asking the question because they just want to make sure they can afford you.

This is where doing your homework will pay off for you, too. Your research will tell you what a reasonable pay range is for that position, in that part of the country. You can easily find out what they should be offering you for this job. If they do try to lowball you, you'll know it and can negotiate...after you have the offer in your hand.

If you feel strongly about not revealing what you make (and many people do), you can absolutely say, "My previous position doesn't really relate to this one, so I'm not comfortable discussing my past salary. But I really want to answer any questions about my skills or qualifications to see if we can agree that I'm the right person for the job, and I'm sure that if we do, we'll be able to come to an agreement on compensation, too. I'm really excited about the possibility of working here."

Or you could turn it around on them: "What is the salary range you're offering for this position? "When they tell you, say "I'm completely comfortable with that range. If I'm offered a salary within that range, I won't turn the offer down because of the money."

But please remember that every situation, every interview is different. A negotiation is a dance, not a step-by-step formula. You've got to take the temperature of your own situation and see what you think you can manage doing. But the more you research ahead of time, the better off you'll be.

Job Interview Question 26:

How was your working relationship with your previous supervisor?

How was your working relationship with your last boss? This is an attitude question for sure. They don't really care about your last boss, they care about **you**. Hiring managers know that past behavior predicts future performance, so they are very interested in your answer. Are you going to trash your old boss? Are you going to complain about how you were misunderstood? Or are you going to talk about how much you learned?

This is a pretty standard job interview question, so make sure you're ready for it.

Hopefully, this is an easy one because you got along great. Even if that's true, it's important that you elaborate a little bit on what you learned from that person that will help you succeed in this new job. The hiring manager doesn't want to only hear, "Great!"

Your being 'coachable' is a big deal to your future manager. They want someone who is willing to learn and who can take criticism and improve.

Even if you didn't get along so well with your last boss, it's important to try to keep this answer positive without lying about it. You should never out and out lie—first, it's just not a good thing and second, very few people can lie without setting off some signal you're lying in the hiring manager's subconscious mind.

Think about the positive things you learned from that relationship and talk about that. There's got to be something. Any kind of negativity from you in the interview only reflects badly on YOU. It makes you look like a whiner or complainer. But you can sort of turn lemons into lemonade.

If there was a real personality clash, you can say, "Our personalities were very different, so at times it was difficult for me, but it taught me a lot about how to adapt to another person's work style and made me a well-rounded person."

You might have to ponder that for a while to be able to come up with something positive if you worked for the Boss from Hell, but it's worth it. Being able to maintain a positive outlook and response even in the face of a difficult or stressful job situation is a huge plus for you.

And always remember that your focus is to sell yourself for this job, so try to bring it back around to how what you learned at that job from that boss will contribute to your success in this one.

If you do have a difficult situation you can't think of a way to talk about positively, consider hiring a career coach to help you.

Job Interview Question 27:

How would you feel about working for someone who knows less than you?

It's not ideal to work for someone who does, in fact, know less than you. In fact, it's kind of aggravating. But typically, they don't know less than you in all areas. There is usually a reason they are where they are. They must know more than you in at least one little area, or they wouldn't be the person in charge. Right?

Even if you can't learn something from them (because for some reason they're The Anointed One), then help them be successful. Because if you help them be successful, typically they will help you be successful. But I digress...

The real crux of the issue this question tries to get at is this: Do you understand that there are people who know more than you and you can learn something from them?

There are some personality types this is a big issue for, but typically the folks who have a problem with this are older employees, the Over-50 crowd, who don't think they can learn anything from some young whippersnapper. If you're an older worker, you have to be aware of this stereotype and be careful of what you say in the interview. If you talk critically about the 'younger generation,' or tell a story about some 25-year-old idiot you worked with last, it will just reflect negatively on you. Even if he was an idiot.

73

This interview question is poking around for your sore spot. (It's similar to the 'how do you handle stressful situations' question.) They're looking for negativity. Are you going to be negative? I hope not.

In some jobs, you are going to go in and work for someone who's younger than you. For some people, that's no big deal and you can tell it's no big deal when you talk to them about it in the interview.

They say things like, "I usually find that even if someone knows less than me in one area, they know more than me in another one. I can learn something useful from just about everyone and I enjoy the process."

For others, who use that snarky tone and say things like "It can be aggravating, but I try to teach them what I know without being too threatening" or something similar that sounds positive but really isn't, what flashes through the interviewer's mind is, "My gosh, I'd hate to be the one managing this person because they are trouble." And your job offer disappears, just like that.

Job Interview Question 28:

How would you go about establishing your credibility quickly with the team?

The best way to go about establishing credibility with anybody in any situation is to ask really great questions and try to understand the situation before trying to do any kind of magic trick.

(Incidentally, this is another benefit of asking questions in the interview...you show what you know by what you ask. If you ask great questions, it helps establish your own credibility as a strong candidate.)

A lot of people think you should jump on the white horse and charge in immediately with a quick, decisive fix, and that's not what's necessary in most cases. You can do more harm than good that way, and make a lot of people angry in the process with your arrogance and inevitable mistakes. What's necessary is to ask the questions that reveal that you do understand the situation. Then you can make a stronger decision based on the evidence, rather than a knee-jerk reaction.

In other situations, the best way to establish credibility is just to buckle down and do your job as best you can as soon as possible. Actions speak louder than words.

For those reasons, this question is a FANTASTIC opening to show the interviewer your 30/60/90-day plan. You can say, "I think I can answer that question best with this: I put together an outline of what I hope to take action on and accomplish in my first 3 months on the job and I'd like to talk it over with you." And you bring out your plan and go over it with the hiring manager.

In case you're not familiar with this, a 30-60-90-day plan is a written outline of the primary actions you would take during your first 3 months on the job. You research the company and the job extensively to put one together, because the more specific the plan, the better off you are. The research helps make you the best-prepared, most knowledgeable candidate, and helps you create a better, more accurate plan. Your plan shows that you are very capable of doing the job, even if you have little to no experience. It shows that you're willing to go above and beyond, if necessary, and it shows that you're a strategic thinker, that you can analyze a situation and prioritize tasks.

Both the plan and the discussion of it that you have with the hiring manager show that would buckle down and execute on those things that would help you establish credibility and be a productive member or leader of the team.

Job Interview Question 29:

I noticed that you are applying for a position that is not as senior as your past positions. Why would you consider a job that is, in effect, a demotion for you?

This is a question you might get asked early on in the process, like in a phone interview. If you have a lot of experience, it's going to be obvious that you're overqualified. So the question is, 'Why would you take a job that's less than what you're qualified for?'

There can be a whole host of reasons you can cite...as long as you never, ever say anything that sounds like, "Because I've been out of work for so long that if I don't get a job soon, I'm going to lose my house." Even if it's true.

That's clearly one of the big things they're worried about when they ask you this question. They're worried that you just want A job, not THIS job, and that as soon as something better comes along, you're gone. Or they're worried that you'll be bored. The job won't be a good fit and you won't be happy...which means that eventually, you'll jump ship. And all the money they've invested in hiring and training you is gone, too.

They want to know that the job is going to be a good fit for you.

Even though taking a job that's considered a step backward in your career is considered to be a little unusual in our super-competitive society, there are plenty of reasons you might want to do it.

Maybe it's a shorter commute. Maybe you tried working in management but what you really enjoy is the hands-on work of your industry. Maybe you just really like this company or the product they make. Maybe there's some experience you can get in this job that you can't get anywhere else. Maybe the culture at this company is a better fit for you. Maybe there are growth opportunities at this company that you can't get at your old one (because that was a small company and this is a big one with lots of room to advance).

Since those reasons aren't readily apparent to others, you'll have to explain. Communicate to the hiring manager why this position at this company is a perfect fit for you.

And then point out that the fact that you're a little overqualified for this job is actually a bonus for them because they're getting someone with lots of experience. In this situation, you almost certainly have more experience than the other candidates and that's a big plus for them. It's another selling point for you, and you should help them to recognize it.

Job Interview Question 30:

If we hire you, what will we know about you a year down the road?

Some candidates might wander off the path they should be on with this question (as many do with "Tell me about yourself") and start talking about how they'll know you like football, that you make a mean cheese dip, or that you never take sick days.

Stay on track and use this question just like you do all the other ones to sell yourself for the job. All your answers to interview questions should be strategically focused on getting you one step closer to the offer. Always be thinking: "How will this answer tell them something relevant about me and how I am perfect for this job?" "How will this answer make them want me more?" Strategically approaching the interview works.

This question helps you paint a brief picture of what life would look like with you in that role. If they can visualize it, you're one step closer to getting the job. It's just like thinking about how a couch will look in your living room or how a car will look in your driveway. The more you think about whatever that is fitting into your life, the easier it is to say 'yes' to the sale. In this case, it's the job offer. Incidentally, that's one of the reasons 30/60/90-day plans are so fantastic. They help that hiring manager 'see' you in the job.

I personally think that the very best answer to this interview question is:

"If you hire me, a year from now you'll know that everything I've said to you in this interview is true."

Want to elaborate a bit on that? Say:

"You'll know and understand why everyone in the past has enjoyed and appreciated my work and would like to have me work for them again." (References are an amazingly effective resource for you and you should always make sure yours are prepared for a phone call about this opportunity.)

Or: "You'll know that I'm sincere when I say that I'm excited about learning more about this job and this company, and thriving and contributing and producing and wanting to do more and help you guys with [insert job responsibility here]."

Or (if you want something more specific): "You'll know that my skills in X, Y, and Z were a perfect fit for this position based on the results I got from _____ / the solution I came up with for _____."

This question is really just another version of "Why should we hire you?" You want them to know that you're going to meet, and even exceed their expectations of you.

Job Interview Question 31:

If you could be any animal, which one would you be and why?

Some hiring managers really like these oddball interview questions. Some think it's going to reveal more about your character, and others just want to know what you really act like when you're under stress or just thrown a curve ball. Questions like these do reveal your thought process and offer you a chance to show off your creativity and inventiveness.

As in all job interview situations, your best bet is to be prepared for anything. Thinking long and hard about the qualities that are necessary to do a job well is actually an excellent exercise to go through before an interview, because it can help you focus your thoughts for how to answer all the interview questions you'll be asked. How does your personality, your background, your experience, or your skill set meet or exceed what this job requires?

For this particular question, it doesn't matter a lot what animal you choose, as long as you can tie it into qualities necessary to perform the job well. Although I would generally stay away from animals that have negative associations, like snakes, hyenas, rats, or chickens. Or spiders.

What are the personality traits that are desirable for someone who's going to fill this role?

Just smile and keep your answer simple and brief. Name the animal, and then explain why. Give one or two qualities that you see in that animal that also describe you.

I have a friend who says you should always try to be like an eagle, which is great if you're a CEO, but that's a bad animal to be if you need to be a team player.

A horse is really strong…able to function alone well or as part of a team.

Ants are hard workers, and the ultimate team player.

Monkeys are quick learners.

An elephant is strong, intelligent, loyal to the group, and unstoppable.

A dolphin is also intelligent, and actually considered one of the smartest animals.

Dogs are seen as Man's Best Friend, so might be good for someone in a support role. With a dog, you get loyalty and friendliness. Also protectiveness, but that's probably only required for bodyguards.

(Sorry, cat lovers. A cat's independence might appeal to you, but they have a bad reputation for not giving a darn about you as long as you're feeding it. That says, "I'm just here to collect my paycheck.")

A fun way to end this discussion is to say, "What animal did you choose when they asked you this question in your interview?"

Job Interview Question 32:

If you could relive the last 10 years of your life, what would you do differently?

Hmmm....what would I do differently?

I wouldn't speed when I was going to get a ticket...

I wouldn't have invested money in those stocks...

I wouldn't have bought those shoes...

Maybe those kinds of things are what come to your mind when you're asked about what you would do differently, but when they ask you that question in a job interview, that's not quite what they mean.

This is another way to ask the 'weakness' question. They're looking for your flaws.

If there's an actual problem or issue in your work history that's obvious (or going to be obvious soon), this is an ideal time to address that situation.

Let's say you took a job and you got laid off...maybe that's why they're asking that question because they see that short-lived role on your resume and this is a way they ask about it without asking directly. You can say, "Well, I regret quitting X job to take Y one. It didn't turn out to be a great move for me. Even though I learned a lot from it and I can see the positives in what I learned from that situation, which would be one that I would change if I could turn back the clock. It wasn't the best decision...but it was the best decision I could have made with the information I had at the time. Hindsight is 20/20, isn't it?"

You can't hide all your issues, but you can frame them in a way that seems more positive. You can tell your story as you like. (As long as you don't lie...if they find out that you lied, you're done.)

If there's no problem and your career's been smooth sailing, then you can be a little more philosophical about this question.

You could try making a deflecting joke: "Gosh, that's a tough one. I know we need to talk about a lot of other things in this interview, so I'm not sure that we have time to go through ALL the things I would do differently..."

If you want to answer it more seriously, say something like:

"If I look at it from a personal perspective, certainly I think we all have moments that we would do differently. But overall, I'm pleased with the direction I've taken, the decisions I've made, and the things that have happened in my career and in my personal life. "

That's a good, non-personal, neutral answer that should serve you just fine.

Job Interview Question 33:

If you had to choose one, would you consider yourself a big-picture person or a detail-oriented person?

This is a 'work style' type of question—but it's a complicated one. Employers really want both.

If you're a big-picture person, they'd like for you to also be able to handle the details. CEOs need to be able to consider the data when they make decisions for long-term plans.

If you're a detail-oriented person, they'd like for you to also be able to recognize the bigger picture and not get tunnel vision, because you need to be contributing toward the larger goal. Organizations need both styles in order to grow.

So the best answer really is, "I'm a _____, but I can also _____."

What you say first should absolutely depend on your job...accountants should be detail-oriented, and CEOs should be big-picture strategic types.

"I'm more of a detail-oriented person, but I can step back and look at the bigger picture, just like you step back and look at a map, to make sure that I'm on track for the larger goal."

"I'm definitely a big-picture person because I think strategically in terms of where the organization needs to be in order to be successful and profitable, but I can focus on whatever necessary details I need to inform those decisions."

And if you have a good story about a time when you used both skills in a successful project, now would be the time to tell it. "I was the group leader for X project, so I had to keep an eye out for what everyone was doing and make sure we were on track for our goal, and keep a checklist of all the details that needed to be taken care of in order to get there. We completed the project on time with excellent results." (And say what those results were.)

Big-picture jobs require strategy, creativity, the ability to see the forest and not get caught up in the individual trees. Generally, the higher up you are in an organization, the more you should be able to see the big picture. So if you're working your way up the ladder into upper management, you should be (or should be learning to be) a big-picture person. Other big picture jobs: consultants, entrepreneurs, writers, counselors.

Detail-oriented jobs are in much greater supply than big-picture jobs. There are always many more soldiers than generals. But as they say, the devil is in the details. You can lose the war for want of a nail. Many of the highest-paying jobs are incredibly detail-oriented, so it's a very valuable skill. Detail oriented jobs: engineers, scientists, mathematicians, surgeons, administrative assistants, researchers, and just about any kind of technology-based job.

Job Interview Question 34:

If you were a tree, what kind of a tree would you be?

This is definitely a wacky question. Sometimes it's "What animal would you be?" or even "What fruit would you be?" You might think it is ridiculous, but you still have to play along, or you'll upset the interviewer.

They're asking because they want to see what you'll do if they throw you off stride by asking a question out of left field like this, or maybe they want an insight into your personality. This type of question checks your creativity, your ability to think on your feet, and just might reveal what you really think about yourself. (They hope.)

What they DON'T want to hear is, "I would be an apple tree because I like apples." That doesn't tell them anything useful, and it really doesn't have anything to do with the interview or the job.

To answer this question (or any kind of question where you have to choose 'what would you be?', think in a broad way about the qualities of whatever it is that you're going to pick and how you would explain your choice. What character or personality traits would be useful for someone in that role to have? Think in terms of the utilitarian productiveness of your choice as it relates to the job you're applying for. What does that job require? And then be careful of the nuances.

For instance, if you were answering the animal question: To you, a cat might seem independent, but one manager told me that to her, they seem lazy. An eagle is always a safe choice for someone who wants to be seen as a leader. Horses are strong, smart and useful. Just don't pick something like an earthworm or a vulture.

If you're answering the tree question, think about how fruit trees are productive, oak trees are strong and reliable, but cottonwood trees spread trash that everyone hates. I wouldn't choose a Weeping willow, because that just seems sad. Sugar maples are productive, too (syrup). Evergreen trees are steady. Palm trees are flexible.

A lot of people go for the oak tree: "I would be an oak tree, because I'm strong and dependable."

If you just can't stand the thought of choosing a tree, you could try saying something like, "I want to be the tree that would be most productive and useful to this organization. That's my goal."

Or maybe you want to research some trees before your next interview.

Job Interview Question 35:

Is there anything I haven't told you about the company that you'd like to know?

Toward the end of the interview, hiring managers will ask some version of, "Do you have any questions for me?" Your answer is ALWAYS going to be "yes."

You always want to have a list of questions to ask in the interview. If you don't have any, it makes you look like you're not that interested in the role.

Here are some examples of great questions to ask:

Why is the position open?

Either the person before you failed so miserably at the role they were fired (in which case you want to know so you don't make the same mistakes), or they were so good at it they got promoted (in which case you want to know so you can see what worked and get a head start on being successful yourself). Or maybe the company is growing, so they've created this new role to deal with that. The answer you get will tell you a lot about what's going on.

When do you want to have it filled?

A few candidates will be afraid to ask this question, but don't be. It is not too bold. You're just getting information that will help you be professional in your follow up. After you send your thank you note, you need to know when you should be calling to check on the status of the job. You need a timeline so you're not left hanging, wondering what's going on. Hopefully, you're following several job leads and have lots of interviews scheduled. You don't want to turn something else down because you're waiting on this one.

How does this role fit in the whole of the company?

This is a great way to find out about advancement opportunities without coming right out and asking about them. And you can find out about what other departments you'll be working with. It might uncover some company culture or organizational issues you need to know before you start.

Where did the person who was in this role before go?

Were they promoted? Where were they promoted to? Is that the advancement track the company generally follows? Do they like to promote from within? All this is great information for you.

Were they fired? Why were they fired? Is there something they did or tried that should be a warning for you?

What is it you like about the company? (Alternative questions: What do you find most impressive about the company? Why do you like working here?)

The answer you get from this question should uncover a lot about the corporate culture, and whether this organization is a good fit for you. It might even uncover some perks that you wouldn't have discovered otherwise….like maybe there's an on-site gym or childcare, or maybe there are stock options you didn't know about that would have an effect on your salary negotiations later.

Job Interview Question 36:

Situational Response Question: An airplane landed in the parking lot. What would you do?

Most situational interview questions are like behavioral questions. They have some direct relation to the job...like, "You're introducing a new policy to the group and facing opposition. How would you handle it?" Or, "How would you handle a situation in which a subordinate was not performing to expectations?"

Others seem like ridiculous, oddball questions that don't have any relevance to the job at all...but what they do for employers is give them a window into **how you think**. How do you approach a challenging situation? That's why they ask these kinds of questions.

You never know what they might ask, and there's really no way to prepare for them. I've seen some crazy questions like:

- How would you move Mount Fuji?
- How many light bulbs are in this building?
- What are 5 uncommon uses of a brick, not including building, layering, or a paper-weight?
- Suppose you had eight identical balls. One of them is slightly heavier and you are given a balance scale.
- What's the fewest number of times you have to use the scale to find the heavier ball?

If you get asked one of these, just take a deep breath and roll with it. The trick is to walk them through your thought process. Talk your way through it, showing how you would approach, think about, or strategize about whatever situation they throw at you.

So if I were asked what I would do if an airplane landed in the parking lot, I would say something like:

"I'm not sure I would do anything. If there are a lot of other people around and they look like they know what they're doing, I think I would stay back and let them handle it. If no one's hurt, I don't see that I have to get involved in that at all, except for maybe calling 911. If someone's hurt, or there's the possibility that someone will be hurt, then I would have to execute something very quickly. But what that would be exactly depends on a lot of things: How big is the plane? Where is it? What do I have access to? There would be a lot of questions that would have to be answered before I decided which action would be the most effective to take."

What I'm doing with this answer is demonstrating that I could evaluate, analyze, and sum up a situation before I decided on which action to take. Immediate, 'charge in on a white horse' action is not always the best move. Sometimes it's more important to stop and create a strategy first.

There's no really wrong answer to these questions. Just take them through your thought process and reason it out. It will be OK.

Job Interview Question 37:

Tell me about a time when you disagreed with your boss about a way that something should be done. How did you handle that?

You can't get away with saying, "That's never happened. I've never disagreed with my boss." Everybody, at some point, has disagreed with a decision the boss made about something. The question-behind-the-question is, how did you handle it? In this case, they're looking to see that you have good communication skills and an understanding of authority. Can you get a competing idea communicated effectively and respectfully (without being rude or obnoxious)? Can you handle conflict in a professional manner?

You can tell your boss that you disagree about the way something should be, if at the same time you offer suggestions about how something should be handled. I personally think that's always the best way: when you disagree, offer an alternative solution. Don't just complain. But if the boss responds by saying, "I appreciate that, but we're going to go in this direction," then if you want to still continue to be employed, you're going to have to give up. They're the boss. (Unless for some reason, it's incredibly unethical…but in most cases it comes down to a simple matter of 'what the boss says, goes.')

The story you tell should be an example of how you handle such a situation respectfully, professionally, and with good communication skills (just like_if your boss disagrees with you). This is a behavioral interview question, so use the STAR structure (Situation or Task, Action you took, Results you got) to tell your story. Just make sure that it's a story that shines a nice light on you when you're finished telling it. You don't want to tell the story about the time when you disagreed but your boss was being a jerk and you just gave in to keep the peace. And you don't want to tell the one where you realized you were wrong. Tell the one where your actions made a positive difference on the outcome of the situation--whether it was a work-related outcome or a more effective and productive working relationship.

Here is a very general example:

"We were working on a big project for X, and my boss decided that we should take Y action. But I could see where that decision would cause us trouble down the road with A, B, and C. So I went to her, told her my concerns, and offered some alternative ideas [state what those were]. She saw my point and liked that I was thinking outside the box. We implemented my idea and it gave us X results."

Job Interview Question 38:

Tell me about a time when you faced a difficult situation with a co-worker.

"Works well with others" is a major skill we're judged on from kindergarten right on into the workplace. (If only we didn't get so many 'opportunities' to hone that particular skill!) That's why you get job interview questions about difficulties working with supervisors, difficulties working on team projects, and how you deal with stressful situations. They're all trying to see if you can get along and be professional (and productive). It's a behavioral question that pokes around in your past to help them predict how you'll behave in the future before they invite you into their environment.

With this question in particular, they're looking for how you deal with problems and confrontations in general and how you come up with solutions. How do you approach a difficult situation? Do you have good communication skills? Are you empathetic? Are you very emotional? Can you remain calm? Can you find a solution?

You should be quick to point out that, "Hey, I try not to get into difficult situations with co-workers." Being able to consistently keep the peace is a great skill.

But you're going to have to tell them something. You can choose to talk about a communication issue you worked through, or a professional challenge you overcame with your initiative, resilience and problem-solving skills.

A communication issue answer might sound like this: "Obviously, there are personalities that I don't do as well with as others. Once when that happened, I just reminded myself that there's a reason they're in that company, that they're a valuable member of the team and I've got to figure out a way to work with them. We had problems because we failed to communicate, which hurt us both. I figured that I must be causing 50% of that problem, so I thought about what I could do to alleviate the situation. So I came up with X, Y, Z solutions that I could use to address this issue, made sure I wasn't coming at it from a position of negativity, and resolved the problem."

Keep your answer emotion-free (don't vent any feelings here), with a happy ending. They just want to see your thought process. They want to see that you can be empathetic and that you are willing and able to negotiate a situation in a peaceful manner with a good outcome.

Job Interview Question 39:

Tell me about a time when you failed.

The key to answering the failure question is that you can't say you've never failed. I know you probably want to, because you don't want to be seen in a bad light. But you can't. And it's OK.

Everybody fails. If you've never failed, it means you've never taken a risk (which means you probably haven't made much progress, either) or you've never made a big mistake (which is impossible).

I've failed lots of times in my career. What's important is that I learn from my failures and I don't make the same mistakes again. And that's what's important for you, too.

This is not like the weakness question. A weakness is a flaw in yourself that could affect your work in the future. A failure is a temporary event that doesn't have to happen again, if you are humble enough to learn a lesson from it.

So first, you have to choose a failure, and second, you have to be able to articulate something you've learned from the mistake so you can transform it into a turnaround story with a happy ending. Everybody loves comeback stories, right?

As in: "Once I failed by missing a deadline for a project, but I reacted to that by taking a course to learn my Outlook program in greater detail so that I could use it to keep myself organized and always on time. I've been much more productive since then, so I'm actually kind of glad that happened because I learned a lot from it and I am providing a greater benefit to my organization."

Or, you could say: "I am naturally optimistic, which is a great thing for my attitude and my ability to work with people, but once it caused me to overlook a possibility for a problem with my project that turned into an actual problem. I learned from that that I can be optimistic, but I should always have a contingency plan in place. And I do. And actually, it allows me even more peace of mind because I know that I've always got a Plan B, just in case."

Do you see? You admit the failure, tell what you learned from it and what action you took to correct it or avoid it going forward, and show why it has made improvements in you and your work. And always bring it back to your selling points so you can continue to be strategic in your interview answers.

Someone who's not afraid to admit they made a mistake and is obviously interested in improving themselves and their performance is always going to be attractive to an employer.

Job Interview Question 40:

Tell me about a time when you had to give someone difficult feedback. How did you handle it?

If you're interviewing for a management-level job, you will almost certainly be asked this question at some point. Nobody likes to give negative feedback, but if you supervise anyone, it's a necessary evil. Managers have to deliver both positive and negative feedback on almost a daily basis, depending on the size of the company and the group who reports to them.

Since delivering even the most constructive criticism can sometimes be a sensitive matter, it requires some higher-level communication skills to do it well. Your future employer will want to know that you have those communication skills so that you can correct undesirable behavior or actions and still run a smooth ship.

They also want to know that you understand the nuances of this situation: how others might take whatever feedback you're giving them. You have to think about how they might perceive what you're saying, what the impact will be on them, what outcome you want, and what you might need to say to preface what you're telling them in order to get that outcome.

They understand, and I hope you do too, that delivering negative feedback well is about being a little more aware than just delivering information. It's thinking about how they will react. Will they receive this information well? It's about what you want them to do with the information once they have it, what you want the long-term effect to be. How do you want them to move forward from here?

You always want to make sure that you ask questions that require them to indicate their understanding of what you said so that you can clarify that you communicated what you wanted to communicate.

So what they're looking for in this question is that you understand that some situations require sensitivity, thinking it through, following up, and maybe even learning from not doing such a good job of giving that feedback.

Give them an example of a time you had to give someone negative feedback, but only as an illustration of your larger philosophical point of what it takes to deliver negative feedback well in order to get the change you're looking for. Show them that you approach it with forethought and sensitivity and with an eye toward communicating well in a positive manner—even though it's a negative subject.

Job Interview Question 41:

Tell me about yourself.

Some people think this is an icebreaker question because it's one of the first questions of the interview (and because in normal circumstances, it *is* an icebreaker question). So they answer it like they would in a social situation and say something along the lines of, "I've got 3 kids, I love to run marathons, I'm a Steelers fan"…whatever. That's a mistake. It's the wrong response because that's not what this question is about.

When they say, "Tell me about yourself," what they really want to know is "Tell me something that will matter to me as I consider you for this job."

This is a golden opportunity for you to set yourself in their minds as a great candidate. It's completely open-ended, so you can say anything you want. So think about the job, the job description, and all the research you did before the interview, and put yourself in that hiring manager's shoes: what is he or she going to be the most impressed by? What is going to get that person's attention and make them sit up and take notice of you for the rest of the interview?

You might start with your education—what's your degree? If you had an especially high GPA, you might mention it—but if you didn't, then don't. Just talk about your degree. If you did coursework that is different from your degree but pertains to this job, this is a good time to mention it.

And then go into your background. Just hit the highlights: promotions, awards, or key accomplishments. Not necessarily the things that you're most proud of—the things that this hiring manager for this job will be most impressed with.

This requires some strategic thinking on your part before you get there—but think of it like tailoring your resume. You tailor that to the job before you submit it, right? And you're going to tailor your answer to this question before you give it. Just think: What parts of my story would be on this hiring manager's list of reasons to hire me? That's what being strategic in the interview is all about.

You don't need to talk longer than a minute or so—just deliver a very targeted message that says to that hiring manager: "I am skilled, I have accomplished some great things, and I can bring that to work here for you."

Job Interview Question 42:

Tell me your life story (more of your personal history).

Hiring managers want to find out as much as they can about you in the interview. It's a bit of a risk-management thing. The more they know, the less likely they'll make a mistake by extending you a job offer. But even if they ask you to specifically reveal more of your personal history, it's still very important that you remember that your focus is not to make a new best friend here...it's to get a job.

For that reason, here's how you want to talk about your personal story in the interview:

Skim over the childhood portion, even though they've asked you for a personal history, because your childhood is probably not relevant for the work you're going to do at this company.

Say something like, "Well, I was born and raised here" or "I'm from X state," or whatever, and then briefly hit the highlights: I graduated high school, went to college, received XYZ degree, immediately was offered a position with ABC Company, and moved on to X Company after that.

But here's the part that trips up most people (I find this with my personal coaching clients all the time): They just want to spit out the history, versus "dressing it up" to sell it a little bit.

Many job seekers almost forget that they are SELLING themselves for the job, not just reciting a career history. Dressing up your answer to make you a more attractive candidate is very simple.

Instead of saying, "I spent 5 years in the military," you could say "I spent 5 years in the military, where I was in a leadership position over 150 soldiers and we executed XYZ."

Instead of saying, "I was the coach of the Whatever-Whatever's," you could say, "I was the coach of the Whatever-Whatever's and I coached them to an ABC championship."

Instead of saying, "I was a lifeguard in college," you could talk about how big the pool was, how many people swam there, what your responsibilities were and how you were rewarded for it.

If you were an account executive in a certain role, point out that you were immediately promoted to a higher position because you were one of the top 5 sales reps in the nation.

Don't just say what happened. **Elaborate** on the things that are important or impressive. Dress it up a bit into 'selling statements' that tell them more about you but also sell you for the job. Focus on making what you're saying a positive thing…something that actively contributes to getting you this job.

Job Interview Question 43:

Tell us about a failed project.

This is a more specific version of "Tell us about a time when you failed." This is a big behavioral interview question. Why do hiring managers want so badly to ask about your failures? It's because we've all failed at one time or another and how we deal with it and react to it says a lot about our character and our work ethic. It gives them another perspective on how you deal with stressful situations, too.

Failures are difficult. I've had a few of them myself.

Basically, how I feel about a failed project is this: a failed project is never a complete failure because you should have learned something from it that will make you smarter the next time around. As long as you don't disappoint your customers and your superiors, then having a failure is not necessarily a negative. In fact, failure can be good for us because it means that we're moving forward, we're trying. A few lumps and bumps on the way are part of the learning process.

I like Michael Jordan's quote: "I've failed over and over again in my life and that is why I succeed." Michael Jordan failed all over the place, but he's also one of the most successful, most accomplished athletes in the world.

We learn a lot from our failures, and that's what the interviewer wants to know that you know. Did you take responsibility? Did you take what you learned and apply it to being better than you were before?

Choose a failure that you learned something from that made you even better at what you do.

105

If it were me, I would choose a project that failed because of something like organization or time management rather than something that was a central skill I need for my job. And I would choose something that happened a long time ago. (Which gives me plenty of time to show that I didn't make that mistake again.)

Give them the background of the story (what was the project, what was going on). Tell them what the mistake was and why you made it. And then tell them what you learned and what steps you took to make sure that it never happened again. You failed, you learned, you improved.

I want everything in your interview to be as positive as you can make it, and that means your answer to the failure question, too.

Job Interview Question 44:

Tell us about a time that you went against corporate directives. Why? How did it turn out?

I once did a survey of job seekers as part of my mock interview program, asking them to give me actual questions they've been asked in job interviews, and this was one of the responses. I almost couldn't believe it. This is not a normal or typical interview question. To me, this is a little like saying, "Tell me about the last time you shoplifted."

I might have disagreed with my boss a time or two, but I never went against corporate directives, and I hope that you haven't, either. Usually, going against corporate directives means that you don't care that much about your job.

(Side note: Don't say that you might have disagreed with your boss but never gone against corporate directives, like I just said above. The natural follow up question to that is, "Oh, really? When?" They might think to ask about your disagreements with your boss, and they might not. But the general rule I would follow is: On negative questions, **don't volunteer more information** than what they're asking for.)

And don't assume they're asking you to describe your independent, maverick spirit, either. Maybe there are some companies where being a maverick is a plus, but I'm not sure that I know who they are. Google's corporate culture is famous for its unorthodox style, but I think that even they would have a problem with someone going directly against Google policies.

It would be a very, very special situation where taking that kind of action would cast you in a positive light with the company (former or prospective). Like maybe some kind of whistleblowing situation. Unless you've got some story about how you saved the company from ruin by going against your evil boss who was bent on destruction, I think I'd pass on answering this question.

I would turn this question (and any other question that seemed overly negative like this one) back to them and say, "I've never gone against corporate directives. Does that happen a lot here in this company? Is that an action that's valued here?"

Maybe you'll get a picture of corporate culture that will either make you think, "Finally…a place for an independent thinker like me!" or will send you running for the hills to get away from what is surely a chaotic environment.

Job Interview Question 45:

There's no right or wrong answer, but if you could be anywhere in the world right now, where would you be?

Let's see....if I could be anywhere in the world, I'd be at Lake Tahoe, or lying on a beach with a fruity drink in my hand, or riding my horse through the mountains, or at the bank counting the millions of dollars I just won in the lottery...all those sound like great places to me.

This is not a typical job interview question. But it's really no more odd than "If you could be any animal, what would you be?" or "If you were a tree, what tree would you be?" Hiring managers ask those kinds of personality questions with dismaying frequency. So why do they ask them? It's because they're trying to get a better idea of who you are. They want insight into your personality and work and they think that maybe you'll let your guard down with this kind of question in a way you wouldn't with something like "What's your greatest weakness?" It's understandable. Their reputation is on the line every time they hire someone. If you're going to be on their team, you're a direct threat to their job if you don't do well. They have a lot at stake.

But you have a lot at stake, too.

Job interviews are hard to come by these days. If you get one, it's a golden opportunity that you HAVE to make the most of. That means that you need to be laser-focused on your goal, which is to get the job offer. To get the offer, you have to sell yourself as the best person for the job. How do you sell yourself for the job? By answering every single interview question (even weird interview questions like this one) in a positive, focused way that adds yet another layer of reasons to hire you.

If you follow that logic along, that means that the best answer to "If you could be anywhere in the world, where would you be?" is going to sound a lot like this one:

"Right where I'm at. For me, the next step in my life and my career is an opportunity like this. And sitting here with you is the best opportunity for me to make the move into this position. So I can't imagine that there is anywhere else I would prefer to be right now."

That's what I mean when I tell candidates to be strategic in the interview.

Because there IS a wrong answer to that interview question, no matter what they say. And the wrong answer is anything other than "Right here."

Job Interview Question 46:

We are looking for someone with experience…or, you don't have enough experience—why should we hire you?

If you're a new graduate, or if you're switching careers, you might get asked this question, especially early on in the process, like in a phone interview. It is a challenge, but don't let it freak you out. They are at least somewhat interested in you, or they wouldn't have even bothered to talk to you. So keep that in mind and maintain your confidence. They are a little concerned, but all you have to do is to sort of help them along in their thinking on this issue.

You've got a couple of good options in this situation:

1. Turn the tables on them.

Remind them that at one point, they didn't have any experience either, and someone gave them a chance. Say something like, "Well, at some point, you didn't have any experience either, when you were first starting out. And obviously, you've been very successful. Would you hire you again?"

At this point, they'll be nodding their heads, remembering and agreeing with you—that's always a good thing! This is a very logical thing to bring up, and it gives you a little bit of a psychological edge in the process.

2. Don't ask about this person's experience (or lack of) directly. Ask about the people they've hired before.

Say, "Of your team, have you ever hired someone who didn't have specific experience in your industry?" They'll probably be nodding their heads with you, and then you can say, "I know there must have been a few times when that didn't work out, but there must also have been some times that it worked out really well."

They're going to say yes, and start telling you about someone who was especially successful even though they didn't have exactly the right education or background or experience. That's your opening. You say, "That's great. I can be that person for you, too. I can take those same skill sets and deliver those same kinds of results." (This is a great time to follow up by showing them your 30-60-90-day plan that spells out for them exactly how you're going to be successful.)

Both of those answers lead that hiring manager around to thinking outside the box a little bit. And you're gaining a psychological edge because you're drawing that connection for them between you and a successful outcome in those reminders of how it's worked out well before.

Keep your confidence, remember that you're a great candidate who learns quickly, and realize that everybody had to start somewhere.

Job Interview Question 47:

What are some of your greatest and/or proudest accomplishments?

This is a great job interview question, but a lot of people don't do it or themselves justice when they answer it.

One of the worst mistakes people make is that they will say that their greatest or proudest accomplishment is something that matters to them personally, like their kids. It doesn't matter if your kids are saints who never fight, spend their weekends feeding the poor, and have just won the Nobel Prize…that's still the wrong answer. Being proud of your kids is fantastic. We all love our kids. But that can't be the answer to this.

Good job interview strategy requires that everything you say must be focused on selling you for the job. That's why you're there.

Your answer to this needs to be something that directly relates to the job, like being awarded X prize for achievement after being in a position for only 18 months…or being recognized as the ABC….or figuring out a solution for a big hairy problem that the company had been struggling with for a long time. It MUST be work-related: awards, accomplishments, successes.

If you fail to say something work-related, you could easily lose out to a candidate who isn't necessarily a better candidate than you, but who does a better job of focusing themselves on the job at hand rather than on their personality or family.

It's also a mistake to say something work-related that isn't especially relevant for this job. For example, you don't want to tell a story about how you solved a technical problem if you're interviewing for a sales job. Even if it was the most complicated technical problem in the world requiring advanced knowledge and serious expertise, they won't care if what they really want to know is, "Can you make a sale?"

Prepare to answer this question before you get to the interview by thinking about your proudest at work and choosing one that would be especially impressive to this company, for this position. Or, come at it another way and read over the job description and then think about impressive things you've done that match up with at least one of those requirements.

When telling the story of your proudest accomplishment, be strategic and choose an example that directly relates to this job. (At the same time, choose another story to keep in your back pocket to help you answer the "What are your greatest strengths?" question.) In your story, provide details. Try to quantify those accomplishments as much as you can because numbers are impressive as hard evidence. Don't be afraid to brag. That's what this question is for.

Job Interview Question 48:

What are your advantages and disadvantages?

This question is another way to get at your greatest strengths and weaknesses as a candidate. But in this particular one, they'd like a list of the pros and cons of hiring you. Don't let it throw you. It is a beautiful thing to be the one in charge of putting together that list (if only during the interview). You can spin this story like a politician and turn it in your favor. Don't lie. Just focus on the positive.

The truth is that they're probably aware of your advantages and disadvantages already. They've read your resume. But this is a golden opportunity to influence their thinking by addressing any shortcomings in your experience or background while explaining why they don't matter that much.

Or look at it another way, and it's an opportunity to show them that your disadvantages or weaknesses aren't relevant or worth even thinking about because your advantages or strengths are so strong that they'd be crazy to pass you up.

115

Remember to sell yourself for this job. You're the "product" that's for sale. The hiring manager of that company is the customer, and your salary is the cost or the price they will pay for the product. Why are you going to be a great value for them?

Be strategic. Answer every question with an eye toward the job description and goals.

Of course, advantages are easy. It's the disadvantages that are going to trip you up. One strategy I like when talking about your disadvantages is using a strength that you could improve on. Another one is using a weakness that either doesn't matter for the job or that helps you with the job.

For instance, if I were asked this question, I'd say that my advantages were that I am intelligent, driven, quick-witted, high-energy, and able to communicate at all levels. Those were all great advantages for me when I was in sales, and also happen to be helpful to me as a career coach and business owner. I communicate very well with an enormous variety of people and can quickly evaluate and analyze what a job seeker's problems are and give them a solution, which saves them time and money.

I would say that my disadvantages are that I'm impatient, not detail-oriented, always want to be a leader. But all of these things are problems that either help me do my job well or don't cause me any problems in performance. See, my impatience is something that causes me a problem in my personal life (just ask my husband and kids) but that serves me very well in driving me to achieve quickly at work. When I say I'm not especially detail-oriented, I would also say "and that's why I take the extra steps of X, Y, and Z to address that issue so I don't miss anything." The leadership piece is another thing that sometimes causes me trouble in social situations but is a very desirable quality in my line of work.

You are in charge of how you present yourself as a candidate, and you can tell your own story in a way that shines the most flattering light on you and your candidacy.

Job Interview Question 49:

What are your hobbies?

Asking about your hobbies and interests seems like an odd interview question, but companies are asking more and more of those 'personality' type questions these days in an effort to make sure you're going to be a good cultural fit for the organization. And the indirectness of this question is also sort of a fishing expedition for them to see if you'll reveal things about yourself that you otherwise wouldn't.

It's not an innocuous question. They will read things into your answer, whether you intend for them to or not, and they will be influenced by what you say.

You've got a couple of strategic opportunities to take advantage of when answering this question. The first one is making a connection with the interviewer. This is a great place to build rapport. For that reason, stick with talking about hobbies that most people can identify with. (You can't build rapport if they can't identify with you.)

So first of all, whatever you do, don't make the mistake of talking about your crocheting or your ultimate fighting championship! Those both can have negative connotations for various audiences. Crocheting makes you seem 'older' and less culturally current, while ultimate fighting will make some hiring managers worry that you have a violent streak. For example, even though I personally like to shoot my pistol in target practice, there are a few people that would not sit well with, so I wouldn't mention that. Instead, I would choose to talk about another hobby, like riding horses.

The second opportunity is a chance to influence how they think of you as a candidate. This is a fantastic place to talk about hobbies that make you look either energetic or smart. Running is good. Hiking or walking are also positive activities. Traveling is always a good one. Reading is great, or any kind of continuing education piece. I always like to hear candidates talk about taking classes to learn something because I think that says something very positive about you, that you're willing to invest in yourself and that you're willing to learn and try new things.

Especially if you're an older candidate, this hobby question can be a strong way for you to communicate that you have a lot of energy or that you're interested in new technology or that you like to learn new things. All of those things go to alleviating any fears they have about your age.

Just remember that even something as small as a hobby can help you build the case for hiring you.

Job Interview Question 50:

What are your least favorite things to do in your role as X?

This is a slightly different version of, "What did you dislike about your previous job?"

They're trying to find out more about you and how you think. If you're transferring roles in a lateral move, your answer will tell them about how you will perform in this new job. If you're making a move up the career ladder, there's not such a direct correlation, but it will still shed light on you, your performance, and even on how much you understand about this new role.

If you choose an answer that happens to be a central component of this job's responsibilities, you've just done yourself some serious damage. You've demonstrated that you haven't done your research, and you clearly don't understand the job.

Make sure you understand the role and choose a 'least favorite thing' that will be only a minor, insignificant component of your task list for this new job.

Another option is to try to choose an answer that anyone would choose. That's an easy way to build rapport and avoid making a mistake. For instance, a common answer to this question for those in management roles is "I hate firing people." No one likes to deliver that kind of bad news. But be sure to say that even though you dislike it, you do it when necessary.

Some answers that I might personally give are:

"I really dislike dealing with failings...even though I always say that failure can be helpful, I still don't enjoy it. I don't like dealing with employees who are failing, a project that's failing, or a situation that's failing. Because I hate it so much, I do everything I can to plan and avoid potential problems in the first place. But I understand that some things can't be avoided, and I do enjoy the feeling that I get when we're able to turn around a bad situation into something positive."

"I don't enjoy paperwork. I enjoy doing things that are going to have a positive impact on my results and performance, but I don't enjoy the monotonous details that are necessary to make that happen in some of those tasks. But I also understand that even if I don't like them, they have to be done. They fall under my job responsibilities. And I'm very driven to make that progress happen, whatever it takes."

As in answering all_job interview questions, be strategic when answering this one. Think about the bigger picture of how you're selling yourself for the job and stay focused on the positive.

Both of these answers are honest, non-cookie-cutter answers that, even though they're answering a negative question, bring the conversation immediately back around to a positive statement about what I will bring to the job.

Job Interview Question 51:

What are your pet peeves?

Why would they ask about your pet peeves in a job interview?

They can actually find out quite a lot about you by what you choose to say when you answer this question:

- Do you get irritated easily? (How long is your list?)
- Will you be a good fit for their company culture? (If you hate being micromanaged and they're very focused on being 'involved' with employee projects, then chances are, you won't.)

I've seen some articles that say you should say that you don't have any pet peeves, but I don't agree with that. Everyone has things that irritate them more than other things. You can downplay your irritation (the interview is not the time to go into a Lewis Black-style rant, for sure), but if you say you don't have one, it just sounds false.

So tell them one. As in all your job interview answers, consider what you're going to say before you say it to make sure it works for you and not against you. Obviously, make sure your pet peeve isn't something you'd run into every day on the job—like, you can't stand team projects when the job is going to require that at least 30% of the time.

Your answer will say as much about you and your attitude as they will about what your actual pet peeve is. So if you say, "I hate blowhards who are all talk and no action. They're also the ones who usually don't

121

pull their own weight on team projects. I hate that, too." That reveals you as someone with a temper, a negative attitude and a tendency to make assumptions about others.

For instance, I might say, "I don't like negative attitudes. It doesn't help anyone, even the person who's being negative. If there's a problem, they should focus on how to fix it." That says that I'm someone who's focused on solutions rather than problems.

Or I might say, "I don't like people who don't work hard at their jobs. I believe that if you've been hired to do something, you should put 100% of your talent and effort into it to be successful and fulfill that contract you've created with the employer." That's an incredibly positive answer that speaks to your work ethic.

A great answer will say something positive about you and add another reason to hire you.

Job Interview Question 52:

What are your salary expectations?

Oh, the dreaded salary question! The good news is that it doesn't have to be a big problem for you if you know how to handle it. The primary strategy I teach my job seekers is, "Do your salary research so that you know what the going rate is for that job in your part of the country, and then deflect naming a number for as long as possible."

Still, there are different approaches to use depending on who asks you this question.

If HR asks, respond with a question: ask what their salary range is for this job. They'll have one. When they tell you, say, "I'm comfortable with that range. If I think this is the right job for me, and you think that I'm the right person for it, we can absolutely come to an agreement. "

If the hiring manager asks, things get a little stickier, but you still have options. It's not always true that "the one who says a number first loses," but you do want to try not to be first.

It's totally appropriate throw the ball back to them, just like you did with HR: "That's a great question. We haven't discussed what the salary and compensation plan for this position is. Can you fill me in on that?"

50% of hiring managers will go ahead and start telling you.

The other 50% really want to know how much you're going to cost. They'll say, "Well, it depends on the candidate. What are **your** requirements?"

So you say, "I am really looking for a challenge, to use my skills in X, Y, and Z. I'm sure that you'll pay a salary that's appropriate for the challenges of this job. What did the company have in mind for that?"

This answer will divert a few more people, but a stubborn manager will say something like, "It really does depend on the candidate. Do you have a range?"

If you can't push back any more, say, "I have to be honest. This is a new position for me. I'd really have to see the total package, the entire compensation plan with all the benefits. My last salary was in the $55,000 range, and this position seems to me to be a rung or two above that in responsibility and in my ability to impact the organization, so I would expect that the salary offer would reflect that."

Salary negotiations are tricky business. One of the best books on the planet on this subject is **Negotiating Your Salary: How to Make $1000 a Minute**, by Jack Chapman. It's a short, easy read and it will fill your brain with all kinds of tips and tactics you can use that work like a charm. Find it and read it.

Salary questions can be difficult, but I want you to remember that your responses really do demonstrate your strength and confidence as a candidate. Stay calm, cool, and confident, and you'll be fine.

Job Interview Question 53:

What are your workplace values?

Asking about your workplace values is similar to asking "What is your work ethic?" Or, "What are your workplace ethics?" They want to know what kind of person you are. What matters to you?

It's really an easy question to answer because your answer should be what your values are. They should speak to your integrity, your character, and your work ethic. As long as you're saying something positive, that's a good thing. But always, keep it tied to your work…they don't care that you love baby seals and spotted owls as a part of your commitment to the environment, unless you're applying for a job with an environmental group.

You can say, "My work place values are the same as my home and personal values" because that shows integrity.

For me, my answer would be "I do what I say I'm going to do, I follow up on my commitments, and I think of others before I think of myself."

Other great answers might sound more like, "I always try to do the very best that I can, because my employer is paying for a service, and I supply that just like I would if I owned a business and that person was my customer. My customer deserves the best I can deliver."

Or, "I believe that everyone who works for a company is part of a team, and it's important for us all to support each other and step up to do what needs doing to get the job done. I try to lead by example in that way."

If you've done your research into the company to see what their corporate values are, you can talk about which of your own values align with theirs. Now, please note that I am NOT saying to lie and just tell them what they want to hear. A lie is always eventually found out, and won't serve you in the end, anyway. You need to know what that company's corporate values are, so you know if you'll be happy working for them or not. Their core values are going to have a major effect on your career. You don't want a toxic corporate environment to hijack your own values and make you miserable. Environment matters.

What you say about your values should give that hiring manager an indication of what kind of a person you are to work with, why he should trust you, why you're going to be a great hire, and anything else that's going to sell him on the idea he should offer you the job.

Job Interview Question 54:

What did you earn at your last job?

For most candidates, "What was your salary?" is a very uncomfortable, Too Much Information-kind of a question. But all potential employers are going to ask at some point in the process, often very early on...sometimes as early as the initial application. So why do they ask? And how do you handle it?

If your recruiter or Human Resources asks, it's because they're trying to make sure you won't embarrass them by refusing an offer over money. If you make $60,000 a year and this job only pays $40,000, chances are you won't take it and they want to know that up front. They get yelled at if they get hiring managers involved with a candidate they can't afford.

If you manage to avoid it during the application process, the hiring manager will probably ask you in the interview. The reasoning is the same. They want to know, "Can we afford you?"

If you feel strongly about not revealing that information, you can try saying something like, "Can you help me understand what information you're really asking for here? I'm not very comfortable discussing my past salary because it doesn't really relate to this job. There are a lot of other factors involved than just straight numbers. I would love to answer questions about my skills and qualifications for this job. I think this is a great company, and I'm excited about the possibility of working here. I know that if we agree that I'm the best fit for the position, we'll be able to come to an agreement on salary."

Or you could avoid answering by asking a question: "What's the salary range for this position?" When they tell you, assure them that you're comfortable with that range and if they make you an offer, you won't refuse it over the money.

If you try to avoid answering, you may face opposition and may even lose the opportunity over it. But if you keep the opportunity and get the offer, then you're in a very strong negotiating position, which is a great place to be.

The whole process is a dance and the steps are not hard-and-fast moves. Take the temperature of your situation and see what you think you can manage doing.

In my personal opinion, it's not a big deal to tell them how much you made at your last job. Why? It's easy to research salary and find out what the going rate is for this job and know if what they're offering is in the ball park. And, it's easy to argue that what you made on your last job doesn't have any bearing to what you'll make at this one, because they're different jobs with different responsibilities. Usually this new job will have more responsibilities and a higher level of authority, so it only makes sense that you'd be paid more.

In my experience as a recruiter, most companies have a range budgeted and they won't make an offer outside of that range, even if what you made before was below it.

If they do try to lowball you, you have options. Now you're in the negotiation process. They want you, but you haven't come to an agreement on the price of doing business yet. I strongly encourage you to read Jack Chapman's book, **Negotiating Your Salary: How to Make $1000 a Minute**. It's the best book I've ever seen for gaining insight on this subject.

Job Interview Question 55:

What did you like or dislike about your previous jobs?

This sounds like a 'get-to-know-you' question, but don't get too comfortable. It's another way to get at your strengths and weaknesses, and you can trip yourself up. Always remember your primary focus is to sell yourself for this job. Be strategic.

Think about things that you especially liked about your past roles and that are related to this job. Think about anything that would support the case for hiring you. What factors or tasks from your past jobs will be crucial to your success in this role?

When you talk about what you disliked, try to choose something that won't be a factor in this new job. Don't unthinkingly tell them something you hated about your last job that is related to one of the main functions of this one. Easy things to choose might be the hours, the commute, the travel time, the limitations of a small company (if you're applying at a large one) or the anonymity of a large corporation (if you're applying at a small company). Try to stay away from things like complaints about your boss or co-workers. Try to be positive.

Obviously, what you disliked will be a negative for you, but you never want to be too negative in what you say when answering job interview questions because that negativity reflects on you. They won't remember the details about your answer, they'll just remember your bad attitude about it. It will influence how they think about you as a candidate.

Here's an answer I would give:

"What I liked about all my previous jobs is that they were all strong communication opportunities where when I worked hard, I was able to make things happen and I was able to be successful.

What I didn't like was when I wasn't able to be successful. Or where I perceived that I wasn't able to be as successful as I should be, or where I had to work through issues that shouldn't have been there. I can't stand bureaucracy, or having anyone stand in the way of the success of the team that I'm on."

That answer tells the interviewer very clearly that I am driven, and very focused on achievement and success. Those qualities were critical to the roles and duties I performed in sales and sales management. In that answer, I added another layer of "here's why you want me for the job." That's what you should try to do in your answer, too.

Job Interview Question 56:

What do people most often criticize about you?

Watch out for this job interview question. This is another way to ask, "What's your greatest weakness?" It is also a fishing expedition to see how well you take criticism. We all have to be open to criticism in order to grow and improve as professionals and as people. Being 'coachable' is a big plus in your favor in the eyes of your future manager or supervisor.

I don't think you can get away with saying, "People don't criticize me, and I can't think of anything." You can't go through life without stepping on toes once in a while, and we all have room for improvement.

You could try to deflect it with humor: "Well, my wife can't stand that I don't put the cap back on the toothpaste." But a serious interviewer is going to press you for a real answer.

When you answer "What do people criticize about you?" (Whether you try the humor angle or not), your big-picture strategy should be to tell them a criticism or weakness that doesn't affect your job performance and in fact, may even help it. Then show them that you can deal with criticism in general in a calm, professional manner.

For example, I have been (and am still, on a regular basis) criticized for being impatient. That's sometimes a problem in my personal life and in my relationships, but that's always been a big plus for my professional drive and success. I know I'm impatient, and I do work to rein that in when dealing with relationships, but I use it in my professional life to propel me further and faster than I would get without it.

Maybe you take things too seriously. You can say, "I've been told I take things too seriously. It's true that I tend to be a serious person. I do have a sense of humor, but I tend to be focus on getting the job done first and having fun later."

If you have a story about how you addressed a criticism and improved, that's even better: "I used to be infamous for being overly critical, which stemmed from my focus on delivering outstanding results. I want all the details to be fantastic. I still am focused on consistently delivering those results, but I have learned to be more tactful and to offer compliments and encouragement with my criticism so that others perceive it as coaching rather than criticizing and it's worked out very well."

Job Interview Question 57:

What do you consider to be your most significant accomplishment?

This is a fantastic job interview question. It sets you up to shine a giant spotlight on yourself as the ideal candidate for this job.

Never, ever answer this question by talking about something you achieved or accomplished outside of work. No stories about your kids, or how you climbed Mount Everest. Always focus your answer on work-related accomplishments.

But don't just choose a work-related answer. Choose an answer relevant to the specific job you're applying for. If you saved the company from bankruptcy in your last job, but you can't find a way to relate the skills you used to accomplish that to the ones you need for this job, it won't do you any good. Go back through your brag book, your performance reviews, everything you've got to think about a story that would highlight your fit for this job.

This is a classic behavioral interview question that requires you to put your answer in the form of a story. Don't just answer it by talking about the end result of your effort, as in "I ranked #1 among sales reps for 5 years in a row" or "I saved my company $5 million dollars last year."

That's fantastic, but if you limit your answer like that, you're missing out on some prime selling time here.

Tell the story. (Use the STAR method—Situation or Task, Action, Result.) Tell how you approached the problem or the goal or whatever it was, how you thought about it, and how you used the resources you had available to start reaching your goal or solving your problem. You can talk about what obstacles you came up against and how you overcame them.

If possible, use your brag book as supporting evidence. (If you're not familiar with these, brag books are simply a collection of "good job" documents: award letters, performance reviews, reference letters, complimentary emails, especially good examples of your work, performance stats that don't fit on your resume, etc.) If you got some award for that achievement, or even a nice email from your supervisor or a customer, show it to the interviewer when you tell what happened. It will make a powerful impression.

With a really good story, you can show your critical thinking skills, your creativity, your work ethic, your skill level—all kinds of things that help sell you for the job.

Job Interview Question 58:

What do you expect from a supervisor?

Be careful when answering this job interview question. There's a line to walk. They're looking to see: (1) do you understand the general supervisor/employee relationship, (2) will your style match with your potential new boss, and (3) will you take this opportunity to badmouth your previous boss?

Don't be too specific, don't be negative, and never, ever badmouth your previous boss.

You probably don't know too much yet about your potential supervisor's management style. If you get too specific, you might step on some toes.

Be positive when you answer this question, and try very hard to keep it neutral and generic. Now is not the time to talk about those things that irritated you about your last boss, and say things like:

"I'd like a boss who doesn't yell at everyone."

"I expect that a supervisor would not play favorites."

"I expect a boss to trust that I'm a good employee who doesn't need to be micromanaged."

You're veering off into negativity with these bad answers, and revealing more about you and how (not well) than you are giving a good answer to the question.

135

What you want to do with this question is to play it safe and think of it like a "wish list" for an ideal. Don't make it a long list...nobody's perfect. Just name two or three noble qualities that your interviewer can imagine that he or she has (maybe they really do), such as good communication skills, a sense of humor, loyalty, fairness, knowledge, leadership skills, a willingness to teach you something. Those are all good traits.

For example, I would say: "I expect a supervisor to communicate clearly, to treat me fairly, and to give me opportunities to do as much as I can for the organization."

That answer also has the added benefit of pointing out my desire to contribute and achieve within that company.

Other good answers might sound like:

"A supervisor should have good leadership and communication skills and should be able to offer constructive criticism."

"I would expect a supervisor to keep the lines of communication open with me and offer feedback when I'm doing a good job and when I have room for improvement."

"I would expect a supervisor to be adaptable to different employee's work styles and communication styles, and be willing to help employees develop additional skills to be more successful."

Job Interview Question 59:

What do you know about this company?

This is a typical interview question. Hiring managers want to know if you've done your homework. Have you done any company research?

You would be surprised at how many candidates can't answer this question. Other candidates get a basic working knowledge of what the company does from reading through the corporate website and think that's enough. If you want to really stand out among the other candidates and have a great chance of getting the job, the corporate website is only your starting point of preparing for your interview.

If you really want to be a "Wow" candidate, you have to uncover as much as you possibly can about the company before you get to the interview. You can't use the excuse that "Well, if the first interview goes well, I'll look into it more deeply then. Why spend a lot of time on something that may not go anywhere?" That's a bit of a self-fulfilling prophecy. If you don't do your research, chances are that the first interview will be your last one because you'll appear to be uninterested in the job. That failed experience will reinforce your behavior for next time, and before you know it, you'll be through several first interviews with no second interview and no job offer.

So where should you go besides the corporate website?

Google – When has the company been in the news? Do they have any plans in the works? Are there any blog articles about it?

LinkedIn – Companies put different information here than they do on their corporate pages. Also look up past and present employees, if you can.

137

Facebook- Companies' Facebook pages have still a different focus and can give you another perspective.

Twitter – Sometimes, employee Tweets tell you a lot.

Competitors – Research the company's competitors to compare.

Ask people – Tap into your network or ask your recruiter for the inside scoop.

Use what you uncover to make yourself a list of information about the company. Then when they ask you, "What do you know about us?" you can talk about their products, services, reputation, place in the market, problems, mission, history, and more. You'll be better-equipped to talk about your skills in relation to their needs, and you'll have more-informed questions to ask in the interview, too.

Then you can say something like, "I know X, Y, and Z, and that's why I am very excited about working here. I think I'm an especially good fit for you because of A, B, and C." And you've just given them another reason to hire you.

Job Interview Question 60:

What do you wish you'd done better?

When you are asked this question in job interview, please be aware that they are referring to your career, not your life. You could say that you wish you'd hired someone to tile your floor instead of doing it yourself, or that you wish you'd planned your vacation better, or you wish you'd studied more before your SATs, but those answers won't satisfy your interviewer. This is a tough job interview question.

What would you do differently in your career? What do you wish you'd done better? This question is a behavioral interview-style way to find out "what's your greatest weakness?" It's also closely-related to "What's your biggest failure?" Hiring managers know that we're onto that question the way it's normally asked, so they just ask it a different way. But with this question, you must have a story to tell.

Asking this question also is a way for them to find out about how you deal with adversity and difficult. They want to know that you are mature and that you can learn from your mistakes. It's a peek into your thought process. What they're hoping you'll be able to do is communicate a story or situation (what happened), say what you wish you'd done better, and then provide an example of when you did do it better. Because that's the ideal kind of employee—one who learns from their mistakes.

Even if you're telling them a real story about a real mistake, try to give them what they want to hear without choosing something that would directly affect your performance at this job. Nobody wants to hire an accountant who had organizational problems at her last job. Nobody wants to hire a sales rep who had an issue with a co-worker that you couldn't work out—because that shows an issue with interpersonal and communication, a fatal flaw for sales reps. So try to talk about a real mistake that you learned something significant from that would never affect your performance at this job.

For instance, that accountant might say, "It's always easier to look back to find room for improvement, isn't it? Once, I was having a disagreement with a co-worker on a project, so I went to my supervisor to try to figure out what I was doing wrong and get to a solution. My intentions were sincere, but the result was that it angered my co-worker because she thought I was trying to get her into trouble. I have learned since then that direct communication is always best, and I am very conscious about those co-worker relationships. It actually was a good experience because I am a much better communicator and team player now."

Now you're an accountant who's also got good communication skills and can be a team player. You've turned a negative into a positive. That's good job interview strategy.

Job Interview Question 61:

What excites you and scares you about this position?

This is a tough question. I think it sounds like another version of "what are your greatest advantages and disadvantages?" or another way to ask about your strengths and weaknesses. They're looking to see if you'll tell them about any issues or problems you might have, while they're assessing your enthusiasm and approach to the job.

As with most interview questions, keep it as positive as you can. I don't normally have a fear when I go into a new job and I don't think that you should voice one, either.

Why not? Well, think about this interaction you're having with this hiring manager. This process you're going through to jobs a sales process. You're the product and he (or she) is the buyer. Why would they want to choose a product that wasn't certain it could do the job? Put yourself in the buyer's shoes: would you buy something at a store that "hoped" it could do what you needed it to do, as long as nothing went wrong? Of course not. You'd buy the product that said, "I can do X...no question. I've done it before and I can do it for you."

For those reasons, the best answer is something like, "Nothing scares me about this job, and everything about it is exciting because I know that I can impact A, B, and C. I know this because I've done it before." ("A, B, and C" are those outcomes the company wants to affect with the tasks of this role.)

If you haven't actually done this job before, you can say, "I've done something very similar before." And make sure you know why and how your skills that you learned in other places transfer to this one.

Another great answer sounds like this: "I can't say that I'm scared at all about this job. I'm excited about the opportunity to exceed your expectations, and I'm excited about what the future holds for me once I do that."

If you're really pressed for an answer to the scared portion of this question, say "The only things that scare me are things that might come up that could cause me to delay my success or make success more difficult to attain. I don't see that happening, but if it did, I would find a solution." That's a positive, confident, can-do attitude.

Stay positive, confident, and focused on what you can do for them. That's what will sell you for the job.

By the way... This question is a great time to introduce your 30-60-90-day plan. Talking about what you're excited about in this job is an ideal segue to what you've put together to be successful in your first 3 months on the job. And it's an amazing bridge for any experience gaps you might have, too.

Job Interview Question 62:

What have you been doing since you got laid off?

I know…this job interview question makes you want to roll your eyes. The painfully obvious answer is, "I've been trying to find a new job!" But you can't say that.

Why would they ask you this question? It turns out, they have several good reasons for asking. There are a lot of questions behind it, and if you know what they are, you can answer it more effectively. Here's what they're really asking:

"Are you able to maintain a positive attitude in a very difficult situation?" We all face difficulties in our lives and in our jobs. They want to know that you can keep going and find solutions even in the face of a difficult situation.

"How much of a go-getter are you when no one's watching?" Do you have the energy level required for this role? If you've just been lying around for several months while you're out of work, the answer is: probably not. If you got a good severance package when you got laid off and took some time for yourself, that's OK. But you should point out to them that you've only recently begun looking: "I've just recently begun my search for a new position, and here I am with you. I am really excited about a job opportunity like this one."

"Are you able to fill your time with constructive tasks when it seems you have nothing to do?" Are you a seeker? If you've been filling your time with retraining yourself or learning something new or even completing some family task you've always wanted to do, that's great and you should talk about it.

In fact, I always recommend that, in order to stay motivated for the job search, job seekers spend no more than 4-5 hours a day actively job searching. After that, do something that helps your mental or physical state: Volunteer, learn a new skill, take a class, and even work out. Job searching is tough and you should take care of yourself while you're in the process. I know of one guy who lost 50 pounds while he was out of work. Not only was that impressive, it did wonders for his attitude and mental outlook while he was job hunting.

All of those other things: volunteering, learning a new skill, or taking a class, are powerful signals to the hiring manager that you are someone who keeps striving. You are a go-getter and if she's smart, she'll jump at the chance to have a self-starter like you on her team.

Job Interview Question 63:

What have you learned from your mistakes?

This job interview question is an opportunity for you to show them that you're a "growth" person...someone who learns from their mistakes and grows from it, developing into a stronger, smarter, better version of yourself.

If you want to keep it general, focus on universal truths or character traits. You can say that you've made mistakes in the past, and realized that there are certain universal tactics that are good to apply in any given situation: Evaluate exactly what's going on. Take in more than one opinion. Sleep on it. Don't make rash decisions. Be persistent. Show that you've matured and learned.

If they press you for an example, you need to be able to provide one, so you better have thought one up. And it should always end on a positive note.

Give your example in the form of a brief story. Use the STAR method to tell it...say what the Situation or Task you faced was, tell the Action you took that resulted in the mistake, and then go into the Results, or what you learned from it. And then take your story to the next level by telling them (if you can) about how you implemented what you learned in a different instance and succeeded. That gives you an even happier ending to your story.

A great story might sound like this: You tried something, it didn't go exactly right, you re-crafted it or made adjustments or did something different based on what you learned from the problems, and then you did it again and succeeded.

If you haven't had a chance to redo that situation with your new-found knowledge, then the story you tell is about what you learned from it and how and why you won't make that mistake again.

Both of these story structures will serve you well in the interview.

When you choose the specifics for your story, be strategic. Don't say anything damaging to the possibility of your performing well in this new role. Choose something that isn't so critical and then say what you learned.

One good example would be, "I made a mistake when I took my last job. I wasn't as critical as I should have been about what the job was really like, and when I got into it, it was completely different than what I should have pursued. Because of that, it cost me some time in my career, and it cost that company as well. I've learned to do quite a bit more research and ask more questions before I commit myself to a position."

Another might be, "I made a mistake when I was supposed to take a customer to X event, and I didn't send the final email. (Or, "I didn't give them my phone number", or whatever.) Because of that lack of communication, we missed the meeting. I learned to be meticulous about my customer communication, because very often it's those tiny details that make or break the whole thing."

Job Interview Question 64:

What is good customer service?

This question will generally be asked in interviews for retail or customer service jobs, but there's really a wide range of jobs that have contact with customers, or people who pay money for a good or service. Engineers, accountants, and manufacturers can have contact with customers, too.

I think that the best explanation of "good customer service" came from a recruiting client of mine who wanted to hire a good customer service rep. When I asked what that meant to them, they said, "Customer delight."

So in my opinion, the best answer to this question would sound like this: "Good customer service is that which delights the customer. It's what the customer says is good. It's not what you say is good. It's not what the company says is good. It's defined by the customer. The most important thing is to make the customer so happy that they will refer you to someone else. So one of the questions I always ask is, "Did I provide what you were looking for today?" because I know how vital it is to make sure I'm providing what they need so they will be delighted with us."

But any answer that indicates you're aware of how important 'customer delight' is would be fantastic. When you're speaking to a customer, you are the face of the company. You are their representative, you are in the front lines of their reputation in that arena. You matter a great deal.

Even a waitress needs to realize that she is the face of that restaurant. Diners don't see the people in the kitchen preparing their food, and they very often don't see the manager, either. They see the waitress. She has a profound impact on their experience at that restaurant, which will show up in how they feel about it, if they come back, and if they recommend it to others.

When I was in sales, I had a policy of treating every customer like I would treat my grandmother…politely, respectfully, and patiently. And I'm not a patient person. But I knew that if they had a good experience with me, they would buy from me again and they would tell others about me and my product. My customer service actions in the field would reflect in my sales numbers.

These attitudes are what you want to show the interviewer with your answer. Don't just say something like, "Good customer service is being friendly and helpful," or "Good customer service is being knowledgeable about my inventory and being able to help my customers make good decisions." Those aren't really bad answers, but you can do much better if you go one step further and talk about this idea of 'customer delight.'

Job Interview Question 65:

What's your greatest weakness?

"What's your greatest weakness?" is possibly the most annoying interview question just because of its sheer ridiculousness...your choices seem to be either to give them an obviously fake weakness (like you're a perfectionist or you work too hard...ugh!), or a real weakness (like you're disorganized or you have a bad temper), which means you might as well kiss your job offer goodbye now.

Most people stick with the safe route and go for the fake one. Do you? It turns out, the 'safe' route is not the best route.

The hiring manager's not just looking for your weakness. He doesn't really think you'll say something terrible about yourself. He's looking, among other things, at how you react to difficult. He knows that you know it's coming, so how prepared are you? And, the answer you choose will give him some insight into you and your personality.

YOU have the power to mold and shape this answer into one that serves you best (while sticking to the truth, of course).

There are several approaches, but this is the one I think will help you find your balance in this difficult answer:

Use an actual weakness that is also a strength in this job. A real weakness that might cause you a problem in other areas of your life but actually helps you achieve in this job. But for the most part, don't ever choose perfectionism, because it's too much of a cliché by now.

For instance, I always used impatience as my weakness. No one can argue that impatience isn't a real weakness. It is, and it's caused me problems. But impatience is also something that's driven me to succeed faster than other people. It's something that made me a better sales rep. I didn't want to wait for that sale, I was pushing to see if I could get it now.

Someone else could answer that they get frustrated with people who don't work as quickly as they do—which says that you work fast and are dedicated.

It seems more honest than talking about a weakness that you've overcome already—that's not your greatest weakness anymore, is it? But you absolutely can talk about ways you deal with and minimize the negative effects of the one you have.

Thinking about the greatest weakness question this way requires a little more creativity and thoughtfulness on your part, but the strategic advantages you'll gain from it in your interview will be worth it.

Job Interview Question 66:

What is your ideal job?

In a personality test, this question may not be so easy to answer. But in a job interview, it's one of the easiest questions you'll be asked.

Question: What's your ideal job?

Answer: This one.

As far as they are concerned, your ideal job is the one you're interviewing for right now.

In asking this question, your interviewer is trying to find out if you'll be happy and productive in this position, with this company, or if you just want anything with a paycheck. So it's a little bit like answering the question, "Why do you want to work here?" They want to know that it's about more than the money.

So you can answer it from that point of view if you want. You can't actually be flip and say, "This one!" but you can talk about certain aspects of this job and how they fulfill personal goals and desires for you and that's why you got into this line of work and then tie it into why this particular job with this particular company is such a good fit for you.

This is yet another place where the company research you do before the interview will benefit you tremendously. If you've done your interview prep right, you can add those elements that make it clear that you are interested in this job, with this company.

"I really believe my ideal job is this one because I love X, Y, and Z, that's why I went into this area as a career. But I particularly am excited about this job with this company, because of what I've learned about how you handle ABC. It seems like an ideal environment to do what I love to do."

Or you could keep it more general and say something like:

My ideal job is one that I enjoy going to each day, where I can make an impact and be rewarded for it, and others notice that I'm making an impact and continue to grow in that way.

Do you see? You're talking about other rewards besides the money that make it worth it for you to get up and come to work every day. It shows that you're thoughtful and sincere and that you've thought about your fit for this role, which almost always means you'll be more successful.

Your answer here will speak to your enthusiasm for the job and ultimately, your success.

Job Interview Question 67:

What is your least favorite managerial task?

With this question, they're trying yet again to get a feel for any potential weaknesses you'll bring to the job, without asking directly about your weaknesses. Hiring managers are fully aware that you'll be ready for the 'weakness' question, but maybe not so prepared for this one...so they hope they'll get an honest answer. Are you irritated by the details? Are you impatient with subordinates and their issues?

A side benefit for the interviewer is that your answer should also give them an idea of your management style. Are you task-oriented? Results-oriented? Focused on mentoring and developing your subordinates? What you don't like will give them a clue about what you do like and how you work.

If you get asked about your least favorite **anything** that has to do with your job, I sincerely hope you pick something that is a very small, insignificant part of your to-do list!

For instance, for a management role, you'd generally never want to say you dislike meetings (which are necessary for planning), filing reports (upper management needs to know what's going on), training employees (your job is to make them better), or sticking to a budget. Key responsibilities differ greatly depending on the job, so you had better do your homework and know very clearly what your job responsibilities will be so that you don't inadvertently say the wrong thing.

I once had a candidate say something that he hated that was actually a key part of his job. Obviously, he didn't get that position.

So, it's got to be a small part, and it's got to be something that everybody can see is distasteful. Here's an answer that I would give:

"For me, my least favorite task has always been firing people. I hate that. It doesn't mean that I would shy away from it if it had to be done, because we all have to do things we don't like to do for the sake of the organization or the goal, and you can make that clear in regard to yourself, too. You don't like it, but you will do the things that are necessary for the organization to be successful."

In fact, any task you choose as your least favorite should be immediately followed up with an acknowledgment of the necessity of doing even those tasks we don't enjoy in order to further the continued success of the organization. This will show your maturity and your professionalism.

Job Interview Question 68:

What kind of money would you be interested in making?

Hiring managers always want to know how much you're going to cost, so they'll ask the salary question a hundred different ways: "How much did you make at your last job?" "What are your salary expectations?" Or this one, "How much money do you want to make?" As much as you would like to say, "I'm interested in making as much money as I can!" you can't say that. Even if it's true. (Wouldn't we all?)

The truth is that for most jobs it doesn't matter so much how much you would be interested in making. This job has a range and it pays what it pays. It's up to you to do your salary research to find out what a reasonable salary range is for this particular position in this particular area of the country. If you have more experience or special skills that you're bringing to the party, you can reasonably expect to be on the high end of the scale. If you don't have that much experience, you're probably going to fall on the lower end.

The only exception would be in sales jobs that work entirely on commission. For those jobs, the salary range really is up to you, and your answer to this question needs to present you as a strong, energetic, driven, determined professional who is willing and able to do what it takes to make the sale and ring that cash register. They will love that answer because the more you make, the more they make. Your success will make your sales manager look great.

Still, the basic idea with all salary negotiation is to try to avoid being the first one to say an actual number. So when they ask you, "How much money do you want to make?" my first piece of advice is to turn it back to them and ask, "What is the salary range you have budgeted for this position?" If they tell you, you can say, "That seems like a reasonable range for this job. If we agree that I'm the best fit for the position, I would be comfortable with an offer in that range."

If they don't let it go and instead press you for an answer, you can say, "I've done some research and I understand that the going rate for this job falls somewhere between X and Y dollars. Is that the range you're offering?" You're still dodging a number, and asking a question that throws it back in their laps. If they tell you that in fact, it is what they're offering, you can again offer reassurance that you would be comfortable with that range if you agree that you're the person for the job.

Job Interview Question 69:

What makes you unique?

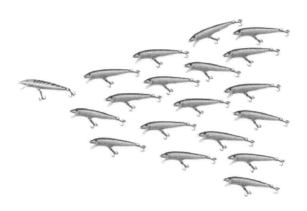

What are hiring managers really asking when they ask about what makes you unique? Well, they don't want to know about what makes you special on a personal level. They want to know what makes you unique in relation to the job you're interviewing for. Essentially, they're asking, "Why should we hire you?" "Why should we choose you over everyone else?" "What makes you different from the other candidates?"

What makes you unique is your individual blend of education, experiences, skill sets, and personality. Sometimes it's not the particular job on your resume that makes you appeal to hiring managers. Sometimes it's an aggregate of the different pieces that you're bringing to the table. Maybe you have strong communication skills, and experience in the industry, and experience in advertising and that ends up being the mix that attracts that hiring manager to you.

Think about what makes you unique and what makes you valuable, and then think about WHY it makes you valuable. You can even quantify your answer of how in the past, your blend of experiences has proven valuable to previous employers.

"Because of my background in X, I was uniquely positioned to take advantage of Y when I worked on ABC project. I completed it faster and with better results than anyone else in the company."

"I believe that my education in X combined with my experience in Y work together to give me an especially great advantage when approaching ABC. I draw on both to solve both every day issues and special challenges. For example, in X Situation, I took Y action and got Z results."

"My background in X is different from most people in the field, and that gives me a unique perspective and the ability to see solutions that are more creative and resourceful. For example, I came up with X solution to solve Y problem, and it worked out beautifully." (A few numbers that prove that success would be outstanding to include here.)

If the quality or the success rate of your work is outstanding, that's valuable to an employer because it saves them time, money, and aggravation. But you have to think about why it is that you are especially successful and be able to articulate that.

Whatever you say, now is the time to brag. You must show that your particular blend of education, experiences, skill sets and personality is the solution they need to solve the problems they have.

Job Interview Question 70:

What motivates you?

What's the one big elephant in the room that MUST be ignored with the motivation question? All together now: "Money."

As much as the money question is a big part of why you work, employers want to think that you're also doing this because you love it. And you should love it. You can make money doing a lot of different things, so you should enjoy the job you choose to do.

The reason hiring managers ask this question is that they want to know what makes you tick and that you have your own reasons for working hard and achieving goals that have nothing to do with them and the paycheck. People who are motivated by some other force than the direct monetary reward work harder and do better at their jobs.

To answer this classic job interview question, be strategic and relate what motivates you to your skill set and your fit for the job. This is an ideal place to show your enthusiasm for the work, and that's very appealing to hiring managers.

A great answer strategy is to try to think about some project that you really enjoyed and pinpoint what it is that really motivated you to work on it and do a good job. Talk about the project and what you enjoyed about it, and how it relates to something that you'd be doing in this job.

If you're in project management, talk about how you love to orchestrate the process of a successful project and see all the different parts and pieces come together to a conclusion and then name a complicated project you worked on, talk briefly about the challenges of it, and tell how it turned out.

If you're in sales, talk about how you are motivated by a sales target because you are so competitive. And then tell about how you met and exceeded your sales numbers last year.

If you are in customer service, talk about how you love to uncover a customer's needs, solve their problem and end the interaction on a positive note. And then you could maybe throw in an example of a particularly difficult customer issue that you solved.

Bottom line: Keep your answer positive and use it to point to a significant accomplishment.

If you do that, you can hit two birds with one stone: You can sell your enthusiasm for the job along with your skill and fit.

Job Interview Question 71:

What questions do you have for us?

By the end of the interview, when they ask if you have any questions for them, you probably feel like you're toast. You're just done, and you want to go home. That's the way most people feel, so the most common response to this question is, "I don't have any questions, I think you've covered everything."

That's bad, bad, bad. It's one of the things you should never say in a job interview. It makes you look uninterested in the job.

The best questions to ask are those that make it clear you've been listening to what their main problems and concerns are. Clarify, elaborate, or dig deeper. There are lots of good questions to ask.

You can ask about the timeline: "How soon do you want to have someone in the role?" That shows you are motivated to get started quickly.

You can ask about the last person who was in this role. If the person who had the position before was promoted, ask, "Is that a traditional track for this job?" If the person who was in the role before wasn't meeting expectations, ask, "Can you tell me how they weren't meeting expectations so I could understand?"

If you're speaking with your direct future boss, ask about the biggest challenges of the job and can he see you meeting those challenges?

If you're speaking with the Human Resources Manager, ask about the company, the growth of the department, where it fits in relation to the rest of the company, and so on.

If you're speaking with upper management, ask questions that demonstrate your understanding of the industry as a whole and this company's place in it and its plans for the future.

This is not the time to ask about anything that would benefit you, like salary, vacations, or perks. At this point, they're like your customer. It's all about them right now, not you. Remember that the job interview is a sales process and you have to keep selling, or keep showing them all the different reasons why you'd be a good fit for them until they say, "yes, we want to hire you." You don't have to keep asking an endless round of more and more questions. Just ask a few more questions that show your interest, enthusiasm, and concern for their problem (which is the job that isn't getting done until they put someone in that role).

Continue the conversation and ask questions to find out more details that will help you move in the direction of uncovering more of their motivations, needs, and wants you can so you can better position yourself as the candidate they want.

Job Interview Question 72:

What salary are you looking for?

I hope that you know beyond a shadow of a doubt that you are never to bring up money in the interview, at any time, until they make you an offer—until they say, "yes, you're the one, let's come to terms." Curbing your enthusiasm until then will serve you in the end.

Bringing up money too soon is a job interview mistake. You'll look like the paycheck is all you care about, and that's a big turnoff for hiring managers, understandably. And if you wait until they feel like they've got to have you, then the money conversation ends up being a lot more in your favor. People are usually willing to pay a little more for a product they're already sold on.

However, it's pretty common for the interviewer to try to pin you down on salary before you get to that point. They are very interested in how much you're going to cost by asking about your salary expectations as soon as they can. It's only natural for them to want to find out as much as they can, but if you let go of that too soon, it can hurt your salary negotiations later.

As in most job interview situations, you've got a couple of good options:

You can try to deflect with some humor by asking: "Does that mean you're making me an offer?"

You can turn the question back to them and say: "What's the range you have set for this position?" When they tell you, you can say, "I'm comfortable with that. If you decide that I'm a good fit for the job and I decide it's a good fit for me, I will be completely fine with discussing a salary in that range."

Or you can be more straightforward and say, "I'm really interested in finding out more about the job and telling you more about me so that we can see if we're a good fit before we start talking about the money."

If that doesn't feel comfortable, you can say, "I'm looking for a great opportunity, and I'm sure you'll offer a salary that's commensurate with the responsibility of this job."

What all of these answers do is help you deflect the question. You want to do overall is to put that discussion off for as long as possible.

You want the focus to be on selling yourself for the job—because if they don't want to hire you, the money doesn't matter anyway. You don't have anything to talk about, really, until they're ready to say yes to hiring you.

Job Interview Question 73:

What type of work environment do you prefer?

The best answer to this job interview question of what work environment do you prefer is the same answer you'd give to "What's your ideal job?" The correct answer is: "This one."

Of course, you need to respond with the type of work environment that they have, or at least close to it, or you're not going to get the job.

But, you don't just want to get the offer...you want to get a job that fits you as well.

Since you don't know exactly what their work environment is like, it's best to answer by talking about how flexible you are, and then following that up with "What would you say the environment is here?" Or, "How would you describe the environment here?"

Here's a good, positive example:

"I have preferred [X-type] of environment in the past, but I love new experiences and what I can learn from them. I see a different type of environment as a new way to develop additional skills. What would you say the work environment is like here?"

The work environment could be fast-paced, technology-based, customer-focused, high-tech, internet-based, retail-based...it could be anything. Maybe they'll say that they are very creative and loose, or highly-structured, or like nothing you've ever seen before.

When they tell you, you'll get either (a) a really good idea that you're going to hate this job and it's a good thing you found out now; or (b) certain words or phrases from them that will make you say, "I thrive in that type of environment."

With a better idea of the type of work environment they have, you can elaborate on your answer to talk about how you are so enthusiastic about being able to be a part of that, or how you have done well in other environments like theirs, and therefore expect to do well in theirs, too.

The job interview really isn't just a hurdle for you to cross in order for you to get the job. It's really supposed to be a way for both parties to get to know one another. They want to know if you're going to fit in, be happy and do well there. Hiring you is an expensive proposition for them, and a risk. Can you do the job? Are you going to be happy in their company culture? And you need to know if this is a place you'll be happy to spend a large portion of your waking time, and if it will be good for your long-term career. This question is a way to have that necessary conversation.

Job Interview Question 74:

What was the last book you read?

It doesn't matter if the last book you read was an actual paper variety with a spine and real pages or the digital version on your Kindle. If you read on a regular basis, it usually means that you're someone who's intelligent, curious, and interested in personal growth and learning. It also usually means you're a good communicator. For some interviewers, that's all they want to know. For others, they are hoping you'll indicate that you're keeping up with the reading in your field…that you're on top of trends, or the latest information. There are so many things we can learn from reading and it's a big plus for most people and most jobs.

The first rule when answering this question is: Do not lie about the last book you read. Ever. Do not name a book unless you have read it. I once interviewed someone who did lie about it and it was horrible. I caught him in the lie because I had just read the book he named. When I asked him what he thought about something in the book, of course he couldn't tell me and was completely embarrassed, and it left me wondering what else he was lying about.

Anticipate that you might get this question and think about a book you can read and talk about. Think about that book a little bit before you go into the interview because you might just get someone like me who reads a lot and will want to discuss it with you.

Ideally, you can talk about a book that pertains to your job or your industry. It can be something you read just for enjoyment, but try not to name a romance novel, "Fifty Shades of Grey," anything from the

"Twilight" series, or anything you might be embarrassed to be seen with in front of your more "educated" friends. It won't make the interviewer see you the way you need to be seen in order to look good in the interview and get this job offer.

I think that one of the best things you can do for your career, and especially in your job search, is to read books that will help you be more knowledgeable about your field. Something that will help you be better than you were before. My best advice is to go find some of those books and start reading. It will give you some interesting material for your next interview.

Job Interview Question 75:

What was your least favorite part of your last job?

Why does the hiring manager want to know about your least favorite part of your last job? Because they want to find out more about you, and they are hoping to uncover any potential problems before they hire you. What you say and the way you say it will tell them a lot more than you think.

The basic job interview strategy you want to follow with answering this question is to keep the emphasis on the positive rather than the negative and be logical (strategic). Don't tell them something you didn't like that you will find in this job. Don't give them a reason not to hire you.

You never want to go too negative with this answer, either, even though it's about things you don't like. Something like, "I didn't like my manager," or "I didn't get along with my co-workers" is always bad because of what it says about you, that maybe you're the one who's difficult to get along with. You never want to talk about how the workload was killing you, even if it really was unreasonable, because it makes you look like you can't handle the job.

But the answer has to be something you didn't like, so try to make sure it is not something that's a factor in this job. If you didn't like that you had no opportunities for promotion, make sure that there are advancement opportunities in the new job. If you weren't given the chance to be creative, make sure there's plenty of creativity built into this job. If you weren't challenged, say, "I didn't have as much of a chance as I wanted to use my skills in X, Y, and Z and expand my knowledge in this field. That's why I'm so looking forward to being able to utilize those skills and grow and develop into greater responsibility here."

Maybe you could even talk about things outside of the job, like "my last job required me to drive an hour every day to get there, and that commute really cuts into my day. This job is just a few minutes from my house. Not only am I really excited about the job itself, but I'm also excited about being so close and getting rid of that commute."

So, the bottom line is, don't make it personal. Give them an answer of something that will automatically change as a result of you getting this job.

Job Interview Question 76:

What was your most difficult work experience and how did you deal with it?

This is a great opportunity to talk about how you've overcome a challenge and ended up a winner! You can talk about how you stepped up to a difficult situation and got a good outcome, or how you overcame something that was holding you back in your job (maybe you learned a new skill).

Because this is a classic behavioral interview question, you want to use the STAR format to talk about this: Describe the Situation or Task (what was going on), the Action you took (what you did) and the Result (what happened). You can also talk about how you would do it differently if you had it to do over.

Basically, you want to describe this difficult work experience, how you analyzed it, how you possibly brought in other resources to solve it, and how it turned out OK. And if you can quantify, it's even better. What do I mean when I say "quantify"?

Quantifying your answer just means adding numbers, dollars, or percentages to your description of it. So instead of saying "I improved sales," you're going to say, "I improved sales by 30%".

- "I wrote customer emails," becomes "I wrote customer emails that brought in 10 new customers per month."

- "I was known for delivering all my projects on time" becomes "My project delivery was 100% on time."
- "I was a top student in my class" becomes "I ranked #2 in a class of 400, with a 3.9 GPA."

It's much more powerful and attention-getting to add those numbers, dollars, and percentages to your accomplishments. You're saying the same thing, but with more preciseness. You're adding evidence. This is a skill you need to know for both your interview answers and your resume, too. Numbers matter.

Then, your answer sounds more like: "Once, I faced X situation. It was a big problem because of ABC. I realized that our biggest obstacle was Y, so I put some thought into it [you'd want to say what that thought process was here] and decided to do Z. It worked out really well. Because of that, we saw a revenue jump of $10,000 that month."

But it doesn't have to be dollars. It could be that you saved time, increased accuracy, decreased loss, increased customer numbers (without naming dollar amounts), or anything that you can describe by saying "how many" or "how much." That's the way to end your answer and be more impressive in the interview.

Job Interview Question 77:

What were the major challenges of your last job and how did you handle them?

This is a tough job interview question to answer because the major challenges of your last job typically are going to be the key job skills that you're bringing to the new one. (The exception being if you're a brand new graduate or transitioning careers). Since most jobs you interview for build on the job you had before, you're actually likely to be talking about the job skills that you're going to take on in this new role.

You always want to be positive about your job skills. If you successfully dodged the weakness question, you don't want to get caught in this one.

The idea you want to go with here is to talk about a few of the major situational challenges you faced in your last role that you handled successfully—using your key job skills, if possible. Or, you could even choose a challenge that you dealt with using your key job skills, plus some other supplementary skill that you bring to the table that makes you a unique and valuable employee.

You want to use the STAR format to put it together. (STAR stands for Situation or Task, Action you took, and Results you got.) There's nothing magic about the format. It just ensures that you give a complete answer, and that you end on a positive note: a result.

First, explain what the challenge was and why it was important. Then take them through your thought process: Did you have to research new information? Did you have to call in additional resources? What resources did you bring in? Then, tell them how it ended up. If you can quantify your result, do it.

If you can, choose challenges that highlight the top skills they want someone to have in this role. You can have a story or two in your mind when you go to the interview if you are very familiar with the job

173

description and the company. (This is yet another reason to do your homework and research the job and the company before you interview.)

With all behavioral interview questions, the hiring manager wants to know how you handled a past situation so that he can see how you might handle a future similar situation. Keep this story positive, don't badmouth anyone when telling it, and focus on the results you got from your actions.

Job Interview Question 78:

What were your responsibilities in your last job?

Your answer to this question about your job responsibilities depends entirely on the role you played in your last job. What were your major responsibilities? You want to list those out.

A reasonable person might think, "Why would they ask about the responsibilities of my last job? It says right there on my resume what my last job was." The trouble is that job titles and the actual work they entail don't always match up the way you think they're going to. One company's Customer Support Specialist might have entirely different duties than another's. Or maybe you would assume that a Manager might do certain things based on that title, but in reality, they don't in that company. It's best never to assume. So they ask. And they want to see your perception of your job, too.

It's a good thing that they do ask, because this is a great opportunity for you to point out what a great fit you are for this job.

Start with the biggest responsibility you had, or the one that is most relevant to the job you're interviewing for. Because you want to sell yourself, right? How you present yourself in the interview is all up to you. Choose wisely the responsibilities you talk about.

So if this role is an operations role, you want to start talking about your operations responsibilities.

If it's a finance role, you want to talk about your finance responsibilities.

You want to make that connection to what matters to this manager. Pick the top 3 or 4 responsibilities, briefly talk about them and say, "I believe that's one of the reasons why I'm a great fit for this job. What I've done before is very similar to what I'd be doing for you. I've been very successful at it, and I can be successful for you, too."

If you've done your research and carefully read the job requirements, this should be easy.

What if your previous job wasn't similar to this one? Well, then, now is the time for you to show your transferable skills. Something you did in your old job developed a skill you can use in this new one. When you answer, connect those dots for the hiring manager and sell yourself for the job.

One warning: Don't lie about your previous job responsibilities. The hiring manager can and most likely will check your references, and when they do, you will be caught. Besides, the best way to prove that you can do the job even though you haven't before is not a lie, it is a 30/60/90-day plan. That's very convincing evidence that you've got what it takes for the job.

Job Interview Question 79:

What will you contribute to this job?

This question is very similar to "Why should we hire you?" Or, "Why do we want you over the other candidates?" The job interview is a sales process in which you are the product and the hiring manager and company is the buyer. Your salary is the price of the product, you and your skill sets. It's fair for them to ask, "What are we going to get for our money?"

If they ask you what you'll contribute, rejoice. This is a softball question. It's an ideal time to sell yourself for the job. If you get this, you're golden.

So how do you approach it? You want to be thinking about what they've asked for in the job description. You should have already connected your skill sets to what they're asking for in this role. You can also get some priceless additional insight into what they're looking for when you ask questions during the interview.

One great question to ask early on in the interview is, "What does your ideal candidate look like?" They'll give you a wish list that might include things that aren't in the description. Take in all that information and talk about how you have what they're looking for plus a little extra. That "plus a little extra" is important.

They're already looking at candidates who meet their requirements. Show them how you meet and exceed those requirements. Maybe that's more experience, additional background that allows you to bring a different perspective, or character traits like your strong work ethic or driven personality. That's "extra" is what's going to set you apart as a unique candidate. Sum that up in a positive way that sells you for the job.

This is also an ideal time to bring out your **30/60/90-day plan.** This plan is an outline for what you will do in the first 3 months on the job. It covers any on-the-job training, getting up to speed, and how you'll become a fully-functioning employee. Hiring managers love these things because they show that you are someone who goes the extra mile and can put some critical thought into the job and how you'll be successful at it. They say, "What will you contribute?" And you say, "I'm so glad you asked. I've written up a plan that shows you how I will bring myself up to speed quickly in the job and start contributing by doing X, Y, and Z." And then you've launched into that conversation, which will elevate your interview conversation in a big way.

Job Interview Question 80:

What will you do if you don't get this position?

This question is mostly likely to be asked when you're interviewing for an internal job or promotion. You're probably going up against other candidates in the company, and maybe even some external candidates, too. They're worried about how you'll take it if you don't get the job, and they want to know if you're more interested in the good of the company or just in your own career advancement.

If this is the case, a good answer would tell them that you're a team player who is interested in the good of the company.

For example: "Of course, I will support whoever you choose to fill this position, and I'll keep doing the great job I always do. But I do think that I'm a great fit for this role because of X, Y, and Z, and that I would be the best choice." (A bad answer would be: "I'll assume that you're never going to appreciate me and I'll be looking for someone who does.")

However, you might get asked this question in a regular job interview, where you're new to the company. Maybe they're fishing to see where else you're applying, maybe they want to know how serious you are about your job search. You don't need to tell them where else you're applying, but by all means let them know that you are committed to getting a new job and that you will be a great asset for someone somewhere. Here's an example:

179

"I would really like to get the job here, because I think I'm a great fit. I'm excited about your company because of the work you do in A, B, and C. But if I don't get the job, I'm going to go on living and breathing, and I'm going to find someone else who's going to appreciate my skill sets, and I'm going to get to work doing what I do best. They're going to really appreciate it, and I'm going to drive their business." (Or increase their productivity, reduce their costs, increase their market share, improve their customer service, whatever it is that would apply in your situation.)

You're going to do all those great things in a role similar to this one in another company. You'd like for it to be here, but if not, it will be somewhere else. You are that determined. You are going to get a job.

That's a strong, positive answer that shows that you are confident in yourself and your abilities.

Job Interview Question 81:

What would you do first at this job?

When they ask you this question in the interview, they want to get a picture of how you would be in the role. How you answer tells them about your personality and your work style. Do you attack it from day one? Do you take it all in and analyze it first?

If it were me, I would answer it like this: "The first thing I would do is get to know all the systems and parts and pieces I need to know in order to be successful at the job. I would want to define what my end goal was and then work backwards from there and make sure that I know everything I need to be successful at this."

And then I would introduce my 30/60/90-day plan: "I'm glad you asked that, because I have been doing a lot of thinking about this question and I came up with a working list of what I would do in the first 3 months. Can I get your input on that to see if I'm on the right track?"

A 306090-day plan is a written outline for what you will do in your first 3 months on the job. It covers any training you need, learning about the company, getting up to speed, and launching off on your own great things. It's very impressive to hiring managers because it shows your knowledge of the job, your drive, energy, and initiative, and your commitment to success.

Using your plan, you walk them though your thought process and you have your discussion about your first 90 days on the job. You talk, you ask questions, they clarify, and you become cemented in their minds as a fantastic candidate. This discussion is guaranteed to be a more in-depth, better conversation about you in that role than any standard list of job interview questions and answers will allow you to have.

(Even if you chicken out and don't bring your actual plan into the interview, you still should do the interview prep work of creating a plan, so that you have something solid to say in answer to this question. They're that good for preparing you and transforming you into the most knowledgeable candidate.)

Just walk them through what you think would make you successful on the job, and ask questions as you go that confirm it and keep you on the right track.

Job Interview Question 82:

What would your friends tell me about you?

This question could also easily be "What would your friends or co-workers tell me about you?" They just want to know what you would say about how other people would describe you.

Asking you about what your friends would tell the interviewer about you seems like an odd question, doesn't it? But there are lots of reasons an interviewer might ask it: (1) they want to know how you will potentially get along with your co-workers; (2) they want to see if what you say makes sense with what they're seeing in you during the interview; and (3) they're just looking for more of your personality to see if you're going to be a good cultural fit for the company.

If it were me, I would say, "My friends would tell you the same thing my references would tell you: that I'm high-energy, I'm competitive, and I'm driven to succeed. I have those same qualities in my personal life as I do in my professional life." Those happen to be great qualities for someone in sales (as I was).

Just choose 3 or 4 positive traits you possess that would be a plus for someone in that job. That's part of a good job interview strategy. Always be able to tie your answer back to something that would recommend you for the job.

Other great qualities employers might be looking for? Reliable, dedicated, hard-working, honest, organized, trustworthy, efficient, positive, dynamic, strategic, detail-oriented, motivated, self-starter, calm, caring, empathetic, loyal, a leader, professional, flexible, adaptable, a quick learner. It depends on you and your job.

The key: Be consistent. Don't say something that your references will contradict. Either the interviewer will notice the distinct lack of a similar response in your references, or they might even just come out and ask, "Do you think Suzie is someone who ___?" And if they get a long pause as a response, you have just damaged your chances very badly.

Here's a hint: Go back though your performance appraisals and look for descriptive words there. An even better idea is to pick a few trusted people (mentors, previous bosses, past or current co-workers) and ask them what impression you give to others. What 3 words would they choose to describe you? You have to be a little bit brave with this one. It can be a difficult question to ask. But the answers you get will help you both answer this question and help you make sure you are projecting the image you want to project in this job search.

Job Interview Question 83:

What would your manager say was the area you needed most development in?

This question might also sound like, "What would your boss say you need to improve on?" No doubt about it…impressing your boss is always important, and we all have things about ourselves that we could improve on. As with all interview questions, be thoughtful and strategic with how you answer it.

This question is an obvious effort to find out more about your weaknesses, so think about it like the weakness question. There are several strategies you can take: name a real weakness that would be irrelevant for this job, or name a strength that could be even better.

If you name a weakness, it must be something that won't matter or have an effect on your performance in this job, and it's even better if the weakness is something that helps you in your job even though it might hold you back in your personal life.

If you name a strength, it must not be an essential strength you need for good performance on this job.

For instance, if you are a project manager, obviously you wouldn't say you needed better organizational skills. But you also don't want to say that you could have better communication skills. That's a pretty big deal for someone who coordinates people, things, and deadlines. Maybe you would say that you needed to improve on your patience, as in, you sometimes get impatient with the pace of progress, because you are so focused on getting the job done.

In my case, I would say something about needing more detail-management (not a factor in whether or not I make the sale, but also something that nearly everyone could benefit from some improvement in), but then I would talk about the steps I am currently taking to either correct or eliminate that as an issue—organizational software, a great app, something. Talk about how you are correcting the problem, and then give an instance where the steps you are taking worked.

If you are lucky enough that your current boss is going to be one of your references, one great strategy is to get with him or her ahead of time and go over what they might say in response to general job interview questions about your strengths, your weaknesses, your greatest accomplishments, etc. Prepping your references before the interview is a fantastic, proactive thing to do. And in this particular instance, you can make sure you're on the same page so that your answers don't conflict.

Job Interview Question 84:

What can you do to make this company better?

There are a million ways for an interviewer to ask "Why should we hire you?" and this is one of them. They want to know what benefits you as an employee are bringing to the table, and it's right for them to ask. The job interview is where you sell yourself for the job. That doesn't mean you have to act like a stereotypical salesman…it just means that you need to know what the needs of this company are…what problems they have that you can solve. And then you have to be able to articulate to them how you can solve them…how you've solved them before, how you've solved similar problems, how you perform in similar situations.

This question is a great place for you to be strategic in your answer. You want to start with the job itself and with your conversation with them about their biggest problems and what they need help with…or what they need changed or what they need a solution for. And hopefully somewhere in your conversation you've asked them what their biggest concerns are for this position and what their biggest goals are. Remind them that you're first going to attack those problems and come up with solutions for them.

And then you say, that's the first way I'll make the company better, because when I take care of those A, B, C things that we talked about, that makes D, E, and F better for you. And then that affects G, H, and I.

So just by doing those things, I'm going to have a positive ripple effect on the company and as I learn more and expand my responsibilities, I will be able to positively impact the company in other ways.

You're painting a verbal picture for them so that they can see you in the job with all the benefits and positive impact you'll bring to the organization in a variety of ways.

You can do this in just your conversation, but this is really an ideal spot to introduce your 30/60/90-day plan, and that will make you into an even stronger candidate, whether you have experience or not. A written-out plan for what you're going to do in the first 90 days will show them that you are someone who can size up a situation, analyze it, and create a plan of action to reach your goals. That's an incredibly impressive skill, and if you go to that much trouble before you even get the job, they will be amazed.

Job Interview Question 85:

Where do you see yourself in 5 years?

In other words, are you going to bail on them in a few months for another job, or stick around and make their training and investment in you pay off? Is this a stepping stone on your career path, or a job to pay the bills until you can do what you really want to do?

This is a tough question. It's difficult to predict that far ahead, and plans change anyway. They do want to hear that you plan to stick around for a while and grow and develop with the company. If you're an "over 50" candidate, don't say that you'll be thinking about retirement. You want to give the impression that you are still looking forward to learning and growing and working, not looking forward to golf.

Many, many people believe that the best answer is some version of: "I see myself in your job!" or, "I want to be in management" because they think it shows ambition. That is not always the best answer.

If you're interviewing with a very large company, it might be just fine for you to talk about your desire to be promoted and to grow within the company. There's room for you to do that in a large corporation.

But if you are interviewing with a smaller company, an answer like that just might be considered a threat to that person's job. If they don't have anywhere to go, they're certainly not going to let you push them out.

A much better answer (in both situations, really) is to say something more along the lines of "I want to grow and develop my skills," or "I want to be all I can be." You can talk about how you look forward to greater responsibility as you learn more about the company, and that you hope to be ready to do more things. Then you can say, "If you are looking at me for a management position at that time, I would be interested in it, but that's not necessarily my end goal. What I really want out of this is to learn, to grow, and to contribute in a meaningful way."

There is no hiring manager who won't be impressed by a strategic job interview answer like that.

Job Interview Question 86:

Who was your best boss and who was your worst?

This question tests several things about you and gives a lot of information to the interviewer:

- Are you adaptable?
- Can you get along with a wide variety of people?
- Do you carry grudges?
- Do you fit their company's cultural style?
- Do you fit your potential hiring manager's leadership?
- How do you react to negative situations?

Your overall goal to keep in mind is to stay positive and communicate that you can work with any boss in any situation.

To do that, you can't get too specific in what you expect in a supervisor when you talk about how great a particular boss was. If your potential boss for this job doesn't match what you say, you won't get hired. At the same time, you can't start in on how bad one boss was. Even if you can tell a story that has people howling with laughter at parties, you can't tell that story here. Any hint of negativity only makes you look like a negative person to the interviewer.

A great answer in response to "Who was your best boss?" sounds something like, "I've been so lucky to have had some great bosses that I've learned a lot from. They have all had some characteristic or habit or knowledge that I've been able to learn so much from." And then maybe you can say something you learned from one boss in particular that touches directly on your fit for this job: maybe it's a skill or a habit or something that makes you extremely good at what you do.

A great response for "Who was your worst boss?" sounds more like, "I did have a boss who I inherited. I didn't choose him and he didn't choose me and our communication styles were very different. We got along OK and I succeeded with him but it wasn't like it was with other managers."

Why is that a good response? Because you've chosen something vague enough that it won't come back to bite you in this interview, and you kept the outcome positive (meaning you hold no grudges, it was just one of those things, and you were still successful). You never want to badmouth a previous boss.

Try to spin any negative experience into a positive learning experience for you that made you better or stronger than you were before, that you will carry right into this new job.

Job Interview Question 87:

Why are you looking to leave your current job?

It's very important that you think about this well before you set foot in an interview. Interviewers always want to know why, and you must have a good answer ready to go.

This can be a delicate subject, because most people don't leave a job that's a positive situation for them. The sticking point is that you never want to appear negative about anything in a job interview because it reflects so badly on you, so you absolutely can't say anything negative in this answer. This is not where you start talking about all the things you don't like about your current job or your current boss. First of all, it doesn't matter, and second of all, it will only make you look like a whiny complainer to this person. And it will make them think, "Wow, if he'll dish all this dirt about them, what will he say about us?"

If you must give a reason, make sure it's something neutral (by 'neutral' I mean: not negative) that is a factor in your old job and is not a factor in your new one.

For instance, if this job requires no travel, you could say, "There's a lot of travel in the old job and I'm ready to be at home in my own bed more often."

Or you could say, if you're moving from a small company to a big one: "I've loved my time at XYZ Company and learned many skills, but there's just not much room for growth at higher levels there and I'm ready to move up."

Or if the new job is in another city, you can say, "I hate to leave that company; they've been very good to me, but I am moving to this area and need something that's closer to home."

Be as brief as you can. Mostly what you want to do here is focus on how it's not that you're running away from that job, it's that you're running to this job. And give them a reason you're running to this job: it is such a great fit, it offers so many things you're looking for, and so on… Be as specific as you can about what it is that you're running to with this company. Why do you like them? Why is it a great fit for you? Tell them that, and you'll have a great answer.

Job Interview Question 88:

Why did you freelance for so long?

A lot of people have taken up freelancing, consulting, or other independent work in the last few years just out of necessity. In many industries, it's been difficult to find a job. Others have struck out on their own because there has been just so much opportunity—especially in consulting, writing, graphic design, web programming, web, and online marketing. Whatever your situation was, employers are going to have questions about your reasons for doing what you did and consequently, why you want to work for their company now. Do your job interview prep and be ready.

Whatever you do, **don't** give an answer like these:

- "I liked it, but I need insurance."
- "No one would hire me, so I did what it took to make money."
- "I didn't really have to work because my spouse made enough money, but now we're getting divorced."

Why are those bad answers? Because they show you running away from a bad situation, not running to their job. No one ever wants to be the consolation prize, and that includes employers. If you don't really want to be there, chances are you're not going to put in your best work.

You want to show that things were just fine and that you aren't being forced to work for them. This is your choice.

For example, say something like, "Frankly I got caught up in it. Things were going well, there really wasn't a problem. I just decided that I would be better served to be in an organization like this one."

And then you can give your reasons for wanting to work for them. Why is that company a good fit for you? Start by giving them a reason that fits your professional skills (maybe you realize how much better you could be with the right resources and infrastructure). Then give them a reason that you personally like the company. This would be a cultural fit reason. You don't have to work just anywhere, you want to work for them because they fit you well. The third reason can be more of a personal reason: you're looking forward to collaborating with people and feeding off each other's ideas so that you can be better and stronger than you've ever been.

The big point you must communicate is that you are not leaving a failing situation. You are excited about bringing your skills and talents to a larger organization and looking forward to the prospect.

Job Interview Question 89:

Why did you leave your last position?

The underlying questions behind "Why did you leave your last position?" are, "Is there something wrong with you?" "Did you get fired for a reason?" "Will I regret hiring you?" Those are the concerns that you need to address when you answer this question.

It's important that you don't say anything negative about the company you were with because any negativity reflects very badly on you, but you still have to give them a reason why you're no longer with that company. Your answer will depend on what happened, but there are ways you can talk about it to put a positive spin on it.

If you were laid off, and you can truthfully say that it was a mass layoff, like they laid off 40% of the sales force, or they laid off 10% of the workforce and the newest employees went first, then say that. It will make them feel better to know that it wasn't just you. They will understand a mass layoff situation, because so many companies have cut back on their numbers the last few years.

If you weren't part of a mass layoff—maybe it was a restructuring, maybe it was just a much smaller number of people, it's very important that you be able to offer references who can speak to your skills and your character. The very best reference in this situation is your old boss. That will ease a lot of doubt.

If that's not possible because you were in fact fired, don't try to act like you weren't. They will almost certainly call your references and your old company to find out the truth. You can say something like, "I have to be honest with you here. That was kind of a bad situation that I'm embarrassed about. It wasn't a good decision to take that job—I did it for the wrong reasons, it wasn't a good fit, etc. I can only say that it was a brief bump in the road of an otherwise great career. I would love to have you speak to some of my references, including my former employer John Smith (who is going to be your boss from a job you've had in the past). They will be able to speak to my qualifications for this job, and my work ethic."

And then make sure you prep and coach those references. They need to know they're about to get a phone call, and they need to know what's most important for them to speak about. Your references are an ideal resource for you to utilize in this particular situation.

Job Interview Question 90:

Why did you take a job that seems to be outside of your career path?

So what happens when your potential employer is reading through your resume and they come across the job that doesn't make sense? You have a job in your history that doesn't fall within the logical progression of jobs in your field. And they want to know why.

What they're looking for here is at least some thought process...some understanding of who you are and where you're going. Why did you take that job? What they are afraid of is that you don't know what you want to do and if they hire you, you might not want to hang around their company very long, either. The hiring and onboarding process is disruptive to companies, and most want to minimize turnover so they can concentrate on making money.

There are actually a lot of valid reasons you could have taken an odd job that don't reflect badly on you and will make sense to them: Maybe you thought that industry experience was going to be really useful; maybe you thought that you could learn a lot from that boss; maybe you thought that skill set you'd pick up there would be a benefit to you. Going after additional skills is a positive. Or, maybe the truth is that you had no other choice: you needed a good job, and this was one. Sometimes practicality is reason enough. Just explain that you have worked your tail off in that job, but now it's time to move on to one that more closely fits your skill sets or your desired outcome as far as a career path goes.

They're looking for you to make them feel better about something that puzzles them. And unless you answer that question where they do feel better about it, you have not done a good job of representing yourself in the interview. So you really need to think this through and put yourself in the shoes of the hiring manager.

Just explain to them what they want to know: Are you being thoughtful about your career? Are you making good decisions? Or are you just impulsively taking any old job that sounds good? Why did you do this? And most importantly, does that have anything to do with why you want this job? Are you going to be happy in this career long-term?

Tell them why you made that decision, tell them what you learned from it, and then come back around to why you'd be a good fit for this job.

Job Interview Question 91:

Why do you believe you are the best fit for this position?

This job interview question closely resembles "Why should we hire you?" It's one question that makes candidates very uncomfortable because it puts them on the spot, but it's really a fantastic question. Why? It allows you free rein to sell.

Remember that every job interview is a sales process. You are the product (and the sales rep), and the hiring manager is the buyer. Why should he or she choose you above all the other products available?

A bad answer focuses on you: "Because I really need the job," "Because I really want the job," or "Because I would be great at it and love it."

A good answer focuses on them: What problems can you solve for them? What solutions do you provide to them? Tie everything to what they have asked for in a candidate, both in what you read in the job description (job interview preparation is essential to answering this question) and what you learned through asking questions in the interview (if you've had a chance to do that yet).

Think about the things a hiring manager is looking for: the skill sets, the relationships, the background, the character traits...everything that is necessary to be successful in this role. Maybe it's going to be an incredible amount of work, so you need to point out your work ethic. Maybe it's going to require tremendous communication skills, so you need to give an example of yours. Maybe it requires a quick learning curve, so you can say why you're going to be able to get up to speed quickly. Maybe it requires a particular background, and you have that.

Know how your skill set equals the skill set required for this position, and then deliver a concise but detailed statement that explains that. Show them that you fit. And provide a few examples of how you have done that in the past (which means that you can do it again for them). What have you achieved or accomplished that make you a great fit for this role?

Here's an example: "I'm the best for this because you said you were looking for A, B, and C: I've got A...we talked about that; I've got B...I showed you that; I've got C...you asked me questions about that. I fit all your requirements. That's why I'm the best fit for this position." You are reiterating what you have talked about and summed it up for them.

Don't be shy...tell them why they need you.

Job Interview Question 92:

Why do you have a big gap in your employment history?

A gap on your resume can be anxiety-inducing for a job seeker, and for the employer who's looking at them for a potential hire. But it's really not as bad as you think. Actually, many people have employment gaps, and they have them for a lot of reasons ranging from the poor economy and mass layoffs in recent years to family obligations of the sandwich generation.

It's not that big of a deal. You just need an explanation. The company wants you to explain the situation to them in a way that makes sense:

- "I took time to stay home with my children."
- "I took time to be with an ailing parent."
- "I took time to be available for a family member with a terminal illness."
- "I was ill / injured and took time to recover."
- "I was laid off and took time to update my skills by taking X classes." (This is a fantastic use of your time!)

They just want you to explain it to them. Be honest. You never ever want to lie or try to fudge your employment dates. They are very likely to check your references and as soon as they see that you lied, you're chances are gone.

But don't just give an abrupt answer like, "I took time to stay with my mother who died of cancer." Give them a little bit more:

"Unfortunately, my mom was terminal with cancer and I wanted to spend time with her and I had the opportunity to do so. I was the person in the family who was responsible for getting her to and from doctors and taking care of her day-to-day needs. It was a very special time. She's passed now, and I am ready to jump back into my career."

Did you stay home with your kids? Say so: "I was a stay-at-home mom. I raised 4 kids. I have them all in school now and I'm now at a point where I have a lot of time and a lot of energy and a lot of drive and desire to put my skill sets to use in a professional capacity. I think this opportunity is an ideal chance for me to use them to help you _____."

That blank needs to be filled with something like, "drive your profits", "increase your revenue", "decrease your costs", "increase your customers", "decrease your production time", or something that sells you to them as an asset that can help them achieve their goals.

Whatever your reason, be strategic and bring it back around to what can contribute to the company. What skills do you have? What problems can you solve? What benefits do you bring?

Give your explanation, focus on the future, stay positive, and you'll be fine.

Job Interview Question 93:

Why do you think you can manage a team without any prior managerial experience?

If you're interviewing for your first management-level job, you will definitely be asked some version of this question. They'll want to know if you think you can do this job and why.

The key here is to explain that at some point, everybody who becomes a manager has to manage a team without any prior managerial experience. Everybody who is a successful manager has made that transition. What then, makes you confident that you are someone who can make that transition? What do you have in common with those people so that you can say, "they did it, and this is why I can do it, too."

I would give an answer that sounds something like this: "What I've seen is that a really successful manager is someone who is extremely driven, has a strong work ethic, has strong communication skills, wants the best for the company as well as for their employees, is willing to train and mentor others, and is someone who lifts people up and helps develop them and removes obstacles from their success. I am that kind of person and I can give you some examples of that. In X role, I did Y. In A role, I did B." The examples you give should show you exhibiting those character traits in various situations.

Maybe you had a role where you had to make people do things but you had no authority over them. That means that you had to be a better manager than someone with the power to actually make them do something. You had no stick, so you had to use only the carrot. That makes extremely strong managerial experience. If you have a story where you were on a team and took on the role of leader to get the team to a goal, then absolutely tell that story. Tell what obstacles you faced, how you resolved them, and what the results were.

I also like turning the question back to them: "So, Mr. Manager, at some point, you didn't have managerial experience, either, right?" They will agree, of course, because they have to. So you say, "What made you think that you were someone who could take on that role?" They will say, "Because I was A, B, and C." You say, "Well, I'm that way, too, and I can be successful, just as you have been."

This question is also an ideal time to introduce your 30/60/90-day plan. It's extremely helpful at management-level interviews because they demonstrate your strategic thinking and problem-solving skills, both of which are essential to a successful manager. And when you write out your goals, you will show them that you do, in fact, know what it takes to be successful in this job and you are completely capable of it.

Job Interview Question 94:

Why do you want to join this company?

The hot button question: Why do you want to work here?

All companies want to know that you want to work for them rather than you just want a job. An enthusiastic employee is a better employee—and more pleasant to work with, too.

A good answer to this question should always be part of your job interview prep. Your answer to this question should sound like, "I want to join this company because…" and then you need to list at least 3 reasons why.

The first one should always show fit in terms of professional skills: "…I can see where my skill sets would benefit you in this particular position. Because they would benefit you, I would also benefit personally, professionally, and financially from that. If I can come in here and fix this problem for you, I'm sure you'll have other problems I can fix down the road, and that looks like a great future for me."

This one tells them why you're excited about what you can do for them. It still places the emphasis on what they're getting out of hiring you.

The second one can show fit, but more of a cultural fit: "Another reason I want to join this company is that I like the culture. It fits me. I like what I've been reading about the company, and it seems like a great fit for my personality and values and who I want to be working for."

The more specific you can be in your answer, the better. It is absolutely critical that you do your company research before the interview so that you can give these specific examples. What does this company do that appeals to you? Is it a top company in its field? Are they known for their cutting-edge products? Do they have a great reputation for customer service? Are they known for being a great place to work? Do they emphasize employee development? Talk about those things that speak to you about the company and your fit for it.

And then you can say something that personalizes it a little more, like: "The job is in a great location for me. I've always wanted to move here." Or, "It's only 5 minutes from my house, and I love that." Or, "I've always used these products, and I just love them and am really excited about being a part of that." Something that gives you another reason of your own for wanting this job.

Show them your sincere enthusiasm. All of these reasons give them one more reason to hire you.

Job Interview Question 95:

Why do you want to switch from an academic field to business/industry?

The one big perception / misconception about academics is that they can't make it in the 'real' world. They are secure in their ivory towers and not coming out any time soon. So if you find yourself trying to leap from your own ivory tower (or ivory laboratory, as the case may be) your interviewer is going to want to know why. What will you have to say for yourself? This question is an excellent jumping-off point for you to talk about your drive, your enthusiasm, and your ambition. Break the stereotype!

If it were me, I would say something like this: "I want to switch because I want to be rewarded for the things that I do. In an academic field I can work day and night, 24 hours, and no one will notice, and I will not be paid any more than my peers are. In a business role, it's my perception that the harder I work and the more that I do, the more the company will reward me. I'll have even more opportunities to take on more responsibility, which will in turn give me more reward."

What can that reward be? Recognition, money, more authority as you climb the ladder, the opportunity to influence others, the chance to be appreciated for what you do, and even the opportunity to be treated differently based on your success.

Anytime you have something in your background that goes against the norm (a gap in your experience, a side-step off your career path, a job that looks like a demotion, and so on) the interviewer will want to know why. All you have to do is provide a reasonable explanation.

You have the power to tell your story in a way that reflects well on you. In this case, the story shows that you want something more for yourself. You are ambitious and energetic and want to be rewarded for your hard work.

In most cases (including moving from academia to industry), you want to tell the story in a way that makes it clear that you aren't running away from whatever situation you were previously in...you are running TO the situation you want to be in. You're not ever going to talk about how bad it was where you were...you're only going to talk about how excited you are to be moving forward. Keep your story positive.

Job Interview Question 96:

Why do you want to work for someone else after owning your own business / freelancing?

LOTS of hiring managers will have a hard time believing that you can start taking orders after being your own boss. It's not a big leap to make…it would be difficult for many people. Your best answer to this difficult job interview question will be honest but positive.

My best answer would sound like this: "I am really good at X, but I'm not good at Y, so I'm ready to move into being part of a company again." X would be whatever technical skill or skill set I have that is going to be required in this job. Y would be whatever business acumen necessary for growing your own business, but not needed in this new job.

As in, "I'm a really good graphic designer, but I'm really not good at getting customers." You can't successfully run a business if you don't have the marketing skill to get customers. But in a larger company, someone else will do that for you. All you have to do is design.

In general, it sounds like this: "I'm better at doing the job than I am at marketing the job, and I wasn't ready to expand and bring other people into my business who could do that for me. What I really want to do is focus on the core skills that I'm very good at. I want the chance to hone them even more and do the things I need to do for an employer in a concentrated fashion. I know that will give me a real sense of achievement, and I know that I will still be financially rewarded for that as a part of this organization."

Another great answer tells them that you're a people person: "I want to be where I can work with others. I'm tired of working by myself all the time. I want to be part of a group, or part of a team."

Or you can keep it simple and say, "I just didn't enjoy self-employment as much as I think you should when you're self-employed. I enjoy being part of a company and having colleagues to learn from, bounce ideas off of, and share the day with."

All of these answers make it clear that it's your choice to come in from the world of self-employment. You're not going to ever talk about how it was a colossal failure, or you can't afford the insurance, or you're about to go bankrupt. You're going to say, "I tried it and decided it was not for me....but this opportunity is."

Job Interview Question 97:

Why have you been out of work for so long?

Boy, I bet you'd like to know the answer to that question, too! The job search can be a very difficult time for many people, but it's important that you show a positive face to everyone. Answer every job interview question with as much positivity and as little negativity as you can. It makes you more appealing to others and puts you in a better spot to receive a job offer.

The worst thing you can do is shrug your shoulders and say something vague about the job market. And you can even do better than saying, "I just haven't found the right opportunity yet." It's better to point out that you were out of work by choice.

If you can, talk about how you took some time for some personal things before you hit the job search (maybe because you had a nice severance package, maybe for some other reason). Why would you want to do that? Because it's helpful to you if you can point out that in reality, you haven't actually been in an active job search for as long as it seems.

So that gives you a 3-6 month cushion of time and then you can say, "So I've only really been actively looking for the last 4 months or so, and I've been on some interviews, but nothing that really was a great fit. But it's REALLY picked up lately, so I don't think that I'm going to be in the search for much longer."

Do you see what I'm doing here? So overall, I'm saying, "Well, first, I didn't start it really as soon as I probably should have because I took that time off, and second, the market's been pretty bad, and third, it just takes a couple of months to really get a good search going. The average time from first contact to job offer, if you're going to get one, is 8 weeks, so the fact that I've only been searching for 4 months is probably the biggest factor."

And then, this is a really **big key point**: say that "based on what I'm seeing, though, it's really picking up and I don't expect to be unemployed for much longer." That's an important psychological tactic to use: everybody wants what someone else wants, so give yourself a little bit of that aura of unattainability by pointing out that you are going to be snapped up soon.

Job Interview Question 98:

Why have you changed jobs so frequently over the past X years?

Job-hopping is not a great habit. When you stay at a job for only a few months or a year, over and over again, you are cultivating an image of someone who can't be depended upon, who doesn't know what they want, and who's probably more than a little immature. Employers question your loyalty, and tend to shy away from hiring you because you look like a very expensive disruption rather than a potentially valuable and stable employee.

Still, there are cases where there are good reasons for job-hopping (or at least where it was no one's fault). If you have a few too many jobs in the last few years on your resume, they're going to ask you about it in the interview. You should have an answer ready to go, and it needs to make sense.

A bad answer is going to reinforce the stereotypes they have about job-hoppers:

- "I get bored easily."
- "I was chasing the money."
- "For some reason, people don't seem to like me."
- "I keep ending up in hostile work environments."
- "I've had a string of bad luck lately."
- "I got fired...over and over again."

All those answers say negative things about you.

A good answer is going to give them a reason that makes sense.

The person who's been laid off should say, "Gosh, I wish I hadn't had to change jobs. It wasn't my choice. With the economy, I was laid off of two different projects, (give a few details). So it's not that I really like it. I wish that hadn't happened, but that's where I find myself now."

"These jobs were contract jobs." (Or other jobs where there wasn't any type of commitment or expectation from the employer.)

"I've been looking for the right position." (The follow up question from them will be, "How do you know this is the right position?" You should be able to give them 3 solid reasons why this position is a great fit for you, professionally, culturally, and personally.)

"The company went out of business."

"Our division was dissolved."

"My spouse is in the military, and we had to move."

All those are good reasons. Some of them show that it wasn't your fault, and if that's true, you should definitely say so. If you can, tell them why your job hopping wasn't a bad thing--talk about what you learned from those experiences that help make you a better-rounded person and a more valuable asset to them as a company.

Job Interview Question 99:

Why haven't you been promoted?

If you're someone with quite a bit of experience but you haven't moved up the career ladder, you can expect to be asked why you haven't been promoted. Employers don't worry about this issue quite as much as if you had been fired, but both situations do make them wonder if you have some secret fault they don't know about yet.

Remember that hiring you is a risk because they'll be investing time and money into training you and getting you up to speed in the job. And they really don't want to have to go through this hiring process again. So this question is yet another way to ask about your weaknesses, or otherwise uncover flaws while they still have the chance.

The best answer is one where you can say, "I was actually offered a promotion, but I wasn't interested. I didn't want to take on that additional responsibility." There could be a lot of reasons for this. Maybe you had small children or other family obligations. Maybe you had something else going on.

Or, "I was offered a promotion, but I wasn't interested in taking on that role." Maybe you just weren't interested in the responsibilities of that job.

Or, "I wanted to move in a different direction in the company. The promotions that were offered to me (or available to me) were going to take me in a direction I didn't want to go." Not every job you qualify for is going to fit neatly into the career path you are following.

All of these answers tell the best story you can tell, which is that it was your choice.

Or, it could be that the lack of promotional opportunities in your old company is exactly why you're in the job search. Maybe you worked for a small company with no room for you to grow and develop. Then it makes perfect sense for you to be looking for advancement opportunities in another organization.

What you don't want to do is give the impression that you're lazy and didn't want to do the work; that you weren't offered a promotion because you're not good at your job; or that you don't have the work ethic or the people skills necessary to move up the chain.

One thing that will help you in this situation or any situation where there's some question about your background: your references. A great reference will counter a lot of doubts the hiring manager has about you. Cultivate good references and prep them before your interview.

Job Interview Question 100:

Why should we give you the job over the other candidates?

This is a tough question. Most people are not that comfortable with the idea of tooting their own horn, but that's exactly what you have to do here. So feel free to brag. They're looking for you to sell yourself for the job. Tell them why they need you.

In order to do that, you have to have done your pre-interview research plus a little self-analysis. Know how your skill set equals the skill set required for this position...and if you can, show how you offer that PLUS a bit more. That little bit extra is helpful to give you the edge over other candidates.

You don't need a lot, just one more thing that makes you special over and above the other candidates. Say what that is and how it's going to help you exceed their expectations for that role. You won't just meet them, you'll exceed them. Talk about one or two specific accomplishments that really highlight you as a great candidate for this role. Talk about how well you fit culturally with the company, and how they're going to see that even more when they talk to your references.

219

(And your references better be outstanding…make sure you prep your references before the interview. Just give them a heads up that you're interviewing and what the job is for and what particular skills or accomplishments would be helpful for them to talk about.)

Everything you talk about should be focused on how you're going to not just meet, but exceed their expectations.

Say something like, "I deserve the job because I have the skills, I meet the qualifications, I fit you culturally, I've done the work before successfully, I'm going to be able to perform successfully in this role, and that's what you want, do you agree?"

It's OK to ask if they agree or if you've answered the question—you need to know if you answered what they were asking, and they deserve an answer to an issue for them. It's easy. Just say, "Do you agree?" or "did that answer your question?" or "did I answer your question completely?" That's just good communication skills that are necessary in a job interview situation.

Job Interview Question 101:

Why would you accept a lesser salary than what you made before? Won't you jump ship when a better offer comes along?

You might very well come across a better opportunity in the future, but now is not the time to talk about it. Now is the time to alleviate the concerns of that hiring manager so that they feel comfortable pulling the trigger to make you an offer!

Your best answer is to say something like this:

"If I take the job with you, I'm not going to just be taking it for the money. I'm looking at the whole picture. I'm interested in more than just the paycheck. I'm interested in the quality of the company, the quality of my work life, the caliber of my manager, the healthcare and other benefits, the unique things that this company has that other companies don't.

Another company could come along and offer me more money…that could happen no matter what. That's not really relevant because I don't take a job just because of the money, I take a job because of all those factors as a whole. I need a job that will meet all my needs. When I look at this job with you, I see a job that will meet all my needs.

Do I want to be paid as highly as I can be for the work that I do? Yes, of course. But if I commit to you for this job, I will be committed and I won't be spending my time looking for a so-called better offer. I will be working hard and performing and exceeding for you.

I don't sign on for short term jobs. You can look at my history, I've been with XYZ organization for a number of years. I won't take a job with an organization that I'm not committed to."

If they've asked you this question, they like you a lot and they're wondering if you're too good to be true. So all you have to do is put their fears to rest by trying to take the money question out of it, or by at least minimizing it as much as possible.

How to Answer Interview Questions – II

101 NEW Questions and Answers

Job Interview Question 1

Are you a leader or a follower?

This is an important interview question meant to measure your personality, and how your personality will fit with this particular job.

To answer this question well, it's important to think about what role you are interviewing for. If you are interviewing for **a leadership role** and you say that you are a follower, you probably won't get that job. If you are interviewing for a role where you would be **part of a team** (not the leader) and you say that you are always the leader, you won't be a good fit for the team because you can't work collaboratively.

You might be tempted to knee-jerk reply to this one: "I'm a leader!" In our society, we tend to revere the ideal of the decisive, powerful leader. However, the truth is that **most jobs require you to be a little of both.** We are (as a society) moving more and more toward collaborative efforts with more fluid lines of leadership. You might easily at various times be part of a team, reporting to a higher-up, leading a team, or heading a project. That doesn't mean that your best answer is always a safe "I'm both." Think about THIS particular job and what it requires to function and be successful.

Whatever your answer, **be prepared to give them an example** of how you have done that.

STAR Format

The STAR format is a great way to help you structure your answers to interview questions when you need to give an example. It helps you include everything you need to in your answer:

Situation or
Task: This is whatever was going on at the time. What were you faced with? What was going on? Set the scene.
Action you took: What did YOU do to affect this situation?
Results: Always, always **finish the story by telling them what happened as a result of your actions**. This is the most important part!

If you are a leader, tell them about a time when you exercised leadership, including the **actions** you took and what the **results** were. This could be an example of **spearheading** a multi-piece project that would demonstrate your project management skills, how you **motivated** a group of people to achieve a goal, or how you had to make a **hard decision** (telling what the circumstances were and what the results were)

Just like in your resume, you want to **quantify** what you are describing wherever possible:

"I led a group of 12 people in a 6-department project where our job was to streamline processes between departments to save time and money. We decided to (X, Y, and Z) and as a result, cut an average of 2 weeks out of each process and saved each of the 6 departments an average of $100,000 a year."

If you are a follower, help them see **how you contributed** to the team and **benefited** the team. Employers need followers in many roles, but they like to see followers who can take initiative. Talk about a successful project and what your role in that was—something you did that had a significant impact on the outcome. If you can **quantify that impact**, that's even better:

225

"My action resulted in a time savings for us, so we got it done 8 days faster."

Or talk about your overall responsibilities and how your contributions ensured **consistently successful outcomes.**

Job Interview Question 2

Are you better at "managing up" or "managing down"?

Are you better at managing up or managing down? Your answer **always needs to be, "I'm good at both."**

Managing up or down is all about extreme **communication** skills. Here's how this works...

If I **manage up** well, then:

• I **spend time** with and **talk** with my manager

• I understand what their **goals and objectives** are and make those mine, as well

• I keep my manager **informed of my progress** on any given project so that they have confidence that things are moving forward toward success

• I know what their **expectations** are and make it my job to **exceed** them

227

- I am **proactive** and try to come up with ideas and solutions to help the organization succeed. I can't do those things if I don't communicate well with my manager.

If I **manage down** well, then:
- I am a **good team leader** and a fantastic **communicator**
- I understand what our **goals** are and how the team works within the framework to achieve those goals
- I choose **great people**
- I **clarify our team goals** for them and give them room to achieve
- I ask for **input** and I **listen**
- I keep the team **moving toward the goal**

Everyone in an organization needs to be good at both—you report to your manager, who reports to the Vice-President, who reports to the President, who reports to the CEO, who reports to the Board of Directors, who report to investors.

You might have direct reports that you need to manage, but even if you don't, you will have times when you are leading a project and need to manage that team for that project.

So, say that you are good at both managing up and managing down, and **give examples** of times when you have done both of those things.

Your answer should be in the form of a **story**: This is what the situation was, this is what happened, this is what I did, this is how it worked out, and this is what the results were.

Use the **STAR** format:
Situation or
Task (Set up the story—what happened? What was your goal?)
Action (What did you choose to do and why?)
Result (What happened as a result of your actions? Quantify this wherever possible.)

See the two examples below.

For managing up:

"My manager's goal for the year was X, and my job was Y. We met weekly to discuss results and plan for the next week. At the end of the year, we had achieved our goal, plus 20%, and our department received recognition from the company."

For managing down:

"I was handpicked to put together a team tasked to do X. I chose 5 people from a cross-department pool, set X goals, and met with them daily for a 15-minute meeting to touch base and answer questions. In 3 months, we met 3 goals and exceeded expectations on the other 2 by X."

Job Interview Question 3

Are you willing to travel?
(How much are you willing to travel?)

If your answer is an unqualified "yes," because you're willing to go wherever, whenever, for however long it takes, then say so. Any other answer ("maybe," "it depends," "I'd rather not") needs to **wait** until you ask: "How much travel is required for this job? Can you tell me about that?"

Always ask what the travel expectations actually are before you rule yourself out. I've had great candidates say, "I'm not willing to travel," and then they find out how great the job is, or that the travel is to someplace they're really interested in, or that the salary would be very generous to compensate for all of the travelling, and then, all of a sudden they are willing to travel. If they've already let the company know they aren't willing to travel, they've knocked themselves out of consideration and it's over.

As a recruiter, I can tell you one of the things I found interesting about this question is that people define "travel" very differently. Is it **overnight** travel, or is it just **day** travel? Do they mean 20% travel, 50% travel, or 90% travel? If they tell you that it's "50% travel", what does that actually mean in practical terms? Does it mean you're out Monday,

Tuesday and Wednesday every week? Does it mean you're in the office one week and out the next?

Get specifics, not just percentages, because those can be a cause of miscommunication. Ask how many nights away per week they're talking about, so you are absolutely clear on what they are asking for.

Companies know that people quit jobs over too much travel, so they are sensitive to that as a big factor in whether you'll be happy on the job or not and stay long-term. It's in their best interests to make sure exactly whether or not you are OK with travel. You can help them by asking them to **be clear** on how much travel they are requiring.

It may be that once you find out what they mean by "travel" that you really are not interested in the job—but you'll never know until you ask, so don't rule yourself out until you do.

Job Interview Question 4

Assume you come to work here. One year from now you go home at the end of the week and think that this is the best job you've ever had. What happened to make you feel that way?

If you ask others about the best job they've ever had, they almost never mention money. (If they do, it's in relation to "I made great money while I was having fun!")

The hiring manager wants to know that you're excited about THIS job, working for THIS company. They want to know that your expectations are clear and align with what you will find here, and that you have their big-picture goals in mind, too.

Does your **vision** for the perfect job match with what their job will actually be like? Will you **enjoy** this job (and stick around in it, creating success) or will you get frustrated and leave? Do you expect to be **successful,** and why?

You have two options here:

One, think about what will be the most **rewarding** parts of this job for you, and talk about those. Focus on what THIS company can do for you or be for you that others can't. At least part of your answer should focus on that **you'll be happy because they will be happy:** "I will know that I am using my skills in X, Y, and Z to make a real, significant contribution to boost our company's growth/market share/profit and I will feel excited and happy about that."

Two, refer to the **job goals** you may have talked about already and talk about how you have **achieved** those (in a year): "I will have accomplished X, Y, and Z, that you said were our primary goals, and …."

Answer either way, incorporating both job accomplishments and your own personal goals and desires, and focus on your success.

Remember that if you are receiving a paycheck, you are achieving a quantifiable goal. That's the only reason a company would hire anyone. So tie your goals and objectives to **quantifiable goals** the company needs to accomplish. For instance, if you know that the company wants to accomplish "X" in a year, you would say that at the end of the year you would have achieved that goal for them and felt a great sense of accomplishment because you did so.

Relate your answer to what they need, but be **sincere** about what would make THIS company a fun place for you to work. Your enthusiasm will show, and make you more attractive to this employer.

Job Interview Question 5

Describe a time when you were asked to do something you weren't trained to do. How did you handle it?

This is a fantastic behavioral interview question that gets at the heart of **how you respond to challenges.** How do you think about them— are you **afraid or excited?** Do you have the **initiative** to tackle something new? How do you **approach the task?** Can you **think critically** and make good, logical decisions? How do you **function without structure?**

In your answer, talk about **resources** you used, **mentors** you called, **books** you read, counterparts you spoke with, **audio** you listened to, YouTube **videos** you watched, or **coaches** you contacted.

How did you train yourself to successfully accomplish the task?

Use the **STAR** format:
Situation or
Task (Set up the story—what happened? What was your goal?)
Action (What did you choose to do and why?)
Result (What happened as a result of your actions? Quantify this wherever possible.)

Here are some sample answers:

****

"X was the situation, and I remembered that I had done something similar in Y, so I did a little research online and figured out how to apply the principles I learned there to achieve this new goal."

****

" I was faced with X, and at first, I didn't know what to do. But I remembered that our overall goals were A, B, and C. So I thought about what course of action would keep us moving toward those goals? After that, it was easy to narrow down the options, and this is what I did. As a result, we had a fantastic outcome, XYZ."

****

"In my last job, X happened. We had no procedures in place to handle that, so I did some research and found some books on the subject. I read those, had a couple of discussions with my mentor, to kick around ideas, and presented my ideas to my team. After some discussion with them, I developed a new set of procedures to handle X. We had such success with it that the company implemented our new procedure throughout all the divisions."

****

"In my first job, X happened. I didn't know the first thing about how to handle it, so I did some research and asked for input from people in a similar position with more experience than I had at that time. I was able to use some of what they told me and incorporated it into a new solution for our problem. As a result, we saw X% increase in sales."

****

The hiring manager wants to know that you can **think on your own** and come up with rational, proactive **solutions** that produce great results for the company.

Job Interview Question 6

Describe a time when your team did not agree.

The cooperation of countless people on teams is how business is done. Yet, no team always gets along perfectly. When that happens, what do you do? How do you handle conflict? Can you lead others to consensus?

Conflict resolution is an important skill. How you deal with any conflict says a lot about you, your personality, and your professionalism.

This question can pertain either to a team that you led (how do you manage people who disagree?), or to a team that you are on (can you mediate between team members and exercise leadership even if you weren't assigned as leader?).

Always, when asked to describe any situation in an interview question, use the **STAR** format:

Situation or
Task (Set up the story—what happened? What was your goal?)
Action (What did you choose to do and why?)
Result (What happened as a result of your actions? Quantify this wherever possible.)

236

Ideally, your story should tell about how you **asked questions** to achieve understanding of the conflict, found **common ground, presented data** to influence the decision-making process, and realized a **productive or profitable outcome.**

Lots of people will tell the story but forget to mention the outcome. **The outcome, or result, of your actions, is what the employer cares about most.** (Include the actual numbers in the story as much as you can—quantification is powerful.)

If your example is a team that you led:

Situation or Task – Briefly set up the situation that led to the conflict. Choose something that was an **actual problem** involving priorities or a budget. (Don't talk about about trivial things, like how the team couldn't agree on where to go to lunch.) **Be brief.** The employer doesn't need to know that much about the details.

Action – How did you approach the team? How did you exercise your leadership? Talk about how you listened (listening is a critical skill), taking into account the emotions of the people on your team, and made a **rational, logical decision** (rather than one based on your own emotions).

Result – This is your real focus here—the **outcome.** What happened as a direct result of your actions? This is a prime spot to **add numerical evidence** for the employer ("As a result of my plan, we were able to reduce overlap by 50%, which also drastically reduced the time spent in X.").

If your example is a team that you were on (but not necessarily leading), you might want to talk about how you **mediated** the conflict, again by listening and taking the emotion out of the equation. Or, you could describe how you took the time to **talk** to each member of the team and hear what they had to say. Talk about how you **rooted out the miscommunication** or found common ground. End with what happened as a **result**—always a **positive** one.

So, you might say,

"I was part of a handpicked cross-department Kaizen team tasked to find ways to become more lean and efficient as a company. But some of the suggestions stepped on the toes of one person in particular who was from X area and caused them to react badly. I took them out for coffee to take some of the group pressure off and we talked. I realized what the real problem was, and helped them present their issue to the group in a different way. As a group, we came up with a new solution

237

that made this person feel much more positive about it and still achieved our goal. The end result of this project was that we streamlined X number of procedures and saved the company as a whole about 40 hours a week, which they valued at $X."

Job Interview Question 7

Describe a time you reduced costs or improved efficiency.

Every single one of our jobs is tied to **money**. Companies are in business to make money, and every cog in the machine needs to work smoothly together toward that goal. If you don't make more money than you cost, you won't hold your job very long.

So, there must be a time when you reduced costs or improved efficiency in any job you've done, and you need to pinpoint what it is and quantify it. (**Quantifying** it means to identify the numbers that describe the savings—you saved 3 hours, you saved $300, you improved it by 30%, etc.)

Here's an example of a gentleman with a great answer to this:

He was working on a machine, with gold wires. In his process, excess gold was actually falling on the floor—very tiny pieces, as scrap. He went to his supervisor and said, "Look, we should not be throwing away these scraps. We should be figuring out a way to get that gold out of those shavings and recycle it for our sales or for something else.

The supervisor thought that was a great idea, so they actually started keeping those shavings and trying how to figure out a way to separate the gold from the other material—and they did. The company rewarded him with a sizable bonus.

This is a great story because it proved that he is someone who takes **initiative**, thinks in a **bigger-picture way** about the company, and can **bring solutions** above and beyond what his job requires—but what makes it better is **quantifying** it. How would he do that?

He would know how much those gold reels cost: $200, $1000, $100,000, $200,000, or whatever it is. Maybe the shavings represent a 10 % loss, and this idea recovered that for the company.

Whatever the numbers are, you should know so you can describe the **money you saved or the efficiency you improved**. Think it all the way through.

Whatever your job is, think about what you have done that **saved time, saved money, improved efficiency, and reduced costs**. It all adds up to a financial benefit for the company that helps to justify the cost of hiring you—your salary. When you talk about it in your interview, they will be thinking that if you did that for another company, you can do that for their company, too.

Key to a Great Interview!

Any story where you received a reward or other recognition should be in your Brag Book.

Your Brag Book is evidence that you can do what you say you can do. Use it to illustrate an interview answer or the quality of your work. It sets you apart as someone who pays attention to details, is achievement-oriented, and cares about giving your best. It's an impressive "wow" factor. To the hiring manager, offering you a job

240

feels like a risk. Many people believe that past performance predicts future behavior, so brag books are a good way to make them feel more comfortable about hiring you.

Start putting your brag book together today. You'll be amazed at how much it helps your interview performance. If you would like help putting yours together, check out **Career Confidential's** Brag Book eReport on Amazon

Job Interview Question 8

Describe a work or school instance where you messed up.

Everybody makes mistakes. You know it, and the interviewer knows it and they will always ask you about them. Why?

(1) They want to reveal your **character**. Are you someone who admits making a mistake or who blames it on others? Are you too perfect to even think of a mistake you made? Or maybe you have such low self-esteem that you can think of hundreds of things that were all your fault.

(2) They want to know if you **learn from your mistakes** and come out of them better than you were before. Or do you keep repeating the same mistakes over and over again?

Think of a time you made a mistake and acted in the situation so that it ended on a positive note.

What are the rules of a good mistake story?

Rule #1: Don't talk about the biggest mistake you ever made that spiraled out of control and had huge repercussions for your company.

If your story takes 3 minutes because of all the times you say, "and THEN this terrible thing happened", you are choosing the wrong story.

Rule #2: Don't talk about a mistake that points to a major flaw.

If you are an accountant, don't talk about the time you transposed a number and didn't catch it until your manager was in the middle of a presentation to the CEO. Instead, talk about the time you had a miscommunication with a co-worker and how you talked it out and improved your communication skills with co-workers.

If you're an administrative assistant, don't talk about the time you failed to communicate vital information and caused your boss to miss an important meeting—talk about the time in your first job that you didn't write down a message because you thought you could remember it and you didn't, and you had to call back, so now you are meticulous about keeping information complete and organized.

Choose a small, work-related mistake that was a problem for you, but not necessarily the company.

Tell what you did to rectify the mistake or address the shortcoming that caused it in the first place.

Show that you improved as a result of the mistake—that you had a growth experience that made you better at your job.

Job Interview Question 9

Describe how you would complete [a typical task on this job].

HINT!

Take paper and pen to your job interviews!

Use it to sketch out ideas to help yourself think and better answer interview questions.

Take notes for your thank you note and second interview.

This behavioral interview question is very job-specific, so the details of your answer depend on the job itself. The primary reason they are asking this is to make sure that you are what you say you are, and that you **understand what the job is** and what you have to do in order to be **successful** at it. However, they also want an insight into your **thinking style** and **problem-solving skills**, and this question helps them get to that.

Think about this question before you answer it.

Break up whatever task it is into maybe 5-10 steps and walk them through the steps.

"If I were going to do this, here's what I would do: [1, 2, 3, 4, and 5]. I would involve X person in this, and let Y person know. I would have ABC contingency plan just in case."

After you walk them through it, you should ask, "Was that correct?" **Ask if you answered the way they were looking for, or if there was something you're missing.** Ask if they would like you to explain anything further.

Clarifying for understanding is something you especially need to do with these types of questions, so that you are sure you answered it to their satisfaction before you move on.

If they communicate to you that your answer wasn't what they were looking for, **ask what you were missing**. Turn it into a learning moment. Have this conversation with them and think it through. They'll get a chance to see how your mind works, and see what it would be like if they were working with you and showing you how to do things on the job.

Key to a Great Interview!

This question is a perfect time to introduce your 30-60-90-day plan! Find out more in the resources at the back of the book!

Communication like this, with interaction, is at a higher level, and it will show someone that you are very **confident, interested, and flexible,** and these are all good things that you want your potential employer to know about you.

Job Interview Question 10

Describe the boss who could get the very best work from you.

This question is looking at **fit**—how you'll fit into the organizational culture, and how you'll fit with the person who would be your boss. Your answer shows your personality, your work style, and your communication skills. It also sheds light on your past relationships.

I would say, "I always give my best work, no matter what. But I would enjoy a boss who...."

Or, "I always give my best work, no matter what, but I've had some great bosses over the years that really inspired me because..."

It's important to note that **you always give your best**, no matter what the circumstances around you are. And then just point out **2-3 things you particularly enjoy** in someone who supervises your work.

The key here is balance. You want to be honest, because you don't want to say you love being micro-managed if you really hate it, because it would affect you and your work negatively. But you also don't want to pin yourself down to a specific list of 'must-haves' in case this person doesn't have them all. Even if you'd be fine working without them, now they feel that you'd be unhappy and a bad fit.

If you are talking about a **future boss**, a nice safe thing to do is to mention **2-3 qualities that are broad enough to fit many people**, and that managers strive for as a general rule: (1) "I love a boss who **communicates** with me on a regular basis, letting me know **expectations and goals**. Or (2), "I love a boss who **knows a lot about the industry**, because I can learn so much from them." Or (3), "I love a boss who **trusts me** enough to let me work independently but **helps me** when I need it."

If you talk about a **boss who inspired you in the past**, mention something they did that helped you be successful in the job, or made you better, stronger, or more effective than you were before:

"I always give my best work, no matter what, but I've had some great bosses over the years that really inspired me. One in particular was a time management genius, and she really showed me how to learn to prioritize my tasks in order to manage my time and increase my productivity."

(Give a specific example of this, with **quantification** of how much your productivity increased.) Your example could be a boss who taught you organization, communication, management skills, or anything else that has resulted in you being better at your job.

Key to a Great Interview
Quantification

$ %

Describe your achievements in terms of **numbers, dollars, and percentages to strengthen your answers**:

"I brought in new clients" or "Brought in 20 new clients in 3 months"

"I delivered product on time and under budget" or "98% on-time delivery of product"

"Maintained accuracy in company database" or "100% accuracy in 50,000-item database over 2 years"

Numbers, dollars, or percentages answer the hiring manager's (interviewer's) primary question: "How can this person benefit MY company?"

Job Interview Question 11

Discuss your educational background.

This seems straightforward, and in one sense, it is—your educational background is a fact. However, there's always a difference between giving a straightforward interview answer and giving **a *job-winning* interview answer**.

If your **degree is completely and obviously related** to the job you're interviewing for, you can say, "My undergraduate is in Chemistry and I have an MBA. What else would you like to know?"

Asking a question like this keeps the conversation going, which is what you want in an interview. Maybe they want to know why you chose this field. If I were answering this question, I'd say:

"I chose Chemistry because I like it, and because not many people go into Chemistry so I knew it would make me stand out. Plus, I knew that as a female, a Chemistry degree would make me stand out even more, because it is unusual. I went on to get the MBA because I knew that the Chemistry degree plus the MBA would make me even more valuable and better at my job. I'm always looking for educational experiences that help me with that goal. Some people would get the MBA because they think it would naturally get them paid more, just because they hold it. I never thought of it that way. My opinion was, if I get an MBA, I will be better at my job—and the value I bring is what will get me paid more for the work that I do."

If your degree is not 100% related to the job you're applying for, then connect those dots for them:

"My degree is in Psychology, which gives me a unique perspective to bring to this job that most people in this field don't have, so I can bring fresh, out-of-the-box thinking along with an understanding of what makes people tick, and I have excellent communication skills."

If you got a minor (or even just a few classes) in something more directly related and helpful to the job you're applying for, mention those:

"My degree is in Philosophy, but I took 3 classes in X that I did very well in and led me to pursue this as a career. The skills I developed in those classes, backed by the solid critical-thinking skills I honed in my major make me especially effective in this arena."

"Education" is not limited to formal classes at a college or university. You can also count **certification** or **training** classes (work-sponsored or not), **programs** you participated in, **mentorships** with someone experienced in your field, even **reading** you've done on your own (being 'self-taught' can be even more impressive, because it shows your level of drive and commitment).

Job Interview Question 12

Discuss your resume.

This is a standard, open-ended interview question a lot like, "Tell me about yourself." They just want you to walk them through your resume. Your job is to be a tour guide, giving them the relevant facts they will be most interested in as they consider you for this job.

Start from your education and go forward, rather than starting with the most recent job at the top of your resume. So, say something like, "Well, my resume is in reverse chronological order, starting with my most recent experience, but let me start from the beginning and go forward. I went to X school and got a degree in Y. My first job was at ABC."

From there, **it's important to have thought about this job** that you are interviewing for and **what parts of your story will be most impressive** to this interviewer.

"From there, I was promoted to X position, where I accomplished Y."

"From there, I went to Acme Corporation as an X, where I was awarded ABC."

251

"From there, I went to XYZ Company where I really honed my skills in A, B, and C so that I was able to move up to [a promotion]."

What you choose to mention as your accomplishment, the award you won, and the skills you **honed should have as much to do with your ability to succeed at THIS job as humanly possible.** For instance, you wouldn't bother mentioning a Customer Service Award if the job you're interviewing for will have you working alone, never speaking to a customer. As great as that may be, mentioning it will throw the hiring manager off track, and start them thinking of you as a Customer Service person who probably wouldn't fit well into this role.

If you have a job in your history that seems oddly **out of place**, or **a job that you were in a very short time**, or anything else that might cause questions, now is the time to **explain your thinking** behind taking/leaving that position, or taking that time off, or whatever it is. Explain how it fit with your overall career path, or how it was a one-time mistake that you learned from or circumstance that won't happen again.

Be strategic and think about **which parts of your story would make this hiring manager want to offer you the job.** And always be thinking about how you can describe parts of your story in terms of **numbers, dollars, or percentages** ("I worked there for 6 months when I was promoted as a result of a program I started that saved $ per year").

Job Interview Question 13

Do you know anyone who works for us?

Many times, the answer to this question is 'yes,' because many of us find out about jobs or get our foot in the door with the help of someone we know.

If they ask you this question, it's probably because they are thinking about asking for **references**. Someone they know (such as someone who works at their company) is going to be a much stronger reference for you than someone they don't.

If you know someone who works in this company, this someone **needs to have an excellent reputation** within the company. If you know that's the case, then go ahead and tell the interviewer who they are. They will associate you with that person they love and you will be in a better position to get the offer. But after you mention this person, bring it back to why you'd be a good fit. For example:

"Yes, I know John Smith. We've worked well together before, and he encouraged me to apply here. Because of that, I did some research on my own, and the more I found out about your company, the more I got excited about the idea of working here, because I believe this is a place where I could really contribute to growth with my skills in X, Y, and Z."

If the person you know is someone having problems, you might not want to mention them because you will be associated with their negative qualities. Or, you can mention them with a caveat:

"I do know John Smith, but that wasn't a factor in my applying here. I applied because I believe that my skills in A, B, and C are a perfect fit for this job, and the more I have learned about the company and your plans for the future, the more excited I am about the possibility of working here."

If you don't know anyone who works for them, then answer the question behind the question (they are interested in your references):

"No, I don't know anyone who works here, but I can absolutely provide you with references, if that's what you're interested in. They can speak to my skill set, work ethic, and value as an X to your company."

Job Interview Question 14

Does a company need B players? Or is it better off only having A players on staff, and why?

A vs B

Any answer to this question other than "A players" means that you are not an A player. **A players like to work with A players.**

I don't know any managers who should be looking for B players. You should always hire the best you can get, and that's an A player. The more A players you have, the more growth and movement you have.

The more A players you have, the more cushion you have in case one of your A players leaves for a better opportunity.

It doesn't make sense to look for B players anyway—in any organization, there will be some who naturally keep their A player status, and some that will land in B or fall into C status.

That's not to say that B players can't be valuable to an organization. They can. They are often the backbone of an organization that can keep the daily details moving—but they tend not to contribute to active growth.

Key to a Great Interview

For more on 'A' and 'B' players, read Brad Smart's book –
Topgrading, 3rd Edition: The Proven Hiring and Promoting
Method That Turbocharges Company Performance

It talks about how hiring managers should always try to get A players, because there will be enough of them that fall to B player status. If you're going to be a manager, you need to read this book.

Job Interview Question 15

Give an example of a political situation you've dealt with on the job.

Office politics are the "people" part of getting things done at work. Every organization is made up of individuals with varying power levels, goals, relationship lines, and personal emotional baggage they carry with them every day.

This question gets at your **interpersonal, communication**, and **conflict-resolution** skills. How do you bring your **emotional intelligence** into play to navigate in situations brimming with the baggage and hidden agendas of the various players?

Maybe even more importantly, can you do this **without bringing your own emotional baggage or reactions** to the situation? This shows your **maturity, self-control and level of professionalism**.

A 'difficult' political situation is going to be one where **the balance of power is not in your favor**. Your example needs to be one where you **exercised diplomacy or tact** to not just come out unharmed, but ideally to make all the players satisfied with the outcome (everybody wins).

So, a great story to tell might be the time you were involved in a **group project** where one member kept throwing up roadblocks that angered the rest of the group, so you took that person aside, asked questions, found areas of agreement, came back in, built consensus, and got the project done.

As much as you can, **keep the story you choose to tell positive**, with you in a **mediator role** rather than in the direct line of fire.

You don't want to talk about how you had to distance yourself from your boss because the CEO hated him, and walk the tightrope until you could get out of Dodge.

You don't want to talk about how your boss wanted you to do something unethical, and you had to tactfully get out of doing it.

Stories like those are too negative, too gossipy, and don't accomplish the goal of every interview answer you give: to show your fit for the job.

Keep it positive and show how you made a positive impact on the situation.

Job Interview Question 16

Give an example of how you set goals and achieve them.

This is a softball behavioral interview question. You have the power to **choose a story that highlights your very best selling qualities** for this job—so use it wisely. Show them how you think, how you approach problems and goals, and how you can succeed. Always choose a **professional example, NOT a personal one**. Choose a story that relates as much as possible to a **skill that is central to this job**, so that they can easily see how your success in this story would transfer to success in this job.

A good goal that you reached could be anything, such as **completing** an important project, **gaining** a key customer, **improving** a system or process, **increasing** sales, **reducing** employee turnover, **implementing** new procedures to improve X, or **improving** the company's reputation for customer service.

Tell your story using a **STAR** format:

Situation or

Task (Set up the story—what happened? What was your goal?)

Action (What did you choose to do and why?)

Result (What happened as a result of your actions? Quantify this wherever possible.)

For example:

Situation –

"I was assigned X project. It was a complicated project with lots of moving parts, and had to be completed in 90 days."

Task or Action –

"I set a goal of getting the project done in 80 days so we'd have time to make corrections or deal with problems that came up along the way. To keep things running as efficiently as possible, I assigned parts of the project to 5 different teams, with check-in meetings every week. I was able to coordinate their tasks and minimize downtime."

Result –

"Because of the way I set it up, we completed the project on time and 10% under budget. Our Vice-President was so impressed, I received a company award and presented my process at the next company meeting so that other managers could learn from it and implement it, too."

Your story should clearly demonstrate how you added value to the organization through your actions. Use **numbers, dollars, or percentages** to quantify this added value and add a lot of strength to your answer.

Key to a Great Interview -
Quantification

$$\# - \$ - \%$$

Describe your achievements in terms of **numbers, dollars, and percentages.** See how **quantification strengthens your answer**:

"I brought in new clients" or "Brought in 20 new clients in 3 months"

"I delivered product on time and under budget" or "98% on-time delivery of product"

"Maintained accuracy in company database" or "100% accuracy in 50,000-item database over 2 years"

Numbers, dollars, or percentages answer the hiring manager's (interviewer's) primary question:
"How can this person benefit MY company?"

261

Job Interview Question 17

Give an example of how you were able to motivate employees or co-workers.

To motivate someone, you need to know them—what motivates one won't motivate another. To know them, you must be a **good communicator.**

Communication is a vital skill. How you communicate and motivate says a lot about your work style and management style.

Tell your story using a **STAR** format:

Situation or

Task (Set up the story—what happened? What was your goal?)

Action (What did you choose to do and why?)

Result (What happened as a result of your actions? Quantify this wherever possible.)

** If you are interviewing for a **management** position:

Talk about how you **developed relationships** with the members of your team, creating a strong, cohesive unit that was able to **achieve X** (X should be a quantified value, like "the highest sales numbers in the company" or "the award for the best customer service in the division" or whatever outcome you achieved.)

Or, you can tell how you **developed an accountability/rewards program** that boosted employee performance by X%.

Or, you can talk about how you go through the process of **setting expectations and providing specific feedback, and what the results of this process are for you.** Choose an example that showcases your successful management style.

** If you are interviewing for a spot on a **team:**

Talk about the time your group had a member who was more focused on **personal issues** than on getting the work done and say what you did to address that issue. Maybe you created a friendly **competition** to get them engaged.

Or, you asked them out to lunch and **developed a relationship** with them, and you realized that they felt they weren't a valued part of the group, so they weren't participating. When you addressed that issue, the person felt better and became a strong part of the team, and you even became friends.

Any of these kinds of answers show that you are a **team player** who keeps an eye on the group as a whole, not just on your individual piece. It sets you apart as a **leader** they can depend on.

Either way, use the STAR format to talk about your example, and try to **quantify the outcome.**

Job Interview Question 18

Give an example of how you worked on a team.

In your new job, you will also at some point be required to work with others—even if your job is primarily as an individual contributor. Companies want to know that you can do this and get the job done with a minimum of conflicts and issues.

This question is trying to get at your **people skills**—communication skills and other 'soft' skills that aren't on your resume but that dramatically affect your ability to do your job well.

At some point in your life, you worked on some kind of a team, whether it was an officially-recognized, formal team or simply a loose group with a common goal.

Try to choose a situation that would be similar to one you might experience in this new job, or a situation that uses a skill that is central to your success in this new job.

Tell your story using a **STAR** format:

Situation or
Task (Set up the story—what happened? What was your goal?)
Action (What did you choose to do and why?)
Result (What happened as a result of your actions? Quantify this wherever possible.)

The Situation or Task

What kind of team was it?
How did you come to be on the team?
Were you chosen specifically for this team, or was it a normal part of your job?
What was the goal of the team?
Were you facing any difficult circumstances?
Were you on a time limit?
Were you on a budget?
Was the team not getting along?
What was going on?

The Action you took

What did you choose to do in response to the situation?
Was this something that you came up with and had to convince others to go along with?
Explain the thought process behind the decision you made.

The Results you achieved

What was the outcome of the action?
Did you get a positive response?
Was your team recognized for your achievement?
Can you quantify it?

> Did you complete your project 5 days ahead of schedule?
> Did you save $10,000?
> Did you cut 5 minutes off of every part, so that you saved 80 hours over a year?

What if you're a **student with no work experience interviewing for your first job? How do you answer this question?

There will be some example from your past where you worked on a team—a **group project, a sports team, or even a school play**. Talk about the teamwork that helped you came together to achieve your common goal.

Job Interview Question 19

Have you ever fired someone?

If you are interviewing for a management role, they are likely to ask you this question. Managers are usually required to both hire and fire as necessary. They want to know how you would handle that—your **thought process**, how you **feel** about it, and if you can make **good, logical, thoughtful choices** about this situation. Can you make **tough choices**?

If your answer is "No," that you have never fired anyone, you need to follow that up with, "But I always live up to my responsibilities, and I know that this is one that comes with the job, as unpleasant as it might be. Although it is probably difficult to make that decision, I know that I would make it with the good of the whole department and the whole company in mind, with any necessary input from HR and my own supervisor."

You want them to know that **you can make difficult decisions that benefit the greater good**, and that you recognize that the company will have procedures that need to be followed in these situations.

If your answer is "Yes," you'll want to describe what happened.

Tell your story using a **STAR** format:

Situation or

Task (Set up the story—what happened? What was your goal?)

Action (What did you choose to do and why?)

Result (What happened as a result of your actions? Quantify this wherever possible.)

For example:

Talk about what was going on with this employee, walk them through the process of how you addressed the situation, and how it ultimately came to firing that person. Mention what happened after that—maybe morale went up because this person was so negative they drug everyone else down, or maybe your production percentages went up because this person wasn't around to gum up the works any longer.

You want them to know that you **didn't take it lightly, went through the proper channels, and ultimately made the hard decision and took care of business.**

Job Interview Question 20

Have you had to turn an employee with a bad attitude into one with a good attitude?

We've all encountered the person in the office who causes trouble—they gossip, bully, or cause dissension; they are disrespectful and uncooperative; they gripe about the company/the workload/the long hours/the ugly office/etc., they spend a lot of time goofing off, spending time on Facebook or Pinterest, taking long lunches, calling in sick constantly, or otherwise not pulling their weight.

Some companies want you to cut those people loose as soon as possible, but some companies want to try to save them. After all, there was a reason they were hired in the first place and they'd like to have *that* person. Besides, the process you have to follow in some companies is long and daunting, and hiring someone new is expensive and time-consuming.

If you have a story where you've taken someone like that and turned them around, it shows you as a tremendous **communicator and motivator** —two excellent qualities in a manager.

They want to see that you can take action when an employee causes a drain on the morale or productivity of your department. These things can snowball and ruin a previously well-running program.

Any number of ways you could have approached this situation is a good story to tell, **as long as the outcome was a positive one**, like these.

The employee was stuck in a job beyond his or her capabilities, so you gave them a personality test, found another position that fit them much better, moved them over, and now everyone is happy and thriving.

The employee had excellent hard skills but sub-par communication skills, so you sent them to a class to improve his communication and he came back a new person.

The company made a mistake in a new policy that negatively affected the employee, and they were legitimately angry. Once you talked about it, you successfully addressed the issue and the employee was satisfied.

Her mother was diagnosed with cancer, so you worked out a flex plan so she could take care of her personal business and still be productive at her job.

You called them into your office, pointed out their behavior in private, and worked out a Personal Improvement Plan. When they realized how their actions were going to hurt them and maybe even get them fired, they straightened up.

Any story you can tell where you assessed the problem, communicated with the employee, came up with a professional, specific, and results-oriented plan of action, executed it and realized success, is a good story to tell here.

Job Interview Question 21

How did you hear about this position?

This is probably an opening question, possibly in a phone interview—but that's no reason not to answer it in a powerful way.

Never say, "I saw it on Monster" (or Career Builder, Indeed, etc.) and leave it at that. This makes it seem as if you are trolling for any job, anywhere, and you don't care what it is as long as you get paid for it.

If you did learn about it on a **job board**, say so, but then follow up with what caused you to apply for it: "I realized as I read through the job description that I am the perfect fit for this job."

Or, you were so excited to find it because you're a great fit for the job because of A, B, and C (your skills) AND because it's somewhere you always wanted to live.

Or you were so excited to find it because you've heard great things about this company for a long time and you're thrilled about the possibility of working there.

Add **something that expresses your fit or enthusiasm**, which will set you apart.

If you found out about the job through a more focused source, such as an industry **newsletter**, a **LinkedIn group post**, or on their own **company website**, say so, and then again, add what it was that caused you to be excited about applying for the job.

If you found out about the job through a **friend or professional contact**, tell them who that person is and why they thought of you for the job (which mentions your fit for it). Then you can say, "And as I found out more about the job, I agreed. And, it's even a great fit because of X. I'm so glad my friend called me!"

If you found out through a **recruiter**, this can be the most powerful source of all, because the recruiter is the person who likely has a relationship with the company, and who definitely has the most objective viewpoint on whether or not you're a good candidate for the job. Again, mention why the recruiter thought you were an especially good fit for the job and why you think so, too.

Even with questions that don't really seem on the surface like a serious job interview question, **don't miss the opportunity you have with it (and every question) to sell yourself for the job.**

Job Interview Question 22

How did you prepare for this interview?

I love, love, LOVE this question. This is an ideal place to **set yourself apart from every other candidate** in a big way.

The **best-prepared candidate is the one who gets the job**, and this is the place to show that you are that person and make it an easy decision to hire you.

A **'good' answer** would be: "I researched the company" and show that you did by asking great questions about the company, its priorities, and future direction.

A GREAT, stand-head-and-shoulders-above-every-other-candidate, "WOW" answer is to say:

"I'm so glad you asked. I created a **30-60-90-day plan** so you can see how I'd approach the job in my first 90 days and be very successful. I'd like you to have all the information you can about me, and I'd like to find out more about you, so we can see if I'd be a good fit for the position. Can we take a few minutes to go over my plan and see what you think?"

No interviewer will say "No" to this. They will all say "Yes," because **they will be incredibly interested** in what you have done. When you show them your plan, **they will clearly see** the level of **preparation** you put into this interview, and the level of **professionalism** and commitment that you'd bring to the job.

To complete your plan, you will have to:

Research the company (your plan should be as specific as possible to that company).

Think about what it takes to be successful in the job.

Organize and **prioritize strategies** to execute for that success.

Key to a Great Interview!

A 30-60-90-day plan in the BEST preparation you can do for any job interview! Find out more in the resources at the back of the book!

Your answers to all their interview questions will be better because of the research you've done to complete your plan.

When you go through your plan, **ask smart, informed questions** about the job. You'll get **priceless feedback** from this manager about what they see as the primary goals for the job, and what they really think of you and your fit for the position. This will be the **best possible preparation** you could do for the interview.

Job Interview Question 23

How do I rate as an interviewer?

There are not many places you can easily use **humor** in a job interview, but this answer is one of them: "I'm not sure. If you're going to move me forward, I'm going to give you a 10; if you're not, I'm going to give you a zero."

Some questions (like this one) are designed to throw you off your rehearsed and prepared interview game. They want to see **how you react in an unexpected situation**, and maybe even to see how you handle an **awkward** one (like evaluating the person who is supposed to be evaluating you).

Your **safest bet** (besides using humor) is to **focus on the positive** parts of the interview—maybe the interviewer smiled and put you at ease when you arrived. Maybe they're asking you great questions or making it easy for you to point out how well you'd do in the role.

Job Interview Question 24

How do you balance life and work?

This question can be a fishing expedition to see what you'll reveal about yourself that they aren't allowed to ask you about directly.

Very often, this question is really the new version of, "Who takes care of your children when they're sick?" The employer wants to know if you are willing to work extra hours, or if you'll be off a lot with personal matters (like sick children), or if you're the kind of person whose desk chair is empty at 5:01 every day, no matter what.

Once in a while, it means that they're actually concerned with your overall health, because they know that a healthy individual is a better contributor who makes better decisions.

Your **best answer** is, **"I am very organized."** You can elaborate by talking about how you fully engage at work and when you get home, you fully engage there—and it wouldn't be a bad idea to talk about how stepping away from work frees your mind so that you often come up with great ideas at home, and keep a notebook handy to jot those down.

You could assume that the employer is asking about what you do in your **spare time** to offset the stress of work, and this would be a good opportunity to mention an **active hobby** such as running, dancing, hiking, tennis, or even traveling, that makes you seem full of energy. I always like to hear candidates talk about how they **take classes** to learn something new, because I believe that is a positive, that you're willing to learn new things.

You might be able to make a connection with the interviewer, if you happen to have the same hobby they do. Play it safe—try to mention common hobbies like running, hiking, etc. rather than unusual ones (like taxidermy).

If you are really unsure about what to say, toss the ball back into their court: "What do other employees here do?" Or, "What do you do?" This will give you an idea of where they are and where you should be aiming when you answer this question.

Keep in mind that even with this question, **every word you say has a purpose—to convince them to hire you.**

Now is not the time to mention any interest you might have in Flex-Time, Job Sharing, working from home, or any other non-traditional arrangement—unless you know they have a program already in place, or unless it is an absolute deal breaker for you. Otherwise, wait until they love you and are closer to an offer (or better yet, after you've worked there for a while).

Job Interview Question 25

How do you compensate for your weaknesses?

Your interviewer knows that if they ask, "What's your greatest weakness?" you'll have an answer ready that doesn't really seem like a weakness and puts you in good light. Asking this way, "How do you compensate for your weaknesses?" might throw you off your game a bit. It drills a little deeper and assumes that you have a weakness and simply asks what you are doing about it.

Give them a weakness that doesn't affect a central, critical part of your job and tell them what you already do to overcome it.

For instance, I would say that I am not particularly detail-oriented, and that's why I take the extra steps of X, Y, and Z so I don't miss anything.

This might be a good opportunity to show that you are coachable, which is a big plus in the eyes of your future supervisor. Say, "I used to have a problem with X, but my mentor gave me a fantastic solution (then describe that). I've been using it ever since with no problems."

Or, this might be a good opportunity to show that **you can train yourself,** when necessary:

"I used to be a little afraid of technology, but then I signed up for some classes on my own to learn what I needed to. I brush up my skills with a new class every few months or so."

It's going to take some thought on your part, but **be strategic** and think of an answer that names a weakness that is not a deal-breaking factor for this job, and a compensation that highlights a **great quality** they would like to see in you.

Think about the company, think about the job itself, and really tailor your answer to fit.

Job Interview Question 26

How do you feel about an income made up totally of commissions?

If they are asking you this question, (1) you know you're interviewing for a sales job; and (2) they're probably going to pay you only commissions, rather than a base plus commissions.

Since **this is a salary question**, your best bet at this point is to just yet. What you're trying to do is move through the process, not knock yourself out of the running by giving the wrong answer.

Your best strategy when faced with this question is to ask questions of your own:

"In the past, my income has been split between base pay, commissions, and bonuses, so I'm not sure. Are all of your positions commissions-only?"

Stay away from what you really think and ask questions to get as much information as you can.

Job Interview Question 27

How do you feel about working for a younger manager?

If you are asked this question, you are an older worker. Job seekers over 50 (sometimes, over 40) have a reputation for not being able to take orders from some young whippersnapper.

Help them feel better about making the decision to hire you, by saying a definitive, "I'd be just fine with that. No problem."

To lend yourself additional credibility, add a follow up statements like one of these.

"There's a reason that person is in a supervisory position, and I know I'd learn something from them, no matter how old they are. I would look forward to their perspective."

"Age doesn't matter to me at all. What matters in a great boss is leadership ability, and knowledge of the business as well as future trends, enthusiasm, and communication skills."

"I usually find that if someone knows a little less than me because they're younger or don't have as much experience, they know more than me in another area. I learn new things from just about everyone and I enjoy it."

Job Interview Question 28

How do you make decisions?

With this question, the interviewer is looking to see what your decision-making process is like. How do you think? How do you approach a problem? Can you think critically about it and come to a rational, data-based solution or decision?

You can walk them through the process of how you go about making a decision—talk about how you gather information, how you learn more about the problem, who you talk to, what books you read, what resources you consult, and what factors you take into account when you decide.

A great way to answer this is to walk them through a difficult decision you made (with a successful outcome).

Maybe it's how you made the decision to **fire** someone, or it's how you made the decision to **assign resources** to a particular function, even though it was unpopular.

Tell your story using a **STAR** format:

Situation or

Task –

Talk about what you were faced with. What was going on? Why was this a problem? What goal were you not hitting that you needed to hit?

Action –

What did you do? Who did you talk to? What did you read? How did you take in information? Did you try any preliminary solutions before you settled on the final one?

Result –

Reinforce that you made the right decision by talking about the positive outcome that happened because of your decision. Maybe your decision on resources made a ton of money for the company, or maybe it set you up to develop a new market where you hadn't been before, or maybe it just got one new customer that has turned into a loyal and profitable long-term relationship.

Let the interviewer know that you have no problem making sound, reasoned decisions, because it's part of your job. Walk them through how you think so they can be comfortable with letting you make decisions for them in their role.

Job Interview Question 29

How do you take advantage of your strengths?

Asking about your strengths is just as common as asking about your weaknesses. Essentially, this is "why should we hire you?" This is a great opening to **highlight your best-fit qualities** for the job.

The job search is, at its core, a sales process. The employer is like a buyer, or customer, looking for the perfect product to buy that will solve a problem or provide a solution. You are the product that's up for 'sale.' But there's no salesman waiting to sing your praises to this hiring manager—that's your task.

Think about what quality, characteristic or skill you have that will help you do this job especially well. Where will you shine? Don't be afraid to brag…that's essentially the point of this question. And don't be too generic: "I'm driven to succeed, so I work harder than everyone else."

They want to know what YOU can do for the organization, so they can decide whether or not to hire you.

Come up with a few **strengths** that you can **quantify** in some way, because the question is 'how do you take advantage of your strengths', and **the point of every job is to make money or save money or time (which is money) for the company**.

You take advantage of your strengths when you use them to accomplish those money-making or money-saving things for the company.

Have some kind of story or example that illustrates or demonstrates how you've used this strength. For instance:

****

"I am a great listener, and that has helped me build especially strong relationships with my customers. My accounts stay with me X times longer than average because of this."

(Or, your listener skill could help you get projects done faster/ more accurately because you pay attention to the nuances/ details/ whatever. Say what benefits come from this, and quantify them.)

****

"I am very detail-oriented, so I am an organizational powerhouse. In my last position, I was able to successfully maintain X% more accounts than everyone else, making me the top performer."

****

"I am comfortable talking to everyone, which makes me especially successful at going after new business. In my last role, I brought in X new customers in 6 months, that were worth about $X."

****

"I have a lot of experience in X, which means that I can hit the ground running for you and start achieving the X, Y, and Z you would like to see immediately."

****

Think about yourself and what YOUR strengths really are. That's the way to make yourself stand out. No one else is going to have your **unique set of strengths, skills, talents, personality traits, education, or training**.

Make sure that the ones you point out are relevant to this position, so the employer will care about them. If you need to, comb through the job description and think about why you'd be good at X or Y that they have listed.

Whatever you say, be able to **point out the benefit to the employer**—either with **something you've done in the past** (with quantification, if you can) or with **something you will be able to do** for them.

Don't be afraid to brag on yourself. They want to hear how fantastic you are, **they want to hear why they should hire you** over someone else, and they won't know unless you tell them.

Key to a Great Interview - Quantification

$$\# - \$ - \%$$

Describe your achievements in terms of **numbers, dollars, and percentages.** See how **quantification strengthens your answer**:

"I brought in new clients"

or

"Brought in 20 new clients in 3 months"

"I delivered product on time and under budget"

or

"98% on-time delivery of product"

"Maintained accuracy in company database"

or

"100% accuracy in 50,000-item database over 2 years"

Numbers, dollars, or percentages answer the hiring manager's (interviewer's) primary question: "How can this person benefit MY company?"

Job Interview Question 30

How does this position compare with others you're applying for?

The question behind this question is,
"Why do you want THIS job, with THIS company?"

They want to know that you are truly interested in this job, or if this one is your 'safety net' in case the one you really want doesn't work out. They're also probing to see if you are applying anywhere else, and trying to get a handle on what it would take to get you. The good news is that if they ask this, they are interested in you.

Don't say, "This is the only one I'm applying for," even if it is.

Is this your only interview?
I hope not! It's extremely rare for one interview to result in a job. Get multiple interviews so you have the CHOICE about which job to take…that is an amazing feeling. See how in my Job Search and Interview Course at https://careerconfidential.com/coaching-memberships-nf/

286

You want them to think that someone else wants you. At the same time, don't overdo it. Letting them think that you've applied all over the place, to anyone who'll have you, is not the way to make yourself seem like a desirable candidate—it just makes you seem desperate for a job, any job.

A great way to handle this question is to breeze past the outright comparison and point out what especially attracts you to this company and this opportunity, following up with why you're a good fit for it:

"It's very competitive. I am talking with a couple of other companies, but what I especially like about this one is X, Y, and Z. I believe it is an especially good fit for me because of A, B, and C."

(Don't give them the idea that you are talking to *a lot* of other companies, because it makes you seem more interested in collecting a paycheck from anyone willing to sign it rather than someone who is truly interested in the work and finding the right fit.)

You could follow up this statement in a couple of ways:

1)   "Do you agree with me so far?"

This is a great time to **ask if they agree that you seem like a good fit**, or some other question that puts the ball back in their court so that you can see what they might be thinking about you.

2)   "How do I compare to the other candidates you're interviewing?"

They're asking what you think about how it's going, so turn it around and ask them how they think it's going.

***   If a recruiter has contacted you about this job, this is the only time it's OK to say, "I am not applying anywhere else. I am happy where I am, but when Recruiter Smith called, it seemed like an exciting opportunity that I wanted to explore a little further." In this case, the employer will realize that they are going to have to sweeten the pot to lure you away from your current employer (where you're very happy).

Job Interview Question 31

How does your previous experience relate to this position?

This is a GREAT question if you can get it. It's another version of, "Why should we hire you?" You have the power here to **highlight your best qualities**. They want to know **why you're a good fit for the job**, and are looking for information that will make their decision an easy one.

If you DO have related experience, this is easy. Just summarize it, pointing out a few pertinent details along the way. If you've already asked, "What does your ideal candidate look like?" then you know what's most important to them, and you can mention relevant things from your own background. If you haven't asked about their ideal candidate, then you can base your answer from what you read in their job description.

But remember: every candidate can explain a direct relationship. **To stand out, add examples with *quantification* to your answer where you can.** For example, if your experience is in retail and this job is in retail, you have plenty of experience. Where you **stand out** is when you also tell them that you boosted sales by **30%** or you won the company customer service award **3 years** in a row or you reduced turnover by **50%** by implementing X program.

**Key to a Great Interview -
Quantification**

- $ - %

Describe your achievements in terms of **numbers, dollars, and percentages.** See how **quantification strengthens your answer**:

"I brought in new clients"
or
"Brought in 20 new clients in 3 months"

"I delivered product on time and under budget"
or
"98% on-time delivery of product"

"Maintained accuracy in company database"
or
"100% accuracy in 50,000-item database over 2 years"

Numbers, dollars, or percentages answer the hiring manager's (interviewer's) primary question: "How can this person benefit MY company?"

If you're a new graduate or switching careers, your experience may not clearly show why you're a good fit for the job, so **connect those dots** for them and explain **how your skills are transferable** to this position. Things you'll typically want to point out are your skills in communication, organization, project management, time management, problem-solving, multitasking, or making professional contacts.

Think about what it is that you have that would make you successful in this job.

In this case, you also want to show that **you can learn new things quickly** by giving them an example of a time that you did: "My job was X, but Y situation came up and they asked me to handle it. Here's how I did it." Walk them through your thought process to show them your **strategic thinking** and **ability to adapt**, both of which are tremendously beneficial in a new role.

Key to a Great Interview!

If they ask you about your experience, they are trying to see you in the role. The best way to help a hiring manager see you in the role is to show them your 30-60-90-Day Plan.

Say, "My experience relates through X, Y, and Z. But to really show you how I could step into THIS role and be successful, I've created a 90-day plan for how I would approach this job with my skills and even fill in the gap that I have in X. Can we take a few minutes to walk through it?"

The interviewer will be curious to see your plan, and happy to see such a substantial answer to this question. They'll be able to see you in the role much more clearly, which puts them further along the road to offering you the job. Find out more in the resources at the back of the book!

Job Interview Question 32

How have you handled difficult situations with employees?

Every hiring manager has had a difficult situation with an employee. With this question, the interviewer is mostly looking for **how you respond to underperformance**, which is the most common difficult situation. A manager who can turn around an underperformer is a **highly valued** piece of any organization.

Think about a time when you had to deal with a problem employee and had a **positive outcome.**

Use the **STAR** format:
    Situation or
    Task
    Action
    Result

Situation or Task

Tell them what was going on with this employee. What was happening? What was the behavior? How long had it been going on? How was it affecting the bigger picture?

Action

Walk them through what you did to address the problem. How did you intervene? Did you have a talk with the employee? Did you set up a Personal Improvement Plan? What was involved in the plan? Was it a simple plan, or a multi-step one? Did that solve it, or did you have to meet with the employee again? Did you have to get anyone else involved? Did you ask anyone for advice? Did you use any resources? What was the employee's reaction to your intervention? Walk them through the action you took so they can see your thought process.

Result

What happened as a result of your actions? Did the employee have a better attitude or increased performance? Maybe you found a better-fitting position within the company for the employee where they are now successful.

Use quantification wherever you can. Did this happen in 2 weeks or 6 months? Did the employee's performance improve by 5% or 80%? Did you save money by not having to train a new employee?

Walk them through a good example with a positive outcome so they can see how you approach a difficult situation like this, how you think, and if your goals line up with them as a company.

Job Interview Question 33

How many tennis balls can you fit into a limousine?

Will you get asked a brainteaser question in your interview? Maybe, maybe not.

Yes, they can seem ridiculous. The method behind the madness is to evaluate how you think and how you approach a problem. The key is to be ready for anything, and don't get flustered.

If they ask you any kind of **brainteaser question**:

How many tennis balls in a limousine?

How would you move Mount Fuji?

How many gas stations are there in the US?

Just remember that you don't have to get the exact right answer. What you need to do is demonstrate that you **don't get flustered, confused, or thrown off your game** by the unexpected, and that you can come up with a **reasoned, logical approach to problem solving**.

So just take a deep breath and **start thinking through the question out loud**. If you need a pen and paper to help you think (I would), then use the ones you brought with you to take notes.

For tennis balls in a limousine, maybe I would say, "I would first have to look up the average cubic feet of the inside of a limo, and then I would do a simple calculation based on that number divided by the size of a tennis ball. Or, I could get a 1 foot cube, fill it with tennis balls, count those, and multiply that by the average cubic square feet of the inside of a limo." So now, I've shown them that I can come up with **multiple ways to approach and solve a problem on the fly**.

If I were asked to move Mount Fuji, I might say, "How far? I need some parameters." (*It's OK to ask questions to clarify or get more information.*) Or I might use humor: "A bulldozer load at a time." Or, if I wanted to be creative, I might say, "I'd have a contest for anyone who could move the biggest bucketful of Mount Fuji 1 mile, and the winner would get a prize."

If I were asked "How many gas stations are there in the U.S?" I'd probably estimate how many gas stations there might be in a small town of say, 10,000 people and start multiplying until I got to the approximately 300 million people there are in the U.S.

In these kinds of questions, **the answer is not the point as much as is the process of getting there.**

HINT!

Take paper and pen to your job interviews!

Use it to sketch out ideas to help yourself think and better answer interview questions.

Take notes for your thank you note and second interview.

Job Interview Question 34

How will you identify problems and opportunities on the job?

This is a great question that allows you to vividly demonstrate your **creativity, critical thinking,** and **problem-solving skills**.

They want you to walk them through **the process you use to identify top issues and opportunities to move the company forward**. You have several ways to address this question.

First, you can answer by giving them an **example** of something you identified in the past and what actions you took to either address it or take advantage of it, and what the results were. This approach is something you can use **if you have a strong, quantified example of something that had a major impact on your company** (such as an innovative new marketing program, an efficiency-boosting scheduling change, or something that *significantly* saved or made the company money).

Tell your story using a **STAR** format:
Situation or
Task (Set up the story—what happened? What was your goal?)
Action (What did you choose to do and why?)
Result (What happened as a result of your actions? Quantify this wherever possible.)

Second, this is a good time to talk about the **80/20 Rule**, and how you use it to determine where you're going to get the most impact from your actions. This is a very important guiding principle that applies to productivity in every area of your life. It is a data-based decision-making process.

80/20 Rule

A long, LONG time ago, an Italian economist named Pareto noticed that 80% of the wealth in Italy was held by 20% of the people. Joseph Juran took Pareto's Principle and successfully applied it to quality management--and the 80/20 Rule was born.

The 80/20 Rule says (among other things) that 80% of sales come from 20% of customers, or that **80% of your results come from 20% of your effort.**

It's about **productivity** and identifying the **significant tasks/actions** that contribute most to it. Prioritize the most important tasks, and you become **super-efficient and effective**. You will spend time on the things that matter.

Third, this is an ideal time to introduce your **30-60-90-Day Plan**: "I'm so glad you asked that, Mr. Manager. I've worked up an outline of how I would approach the job in the first 90 days, and it includes how I intend to go about identifying areas where I can make the most impact in terms of solving your problems and implementing actions to help us grow." And then get out your plan and start going over it with the hiring manager.

Key to a Great Interview!

Introducing your 30-60-90-day plan is an excellent answer to a forward-thinking question like this one. They want to know what life is going to look like with you on the job and how they can expect you to **tackle problems, identify opportunities, and contribute to the growth of the company**. The 90-day plan demonstrates how you'll hit the ground running to do just that. Find out more in the resources at the back of the book!

Job Interview Question 35

How would people you have worked with describe you?

This is an important question, for two reasons:

1) This is actually going to be **how you describe yourself**.

What you say should be very **positive**: "They would say that I am a hard worker, who is very thoughtful and strategic about the work that I do, that I am proud of my work and what I've accomplished. They would say that I never want to let anyone down, and that I always want to exceed the expectations of the people I am working for. And they would say that I am someone they can trust, rely on, and call on when they are having issues, that I am someone who goes above and beyond."

Whatever you say, **be prepared to give examples** that illustrate what you just said. If you say that you are someone who goes above and beyond, you need to have an example of a time that you did that. If you don't have an example, you will be in trouble.

2) What you say needs to be **close to what your references will say** about you, because they will ask.

If what you say is miles away from what they actually say about you, you will seem very out of touch with how you are perceived by others, which doesn't say good things for your communication skills. (Always know what your references will say about you.)

This is a great time to thumb over to the section in your **brag book** where you have printed out **emails or notes from bosses, colleagues, or even clients to actually show them what others have said about you**. If there are especially positive comments in your **performance reviews, or any awards letters,** those would be good to show, also.

Key to a Great Interview!

If you have anything **tangible** that illustrates your story, put it in your **brag book** and point to it while you answer this question. What could this be? The possibilities are many:

-A **brochure** you developed, to show what you can do

-A **note from your boss thanking you** for the suggestion and talking about how it turned out

-**Sales numbers** pre- and post-suggestion

-**Any workplace improvements** pre- and post-suggestion

-**A note from a customer thrilled** with your new system/procedure

-The outline of a **training process you created**

Providing evidence to back up your story or example is a powerful way to stand out from every other candidate.

If you would like help putting yours together, check out my <u>Brag Book eReport on Amazon</u>

Job Interview Question 36

How would you guide an alien through making a peanut butter sandwich?

This seems like a silly question, but it actually gets right to the heart of how you **think and communicate**.

How well can you teach someone else?

Can you step back from something as completely basic as a peanut butter sandwich and remember to **explain the steps** to someone who knows absolutely nothing?

Can you **put yourself in their shoes**?

Are you a good **communicator**?

So, I would say,

"First of all, we have to assume nothing. So there's an alien sitting at the table. Does he know he's hungry, or do we have to explain that, as well? Here on Earth, when we are hungry, we have to physically eat food or drink, something that has calories in it, or we have a big problem. Then I would show him what peanut butter looks like, and what bread looks like, and what a knife looks like.

I would show him how to twist the lid on the jar of peanut butter to the right to open it, and let him practice. Then I would show him how to open the package of bread and get two slices, and lay them side-by-side on the table. I would demonstrate how to hold the knife, and let him have it. Then I would tell him to dip the knife in the peanut butter and draw it out.

Then I would tell him to apply the peanut butter to one side of a piece of bread, and spread it around. Then I would tell him to place the other piece of bread on top of that one, so that the peanut butter is in the interior of the sandwich. That's how I would guide an alien through making a peanut butter sandwich."

You want to **talk about everything and assume nothing.** They are looking to see how you communicate.

When you are training people at work, you have to make sure you **stop and explain everything**, even if you think it's self-explanatory. There's no telling what your trainee might be bringing to this process in terms of past experience, so you need to make sure there are no misunderstandings.

Job Interview Question 37

I see you had an internship. Did you pursue a full-time job with them? What happened?

Internships are fantastic opportunities, and if you've had one, that puts you ahead of someone who didn't.

Very often when someone has an internship, it turns into a full-time job for them. So if yours didn't, why not? Did that company have a problem with you? (Which means, will they have a problem with you?)

They are looking for reassurance that there is no risk in hiring you, so what you are trying to do in answering this question is to **eliminate any perceived risks**.

If you did NOT pursue a full-time job with them, that's no problem. There are lots of reasons why you might not have, not all of them negative. For now, talk about what a **great relationship** you had, and what a great internship it was. If you can, mention that they could even give a **reference** for you. If they will give you a good reference, the risk of hiring you is gone.

If you DID pursue a full-time job with them, and it didn't work out, make sure the interviewer understands **it wasn't you**; it was them (the company). You could say that they didn't have an opening at the

302

time, or that they cut back on new hires and didn't hire any interns, or that they were in the middle of a layoff and weren't bringing in any new staff. You could say that they didn't have a position open in your area or in your preferred geographical location. **They would have liked to hire you**, but it just didn't work out. Again, if they can give you a good **reference**, that is a complete risk-eliminator.

If you pursued the job with them because they did have open position and you just didn't get it, maybe you could speak about the fact that you didn't have some sort of an experience that now you do have. Something needs to have changed in you or on your part between when they decided they didn't want you and now. **Whatever it was that made you a risk before should be gone**, so that you are not a risk to your new company.

Job Interview Question 38

If I were to ask your current boss to tell me one thing you do that drives them crazy, what would they say?

Even though you're spending the whole interview singing your praises, the interviewer knows you're not perfect. They know you've got a wart or two, and want to find it before they hire you—so, they ask about your flaws. The usual question is, "What is your greatest weakness?" but some interviewers get creative and ask this one.

As with the weakness question, you need to **choose a real weakness that does not directly affect your success on this job**—nothing that would have a major impact on your performance.

Things to **stay far, far away from**:

"I ask for too much direction." - This gives the impression that you don't know what you're doing.

"I run late on projects." - A manager can't rely on someone who commits to something and doesn't meet it—over and over again.

"My boss was mad because I didn't tell her about a problem fast enough."

You might feel justified because you were trying to handle it yourself, but this interviewer doesn't want to think that you ignore problems until they are causing a major and maybe unfixable issue.

****

Whatever you choose to say, follow it up with some statement indicating that you either are **taking steps to improve**, or that even though it's not necessarily a saint-like quality, it does **help you succeed in your job**.

For instance, my bosses would have told you that I am very **impatient**. At times, it causes me a problem socially and in my family life. But that same impatience is what drove me to be a top sales rep and helped me climb the ladder to management very quickly.

Maybe your **desk is messy** and your boss is a neat freak. Unless you are directly dealing with clients or lose things, it shouldn't be a problem. This is a case where it might drive your boss crazy personally, but it doesn't affect your work.

Maybe you get so involved in your work you **lose track of time** and you've been late to a few internal meetings (not great, but not the worst reason to be late). That's something your boss can't stand, so you started setting **an alarm on your phone** and you haven't been late since.

Don't choose a clichéd answer, like you're a perfectionist or you work too hard, but choose something either completely insignificant to your success in this job.

The one exception to this would be if you were actually fired for cause. They will be talking to your former boss. This is your chance to soften the story, present your side, and tell why whatever got you fired is never, ever going to be a problem again.

Job Interview Question 39

If I were to ask your current boss what your greatest strength is, what would they say?

If you had to choose only one quality of yours to explain why they need to hire you, and your entire interview was limited to talking about that one quality, which one would you choose? That is the one you should mention in this answer.

I might try to stack the deck and include a few more in my answer anyway: "My boss would have a hard time choosing between my people skills, my work ethic, or X."

"X" would depend on your individual situation and the job description. It could be:

-"My ability to take steps out of almost any process and make it more efficient."

-"My ability to see the big picture and set smart strategies."

-"My meticulous attention to detail."

-"My ability to take the lead on almost any team project and get everyone working together."

-"My ability to fit into almost any team, get along with everyone, and accomplish our goal."

-"My creativity, combined with my business sense."

-"My knack for finishing projects on time and under budget every time."

-"My nose for finding new opportunities to generate revenue."

Whatever you say, **follow it up with a story** that tells about a time you did this, to give an example: "Recently, I did X and my boss was so thrilled that she mentioned me to the VP and I got a mention in the monthly meeting as an example to follow." This is going to help them **visualize** you in action on the job and get comfortable with the idea of working with you.

Always try to **quantify your answer**. Provide **numbers, dollars, or percentages** to describe what happened, what action you took, or what the outcome was. Let's say you said your greatest strength was your nose for finding new opportunities to generate revenue: "Last year, I realized that our product would be perfect for X market, and we hadn't ventured there yet. So I told my boss and together we came up with a plan that ended up generating $X in sales in the first 6 months."

Whatever your example is, tell a story that provides this quantification for your interviewer. This is powerful **evidence** that you can do what you say you can do, and you understand that your role in this company (and any role in any company) is to make **measurable progress** or provide **measurable results** that help them grow **financially**.

Job Interview Question 40

If you are employed, how are you managing time to interview?

Why would they ask you this question? It's because they are trying to find out if you are lying to or 'cheating on' your current employer. Are you **honest**? Do they know you're looking? Are you a sneak? Did you tell them you were sick? (I hope not.)

Always **answer this question briefly**: "I am taking personal time to do this today."

If there is a need for you to elaborate, you can say: "I am selective about where I interview, because I only want to consider jobs that would be a perfect fit, so it's not taking much time away from work."

Job Interview Question 41

If you could choose any company to work for, which one would it be?

This is a question of **fit**. Will you fit within this organization?

With this question, they are looking to see **how you think**, and if you have **thoughtfully considered** where you want to work, and **what kind of environment** you want to be in. It's a way for them to understand your **character** and your **thought process**. Are you in this for your career, or for just a paycheck?

Ideally, you want to **describe a company with characteristics similar to the one you're interviewing with,** and talk about the characteristics of this company that are most **appealing** to you. Talk about how you are looking for a company that has growth opportunities, that has the same values and ethics that you have, or that will use your skill sets (whether yours are in Accounting or Sales or Operations or whatever). **Help them see how their company is a good fit for you.**

Maybe the company you want to work for is simply in a **specific industry** (medical, beverages, transportation, information technology). Are you looking for a **small company or a large one?** A **public or private** company? **Profit or non-profit? Government or private-sector?**

Say what it is about it that appeals to you: "I want to work for a small company because small companies generally tend to be more fluid, more innovative, and more growth-oriented, and I think that's exciting."

Stay away from saying anything bad about your previous companies: "As long as a company doesn't do X (whatever X was that was so awful), then I'll be thrilled." That's a very negative statement that indicates you are running AWAY from somewhere, rather than running TO somewhere. If you are running away, it doesn't matter so much where you end up. If you are running TO somewhere, it does. You have a goal. It's a positive thing.

Always Remember: Under no circumstances do you name a specific company that is not this one—even as a joke.

If this is your ideal company, by all means, say so (and tell them why) and let your natural enthusiasm shine through. That's a very appealing quality in someone interviewing for a job.

If you get the job, how could you lose or make money for me?

This question really gets at, "Do you understand the job and what it takes to be successful?"

You might be tempted to say, "There's no way I could lose money for you!" But the truth is that everyone can make mistakes, and it's good to show that you recognize where those pitfalls are and that you know how to avoid them.

You could say, "In this position, someone could lose money by making a mistake in X, Y, or Z."

Follow this up with, "I could make money for you first by avoiding those mistakes, and then by being successful at A, B, and C."

"A, B, and C" should be those tasks or actions that are **central to your success in this job**.

Every position in every company has an impact on the company's financial success—even the janitor, because that's the person who keeps the facility clean and attractive. The facility's attractiveness helps to make it a pleasant place to work, so that top performers in the field enjoy working there. Cleanliness helps keep accidents down, so the company isn't paying out in worker's comp. And, it sets the company in the customer's or client's mind as not only a nice place to do business, but reassures them that this company takes care of details as well as the big picture.

Give an example (**quantified**, if you can) to illustrate how you can make money: "I did this at my last job, where I created XYZ that was responsible for pushing us over the top on our performance goals for the year by 30%."

Once you answer the question, this is an **excellent** place to bring up your **30-60-90-Day Plan:**

"I've thought a lot about how I could make money for you and be successful at this job. I worked up an outline of what I would do in the first 90 days to really hit the ground running. Would you like to see my ideas?"

Key to a Great Interview!

A 30-60-90-day plan helps make it an easy decision to hire you!

Find out more in the resources at the back of the book!

Any good interviewer or hiring manager is going to be intensely curious about you and your plan you've put together. This will give them much more information about you and how you think so they can make a good decision about whether or not to offer you the job. As you go through the plan, you'll be **discussing ways you can make money for the company** and getting this hiring manager's input on how you can be super-successful in this role.

Job Interview Question 43

If you knew things at your company were rocky, why didn't you get out sooner?

You may get asked this question if you were laid off in a massive restructuring, downsizing, or other shakeup, and you need to have a good answer.

This is a good place to **underscore your loyalty** to the company you work for:

"I was so focused on doing my job well and taking up the slack where others had left or been laid off that I just didn't have the time to look around for another job. I was hoping that it would turn around, because that was a great company, and a great place to work for many years."

You would **never** want to answer this question by giving the idea that you were clueless ("I didn't know it was as rocky as it turned out to be") or helpless ("I tried to look for something else, but no one else was hiring"). Both of those kinds of answers make you seem weak and less-than-desirable as a new hire.

Always answer questions like these in a **positive way** that shows that it was **your choice**, that you stayed out of loyalty, and that you fought until the bitter end.

Job Interview Question 44

If you were at a business lunch and you ordered a rare steak and they brought it to you well-done, what would you do?

This is not just a question of dining etiquette, it's also a question about **how you respond to mistakes or problems** and how concerned you are with the comfort of your clients or customers.

"Mistakes happen. I would be disappointed, but because that's simply a preference of mine, it would not be worth making the other person feel uncomfortable eating without me or having to wait until my food came back. So, if it isn't going to give me food poisoning, I would just eat it."

If you were running a company that produces X and the market was tanking for that product, what would you do?

This question probes for how you think—are you **strategic**? How do you **approach problems** and come up with **solutions**?

This is like any other behavioral interview question, only it's more realistic than "If an airplane landed in the parking lot, what would you do?"

In this case, you are pretending to run the company.

A good CEO **thinks through problems, gathers and develops resources, looks at the data, makes thoughtful, strategic decisions, and works to position her company to succeed now and in the future**

So a good answer might be:

"I would look at why the market was tanking—is it a temporary situation or does it look permanent? Is it the economy? Is it a change in social trends? I might try to conduct a survey of my customers to see what they're thinking. Based on all the information I gathered, I would look at my product to see if it could be improved or modified to fit the new paradigm, or if maybe it just needed to be marketed with a fresh approach. In addition, I would look at other potential markets for my product that we hadn't yet explored."

If you have questions, ask them. It's perfectly acceptable to **gather more information** before you decide on a plan of action. Walk them through your thought process. **Help them see your problem-solving approach and solution-producing abilities.**

Job Interview Question 46

If you were the CEO of this company, what are the top 2 things you would do?

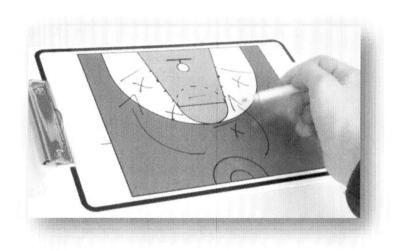

This is another situational interview question, or behavioral interview question, that delves into not just how you think and how you approach problems, but also into how well you've prepared for this interview.

How well do you know this company?

Have you done your homework?

Do your goals and thinking line up with theirs?

They won't want to hear that you would come in with big, sweeping changes to radically transform everything—for one, that's threatening, and two, if you thought the company was that off-track, why would you want to work there?

They also don't want to hear that everything is great and you would change or improve nothing—if that were so, they why would they need you?

If you have done your homework and looked the company up in terms of **news releases, LinkedIn** pages or discussions, **Facebook** pages, or contacting **current or previous employees.**

Then, you would have some idea of the direction the company is going, and you could contribute an idea or comment to that.

If this question is coming after some discussion already in the interview, you could work that into your answer:

"**Based on our discussion** about X, I think that a good direction would be to look into Y—depending on how A, B, and C factor into it."

Anything you would suggest needs to have some **financial benefit** for the company. I would **stay away from** talking about implementing 'feel-good' initiatives like flextime or a company health club and focus instead on things that relate to the primary objective of the company.

Maybe you don't have anything concrete to contribute. In that case, you could talk about **how you would approach a problem** like that:

"First, I would make sure I knew everything I needed to know about what is currently going on, I would talk to people in the company, I would see what the projections are for the next year, and then I would start evaluating different plans of action, based on that data."

Then, here's the **killer follow up** to that statement:

"But that's more theoretical. If you'd like to know how I would approach a new role in the here and now, I have put together a 90 day plan for what I would do in the first 3 months in this job. As we go through it together, you'll see my thought process and learn a lot more about me. Would you like to see it?"

The discussion of your first 90 days in this job will have a much bigger impact on how they see you and your success in this role than the answer to this theoretical question.

Key to a Great Interview!
A 30-60-90-Day Plan is a sure-fire way to show how you think strategically, and you could step into the role and be successful immediately. This plan makes it an easy decision for them to hire you. Find out more in the resources at the back of the book!

Job Interview Question 47

If you won the lottery, would you still work?

Asking this personality interview question is a way for the interviewer to try to establish rapport and get to know the 'real' you. It's also a vehicle they try to use to determine your work ethic, and whether you do this work because you're sincerely enthusiastic about the job, or because it pays for your food, shelter, and hobbies.

There are 3 viable ways you could answer this question:

One - "**I don't know.** It's easy to guess as to what we would do in an extraordinary situation like that, but it's very hard to actually know. If I told you I'd keep working, you might not believe me, but I truly enjoy what I do and get a lot of personal satisfaction in a job well done. It would be hard to walk away from that feeling of getting up every morning and feeling challenged by my day and successful at the end of it."

This answer at least lets them know that **you care about your job** and you enjoy being successful at it, for reasons other than money.

Two - "We all have fantasies of relaxing on the beach, but I am someone who likes to keep growing, learning, and accomplishing. So if I didn't work anymore, I would at least explore some of the **things I've**

always wanted to do, like travel or learn how to do X. I certainly wouldn't run out of ideas for new things to do!"

This answer shows that you are someone who is **energetic, curious, and constantly growing**—all great qualities.

Three - You could answer this one with **humor** and a big smile on my face (one of my favorite tactics): "I don't know if I'd still work, but I'd definitely buy everyone I knew a car to celebrate. Would I know you by then because of our long and successful working relationship?"

This answer ought to make them laugh and relax with you, which is always a good thing in an interview.

Job Interview Question 48

Is it more important to be lucky or skillful?

This question is an **attitude** question. How you answer it will tell the interviewer a lot about **how you look at the world**. Are you an optimist or a pessimist? Do you consider yourself someone with good things going on in their life, or bad things?

It's important to **be positive** in your answer.

You never want to sound like, "Well, it must be more important to be lucky, because those are the people who catch all the breaks!" This shows them that you consider yourself unlucky and are more than a little resentful of that.

My personal answer is:

"I think that if you're skillful, then you create your own luck. You get to be skillful by putting yourself out there, developing those skills, and when you do that, opportunities show up. When you are prepared for those opportunities with what you need to take advantage of them, that's what most people call 'luck.'"

Or you could say something else that shows you have a positive attitude and you work hard, such as:

"I think I was very lucky to have been born into a family that valued education and taught me how to work hard. That background led me to develop the skills I need to do this job, which put me in this conversation with you today. So in that sense, I've been both."

If you have some kind of an **issue** in your background, such as a **career setback**, an **illness** or an **illness of a family member** that's kept you out of the workforce for a few years, this might be the time to talk a little more philosophically about luck and skill:

"Well, I've dealt with adversity in the form of X, that I felt made me very unlucky at the time. But I learned A, B, and C from that which is helping me today to be better at Y and Z. So while I wouldn't have wished that on anyone, I think that it's developed more confidence/a better attitude/a more positive outlook that will help me to be stronger than ever before."

Whatever you say, keep your answer positive.

Job Interview Question 49

Is there any question I haven't asked you that I should?

This question makes me want to use humor to answer it. Smile and say, "I think you should ask me 'When can you start?'"

This is a great time to 'close' for the job. If you don't know what closing is, it's a sales technique for sealing the deal. When you close, you are at the 'rubber meets the road' point where they're either in or out, and you need to know which.

If you say, "I think you should ask me when I can start," and they **smile** or otherwise indicate that they are thinking along those same lines, then you know you've done a good job in this interview.

If they start briskly backpedaling, you know they are leaning toward going with someone else, and you should say (with surprise), "Oh, that doesn't sound good. Is there some reason you wouldn't move me forward?" This gets them to **tell you what problem or doubt they do have**, and you might have a chance to address it and resolve it right there, and possibly **save your job offer**.

This is a great opportunity to plug any holes you might have in your discussion about your experience or fit for the job.

If they haven't asked you about something that you know would impress them, now's the time to bring that up. Make this a great story that is **quantified** and **demonstrates your value**. Your story might also be part of your attempt to eliminate their doubts about hiring you.

Tell your story using the **STAR** format:
   Situation or
   Task (Set up the story—what happened? What was your goal?)
   Action (What did you choose to do and why?)
   Result (What happened as a result of your actions? Quantify this wherever possible.)
Everything I've said so far, though, assumes that you've already gone over your 30-60-90-day plan in your interview. If you have not had a chance to discuss that with the hiring manager, now is the time:

"I think you should ask me how I would approach this job and be successful in my first 3 months, because I've worked up a very nice outline with some great ideas that I'd love to talk over with you and get your take on."

Key to a Great Interview!

A 30-60-90-day plan helps make it an easy decision to hire you!
Find out more in the resources at the back of the book!

Job Interview Question 50

It's your dime. (Interviewer doesn't ask questions)

I once had a candidate go to a **sales interview,** sit down and….nothing. The hiring manager just ignored her and played with a pen. That's enough to rattle the most skilled and experienced person.

The **wrong thing to do** would have been to get rattled, and just sit there, too. It wouldn't take long before the manager would have gotten up and invited her to leave—or even walked out without saying anything.

However, this woman was unflappable. She smiled at the 'interviewer' and said, "I'm so happy to meet with you today. I understand that you are in the market for a new sales rep. What are the most important qualities you're looking for in someone for this job?"

With that question, she got the hiring manager talking, they went on with the interview, and she got the job.

What the hiring manager was looking for was someone who had a strong enough personality and **confidence** to walk into a cold-call situation and **make the sale**. If this woman had shown that she couldn't even step out of her comfort zone to stand up for herself, how would she ever find the strength to stand up for the company's product in the face of an initially disinterested customer?

I've seen a lot of companies "play" with candidates this way—put them in uncomfortable situations to see what they're made of. One company routinely had a cab collect interviewees from the airport and then drop them off at an incorrect location. Another company did something similar—they had the cabbie deliberately take a long and winding route to the interview, making the interviewee late. They learned a lot about their candidates by **seeing how they reacted under pressure,** how they treated the cabbie (who was in full cahoots with them), **and what they did to rectify the situation.**

Never let anything make you lose your composure in an interview situation. Even if you think something is just too weird, it may be a play to rattle you and see what you'll do. Just smile at the attempt, keep your cool, and keep moving toward your goal.

Job Interview Question 51

Tell me a suggestion you have made that was implemented.

Are you just collecting a paycheck, or do you actively try to improve things in your job? Are you creative enough or strategic enough to come up with a better way of doing something? How have you made a difference at your job? Can you identify problems, analyze the situation, and provide a viable solution?

These are the questions in the interviewer's mind as they ask you about your suggestions that have been implemented. Your suggestion doesn't have to be something earth-shattering that changed the direction of the company forever. It can be a simple one—as long as it provided a **useful benefit**. Choose a suggestion to talk about that illustrates something that would be a positive selling point for you in this job.

Tell them about it using **the STAR format:**

Situation or Task –

What was going on? **Was it a crisis or an ongoing problem?** What did you see that could be accomplished **more efficiently, more profitably, faster,** or otherwise **better than before?** How did you **identify** it? How did you **analyze** it?

Action –

What was your suggestion? What made you think of it? Were you able to come up with the suggestion because of your **previous experience?** Did you have to **persuade** your boss, or just mention it and they thought it was a **great idea?**

Result –

What happened as a result of implementing your suggestion? How did the situation **improve?** What got better? How much better? Can you **quantify** what happened (use numbers, dollars, or percentages to describe it)?

Here's an example of a great story using quantification:

A woman wrote a software program code for a call center that **saved them 1.2 seconds every time** they logged in, which in a call center, means millions of times. This 1.2 second time savings added up over the thousands of times they answered the phone every day, and that translated into **savings of millions of dollars** for the company over a short amount of time. So when she describes this, she says (using quantification): "I wrote a program code that saved 1.2 seconds for every login, which saved the company $X every year."

Key to a Great Interview!

If you have anything **tangible** that illustrates your story, put it in your **brag book** and point to it while you answer this question. What could this be? The possibilities are many:

-A **brochure** you developed, to show what you can do

-A **note from your boss thanking you** for the suggestion and talking about how it turned out

-**Sales numbers** pre- and post-suggestion

-Any workplace improvements pre- and post-suggestion
-A note from a customer thrilled with your new system/procedure
-The outline of a **training process you created**

-Providing evidence to back up your story or example is a powerful way to stand out from every other candidate.

If you would like help putting yours together, check out my <u>Brag Book eReport on Amazon</u>

Job Interview Question 52

Tell me about a time when you helped someone.

It would make the most sense that this question would be asked in service-related jobs, where you've **helped a customer or client**, but it could be asked in relation to other jobs if they want to find out more about your **personality or character**, or whether or not you're **a team player.**

If you are in a service-related job, answer this as **an example of how you work.** Set up the situation, talk about what you did (action) and then tell what happened (result).

A great example to choose is one where the customer or client was unhappy and you turned the situation around.

If you suspect that this is a **personality or character question,** then you can choose almost anything. But be prepared to talk about specifics, and tell the story.

Tell your story using the **STAR** format:

    Situation or

    Task (Set up the story—what happened? What was your goal?)

    Action (What did you choose to do and why?)

    Result (What happened as a result of your actions? Quantify this wherever possible.)

If you'd like to **highlight that you are a team player**, choose to tell about a time that you helped someone on your team—maybe this would be to finish a project, or maybe this would be helping train them to be better at their job.

If you are in management, you could choose to talk about a time you helped an employee having a hard time—maybe you saved their job and turned them into one of your better performers.

    *** **It's best to come up with a *work-related* answer.**

You might hesitate over your answer to this question because it feels like bragging. You have to get past that feeling. They asked you and they are looking for a sincere answer—so give them one.

Job Interview Question 53

Tell me about a time when you misjudged a person.

Do not make this story a serious example of how you misjudged them with a severe negative impact. **Keep this story as positive as possible, with the least amount of repercussions.**

My story is this one:

"When I was promoted to Regional Product Manager, my first task was to visit all of my newly-inherited sales reps to evaluate their performance. I flew Southwest out to Orange County, California. I stepped out of the plane to go down the steps to the tarmac (pre-9/11) in my very conservative navy suit with my very conservative background and saw my sales rep waiting for me on the tarmac wearing a pink chiffon scarf waving in the wind 8 feet out behind her.

I thought, 'Oh, no—what am I going to do about this?' I knew that several people had talked about her very positively, and I had had great conversations with her on the phone. It didn't matter. I saw that scarf and made an immediate and negative judgment about her—that she was not a serious sales rep, that she was less competent than what I would want to see, and that she wasn't very business savvy.

As I drove her sales route with her and watched her interact with her customers, I changed my mind. This woman was a fantastic sales rep. She had a warm, friendly style that was very different from my approach, but very effective. She talked to them about their grandkids while she picked up their purchase orders. She was obviously good at her business and was clearly driving business forward. My report was that she was very different, but that she was an outstanding member of the team.

I knew that other sales managers in my company would force this woman to change her style anyway, to fit in with the established company image, but I decided to be open minded and let it go. This woman went on to be one of the top reps in the region."

You could tell the story of how you thought someone at work didn't like you until you realized that this person acted like that toward everyone. You were able to stop taking it personally, and got along just fine with that person with no problems. Since then, you try not to jump to conclusions about other people's motivations before you've gathered more information first.

Tell a brief, innocuous story that taught you a lesson in people skills and made you a better and wiser person today.

Job Interview Question 54

Tell me about a time you conveyed technical information to a non-technical audience.

As in any behavioral interview question, **use the STAR format to tell this story**:

Situation – Set up the story. What was going on? What were the circumstances? Why was this important?

In this case, I was with the American Association of Clinical Chemistry, where I was supposed to speak about oncology. There were 400 people in the audience, divided among approximately 75% press people (not technical chemistry or medical people) who wouldn't have the background to understand all the technical jargon, and about 25% extremely technical medical folks who would have been bored and even insulted if I had simplified it too much.

Action – What did you do to address this situation?

I decided to use a PowerPoint presentation to give my talk, with a lot of examples related to their world to illustrate what I was talking about.

Result – How do you know that you were successful? What happened, and can it be quantified in any way?

It was an extremely well-received speech and I was actually graded on it by the folks who put the symposium on and was given a 94% satisfaction with the topic. What they really liked and what they really commented about was my ability to convey extremely technical information to a non-technical audience.

What does this example communicate to the interviewer?

I said what I did, and gave them a **third-party source for the result**. (The symposium leaders said I did great.) The third-party reference is very **powerful**, and the **numbers** that I gave in the 94% satisfaction rate are also very powerful. I could have said that I did well and got great reviews, but that doesn't mean as much as "94% satisfaction."

Even the number that I gave in the beginning, 400 people, is powerful. It provides a **frame of reference** for the story, and is impressive on its own. Some people couldn't give a speech in front of that many people, or would even have the chance to give that speech. If this was your story, and the number was 30 people or 50 people, it would still be powerful with the actual number included.

I've told them about the **situation—what it was and why it was too technical for the audience,** I've told them **what I did to address it,** and I've said **what the result was.** This is a great answer to this question.

Key to a Great Interview - Quantification

Describe your achievements in terms of **numbers, dollars, and percentages.** See how **quantification strengthens your answer:**

"I brought in new clients"

or

"Brought in 20 new clients in 3 months"

"I delivered product on time and under budget"

or

"98% on-time delivery of product"

"Maintained accuracy in company database"

or

"100% accuracy in 50,000-item database over 2 years"

Numbers, dollars, or percentages answer the hiring manager's (interviewer's) primary question: "How can this person benefit MY company?"

Job Interview Question 55

Tell me about a time you had to take initiative.

Employers want someone who can **take initiative.** Do you have **creativity** to come up with good ideas? Do you have the **decision-making ability** and **good judgment** to take appropriate initiative and the **skill set** to execute on it and be successful?

Use the STAR format:
Situation or Task –
Often in this situation, there would be some sort of **urgency** where there's **no time to discuss** a solution with your boss—but not always. This could be a **nagging problem** or some other situation where you thought, "Hey, I can fix this."
Action –
What plan did you come up with? How did you **think through it**? Did you consider other options? What made you decide to choose the one you did?
Result –
How did the situation **improve or resolve**? Can you **quantify** it?

For instance:

"I once had a very angry customer come to me with an unusual problem, X. This wasn't something I had been trained to deal with, but based on our process for handling similar situations, I realized that I could offer a new solution for this particular customer's problem without costing the company any extra money. [Give details about the solution here.] So, the company didn't lose any money, and we kept an important customer, who later came back and ordered another $5000 worth of products."

Or,

"I had been in my job for about 3 months when I realized that we kept stumbling over the same problem [X]. I mentioned it to my boss, but he was locked into a big project and didn't have time to do anything about it, or really even discuss it with me. I talked to some counterparts in other divisions of the company to see what they were doing, realized they had a similar problem with no solution, so then I went to work. I did some online research to get a stronger understanding of what was going on, and I found a book that related to the topic. I started a discussion about it in a LinkedIn group, and ended up with quite a few helpful insights and ideas.

With that information, I came up with a plan of attack and presented it to my boss, who thought it was terrific and gave me the go ahead. I presented it to my group with a PowerPoint presentation and got them on board. We began implementing it the next day, and it worked like a charm. It improved our X by X% and actually freed up enough time for us as a whole that we were also able to accomplish XYZ where we'd never had time for that before."

Your answer shouldn't take more than a minute to two at the most. **Walk them through the story, give them the details that help them see your value, and end on a positive note.**

Job Interview Question 56

Tell me about a time you planned and coordinated a project from start to finish.

With this question, they want to see your thought process in action—planning, strategic thinking, decision-making, etc. Don't just say, "I once coordinated X and it turned out great." Use the STAR format, walk them through the steps, and include details in your story.

Ideally, you'll choose a work project to talk about, but if you *really* don't have a good example, then use a project from volunteer work of some kind—something where you coordinated something with moving parts or multiple facets, whether that was people, places, or things, and has a successful outcome.

Situation or Task –

What was the project? Why were you doing it? Why were you in charge? What was your goal?

Talk about how you **gathered information** and **used resources** to help you get this done. Did you have to **learn anything new** to complete this project? How did you do that? Did you read a **book,** watch an online **video,** or **talk to someone?**

Talk about the **scope** of the project. **How many people** or groups participated in it? What was the **budget?** What was the **timeline?**

Action –

What did you do? How did you **delegate tasks?** How did you **coordinate** the project? Did you use special **software?** Did you use **Excel spreadsheets?** How did you stay **organized?** Did you encounter any **problems** along the way? How did you decide to address them?

Result –

Did you get the project done **on time?** Did you meet your **goals?** Did you **exceed** your goals? If so, by how much? What did the project **accomplish** for you?

Quantify this as much as you can—maybe you raised $X in a fundraiser, or you came in under budget by 5%, or you completed it X days faster because you took some specific action.

Job Interview Question 57

Tell me about a work incident in which you were totally honest, despite a potential risk or downside.

This question explores not only your **honesty**, but also your **courage**, your **judgment**, your **conflict-resolution** skills, your company **loyalty** and whether or not you have the **tact** and **communication** skills to handle delicate situations.

The overriding rules for anything you choose to tell here are:
--Make sure the downside would have been a negative effect for YOU, not your boss or the company.
--Make sure the benefit gained would be for the COMPANY or your boss, not you.

This situation could be anything. Maybe you were the only "Negative Nelly" in the group on a project that everyone was enthusiastic about, because you saw the downside that no one else did—and ended up coming up with a better solution that avoided an expensive mistake.

Or, maybe you stood up against the group who wanted to hire a particular person, and later found out that the person had caused major trouble in their last job.

Or perhaps you unintentionally caused a problem that you brought to your boss immediately because you knew you couldn't fix it alone, despite the fact that it was going to make you look bad. You did this because you know that it's more important to take action to correct a problem sooner rather than later, when it could become a much bigger issue.

Use the STAR format:

Situation or
Task –
What was the problem you faced? What were the choices in front of you? What were the possible negative outcomes or repercussions of this situation? Did you cause it? Why?

Action –
Why did you decide to be totally honest? What did you say? What did you do? How did you handle it? Did you take them aside to discuss it? If this was in a group discussion, did you try to help someone save face? Did you ask questions until they came to their own conclusion? Or did you lay out your thoughts and follow them through?

Result –
What was the reaction to your honesty? What was decided? What happened as a result of that? Did you learn a lesson that affects how you do your job more successfully today?

Be careful here—if you talk about a problem that you caused, make it a problem that does not directly affect the central responsibilities of the job you are applying for. Learning from a mistake is fantastic, but *causing* a mistake that indicates you are incompetent at your job is not.

Job Interview Question 58

Tell me about the last time you were angry or upset at work. What happened?

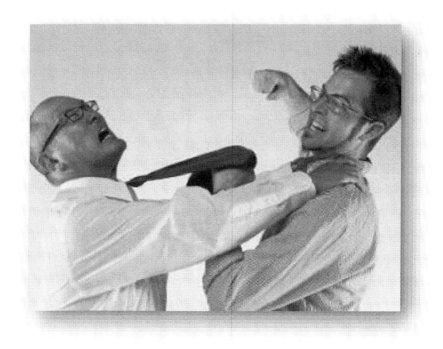

Emotional stability is a huge factor in your professionalism at work. No employer wants drama. They want to know that you are in charge of yourself and your emotions and that you do not lose control.

That being said, we all get upset or angry. We are all under a lot of pressure at work, stressful things happen, and just because we try to stay in control at all times doesn't mean that others do, and their actions and reactions have a powerful effect on us.

So the question is not IF you get angry at work, it's WHEN you get angry at work. What do you do? How do you handle that? In this question, they are asking for an example.

Your overall response needs to talk about **how you successfully deal with negative emotions** like this:

"In any stressful, negative, or upsetting situation, I take a step back, take a deep breath, and think it through. It never helps to lash out, and

I know that my working relationships are going to have to last a long time, so I never want to do anything to damage them out of anger."

So then, your example might be:

"The last time I got angry was when a co-worker got upset and lashed out at me. I was tempted to retaliate but I know it would have just escalated the situation and not accomplished anything. I knew that she and I normally always get along, and that this was unusual behavior. I looked for what might be causing her anger and realized she was completely stressed out because of X project. I offered to help her with a particularly nasty sticking point, and she was glad of the help and ended up apologizing. We still work well together on a regular basis."

Or,

"The last time I got angry at work was when I was working on a particularly detailed and important project and kept getting interrupted. I was on a deadline, so every interruption put me that much farther behind. I could feel myself getting angry, so I stepped back, took a deep breath, and thought about what I could do to solve the problem. I let everyone know that I had to have this done by 2pm so I was shutting my door and turning off my phone until that time. After that, I would be available. I got my project done on time."

Job Interview Question 59

Tell me about the toughest negotiation you've ever been in.

This is a common interview question for anyone in a position to buy or sell for their company.

When you answer this question, think about what skills you are highlighting about yourself in your answer. You want to try and focus on your understanding of **basic** and **advanced negotiation techniques** along with higher-level skills, such as **influencing** and **persuading**. You want the end of your negotiation story (and really, any negotiation you enter) to be a **positive** one for everyone.

So, the story you want to tell does not need to be the story of how you simply dug your heels in until they gave up. Persistence is good, but you haven't shown any of those higher-level skills that demonstrate your skill at negotiating.

Use the STAR format:
Situation or Task –

What was going on? Did you need a great deal on material? Did your supplier come to you with an unexpected delay or price increase because they thought they had you all sewn up? Did your company run into a problem that made your supplier or vendor come back demanding a new agreement? Did you have an important but tough customer demanding things you couldn't deliver and keep any sort of a profit?

Action –

What did you do? Did you stall, or come up with an alternative agreement? Did you say you were about to go with someone else? Did you say that at that price, you would be better off producing this in-house? How did you persuade them? What did you bring into the conversation? Did you have to bluff? Did you use any particular negotiating technique? Did you ask questions? What new benefits did you offer? What concessions did you offer and why?

Result –

What was the final agreement? How did it **benefit** you, and why was the other party happy with it—or at least accepting of it? What did they get out of it?

Quantify as much as possible throughout your story, and make sure you end your story on a **positive** note, with a **win** for your company.

Job Interview Question 60

Tell me about the worst boss you've ever had.

It's OK to say, "I've never had a bad boss." That's the safest answer.

It's also OK to mention an example that is **vague and neutral**: "I inherited a boss and it happened that our communication styles were very different. I was still as successful at my job as I had ever been, but because I didn't choose him and he didn't choose me, we never really clicked as well as I had done with other managers."

So, what if you had the misfortune to work for a tyrannical, backstabbing, manipulative psycho? Don't mention it. **No interviewer wants to hear you talk badly about previous bosses**. It reflects negatively on you and plants the seed in their mind that you are a complainer who won't be happy there, either, and will end up badmouthing them when you leave.

Job Interview Question 61

Tell me about your current (most recent) employer (i.e. what do they do, how long they've been in business, etc.).

This question is looking to see how well you know the company you work for (and if you might also learn as much about them). It's a nice vehicle for talking about **how the company fits into the bigger industry** and who all the players are to demonstrate your **higher-level understanding of the arena.** How you choose to answer it also shows how **detail-oriented** you are and if you can **summarize** effectively.

For instance, a **bad answer** would be: "We are a marketing firm."

A much better answer would be: "ABC Marketing firm is a large regional company focused in the Southwest that's been in business for X years. We handle multi-media campaigns for a wide variety of businesses, from tech corporations, educational institutions, and food companies. Our major competitor is XYZ. They are a similar company, but the critical difference is X."

Under what circumstances have you found it acceptable to break confidence?

This question is looking at your **ethics** and **values**. There should be very few circumstances in which you would ever break a confidence.

Your answer should be, "I would only ever break a confidence if the person was doing something illegal or unethical and I couldn't talk them into stopping and correcting the behavior."

Job Interview Question 63

Walk me through your career from the start to where it is now.

This is a very common interview question similar to "Tell me about yourself" or "Walk me through your resume." This will most likely be asked in the beginning of your interview.

With this question, they get a good **overview** of you as a candidate, they see where you feel that your **greatest strengths** are, and they see whether or not you'd be a **good cultural fit** in the company. This is your chance to **sum up why you're a great candidate** for this job.

The key is to stay focused on the things that will help explain why you are here right now and **why they want to consider hiring you**. Don't get off track into a story that doesn't help you get to that goal, and **don't bring up any personal information**, because it isn't relevant here and won't get you to your goal, either.

They want to know what you did, how one thing led to another, and **why you made decisions to take certain jobs** (especially if one seems to be outside a typical career path) or why you might have a gap of time where you didn't work. Keep your answer to less than 2 minutes.

Start with your **education**: "I got my degree in X from State University and my first job at Acme Corporation in ABC."

Continue with your **background**, mentioning any **jobs, skills, or accomplishments that are particularly relevant** for this job. This requires some strategic thinking to identify what parts of your history would be the biggest "selling points" for you in this job.

What things could you point out that would give this hiring manager **another reason to offer you the job?** (And what things might make him or her nervous, so what could you say that would alleviate those doubts?)

You might say, "I took some time off to deal with a family matter (or whatever it was), and when that was resolved, I got back to work." Whatever you learned along the way that makes you an especially good fit for this job, be sure to mention it.

Point out what it was that made you move from one job to another, showing that you were moving TOWARD something in each job that **added to your growth, skill set, or value** in your field.

Never mention that you left a job because it was horrible, or the boss was a jerk. **Always be positive.** Talk about how you moved toward something, not away from something.

Wrap it up with, "And all that led me here. I believe this job is a fantastic place for me to grow professionally even further, and I know that I could move you forward as well, with my experience in X, Y, and Z."

Job Interview Question 64

What are some of your leadership experiences?

Any job where you will be managing others or even leading a team will be very interested in previous leadership experiences.

They want to know:

- **what kind of leader** you are
- how you **motivate** others
- how you **manage the details**—as well as the people.

If you already have some experience managing others or leading a team, that's great. If you do not already have management experience, that's OK. Think of any time when you organized a project or were placed in charge of getting something done, either at work, at school, or in a volunteer setting.

Use the STAR format to talk about these experiences:
Situation or Task –

Were you **placed in charge** of a project? Did you **volunteer** to spearhead a project from start to finish? What was the **scope** of the project? **How many people** did you lead (**quantification**)? What was your **goal**?

Action –

How did you start? **How did you decide** who should do what? How did you **communicate** with your team? Did you have to **train** anyone? If this was a volunteer experience, it can be an even stronger example of your leadership ability, because no one was compelled to follow your leadership. What **obstacles** did you face, and how did you **resolve** them?

Result –

Tell them about the **successful outcome** of your project. Did you get it done **on time or early**? Did you **reach your goal**? Did you **exceed your goal**? By how much?

Be brief, since you will be talking about multiple experiences, add details, quantify what you can, and be positive and tell stories with a successful outcome.

Job Interview Question 65

What are the most important qualities of successful people? How do you rate yourself in those areas?

For an overall strategy: I would **choose 5 qualities** and rate myself very good on 2-3 and good with room for improvement on the rest.

I would never say that I was outstanding in all 5 areas, because that means that you don't believe you have room to learn and grow, and I believe we all do.

Here are some qualities you could choose:

Dedication –

To be successful, you must want it and be willing to work at it even when it is difficult and you'd rather be doing something else.

Persistence –

It takes self-discipline to be persistent in the face of adversity, but we will always face adversity. The only way to get past it to success is to never give up.

Positive Attitude –

A positive attitude contributes to your success in a thousand ways — in interactions with others, your ability to keep going in the face of obstacles, in your physical health so that you can keep going, and in your expectations. If you can **visualize and expect success**, you are more likely to experience it.

Anyone can develop a positive attitude—and you'll have a better life for it. Read the National Bestseller –
<u>Learned Optimism</u>
by Martin E. P. Seligman, Ph.D.

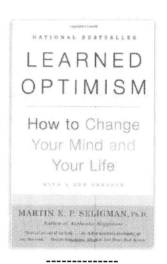

Willingness to Listen to Others and Learn –

You can **never stop learning and growing** if you want to be successful. You can learn a lot by reading, and by talking with and listening to others who have also been successful.

A Desire to be a Subject Matter Expert –

To be successful, you need to **know what you're doing**. You should always be moving toward a being a SME in your field—by reading, listening, and learning.

They Choose Good Mentors –

I have always kept a group of 5 people who know more than me in various areas that I take the time to go have lunch or coffee with on a regular basis. Their advice has absolutely made me **more successful than I would have been without it**.

They Build and Maintain Good Networks –

Your network is there for you when you need to know something, when you need a new job, when you need a new connection. I always recommend that you reach out to contact everyone in your network with a quick email or phone call every 3-6 months, just to say Hi or give them something useful, to maintain that connection.

They Manage Their Emotions –

One of the worst things you can do in a professional setting is lose your temper or cry, no matter what the provocation might be. Successful people practice **self-control**.

They Are Results-Oriented, Not Action-Oriented –

You can do a lot of things and not make any progress or see any results from them. It's never about how hard you work, it's about your results. What works? Successful people plan their next move based on what works and are known not so much for working hard as for getting the job done.

As in all your job interview answers, **be strategic**. Even if you have all of these qualities in abundance, which ones will have **the most impact on your success in THIS job**? Choose those to talk about and point out to your interviewer.

Job Interview Question 66

What are your long-term career goals?

The best answer to this really does depend on the company you're interviewing with—is it a flat company or a structured company? Some companies want you to be planning ahead, and others don't have anywhere for you to go—so they will be threatened if you aggressively talk about advancement, promotions, etc.

Either way, don't give the impression that your entire focus is on getting to the CEO's seat, and don't give the impression that your long-term goal is completely different from this job. Both imply that you may not give your best work because your focus won't be here.

Keep your answer **general**: "It's difficult to predict exactly where I'll want to be long-term, but I know I want to continue to learn and develop my skills and achieve in this field. I am good at what I do, and that is rewarding. I know that as I grow more, I'll want to move into roles of greater responsibility, whether that's added responsibility in this position or in a higher-level position down the line."

Job Interview Question 67

What changes have you made in working with others to be more effective at work?

This question looks at your willingness to **recognize areas where you need to improve** and execute those necessary changes in a successful way. Don't choose things you were weak on that are central to your success in this job. There's no reason to insert doubts about your ability to do the job into this conversation. Choose **small things that you improved on because you wanted to** (not because your boss told you to) that had a positive, lasting impact for you.

Here are a few examples:

I improved my **communication skills** by becoming a better listener, and I have developed excellent working relationships with my colleagues.

I learned about a **technical area** I had no experience in so that I could **communicate better** with our support department. They seem to appreciate it.

When I first started out, I used to get upset by others' disagreements and arguments in the office. I learned to step back and distance myself in order to **keep calm** and not let it affect my work or my **positive outlook**. It's kept me on good terms with everyone in the office, too!

At one time, I was constantly interrupted and pulled every which way by a variety of people coming to me with various requests. So I learned to **set priorities**, and instead of immediately moving to address whatever problem they came to me with, I looked at how that fit into my priority list for the day and planned accordingly. As a result, I am much less stressed and much **more productive**. It wasn't necessarily a problem for me, but I am **always looking for ways to improve** and so I realized that I could become a better **time manager**. I looked at my day, figured out where I tended to be most productive at which tasks, and set up a routine. This helped me plan more effectively for meetings with colleagues, and give more accurate dates for completion of projects. It's worked well. I'm very **organized, productive, and easy for others to work with**.

Job Interview Question 68

What circumstances bring you here today?

This is a great opening interview question, maybe better than "Tell me about yourself." This question gives them a lot of insight into what will make you happy and what has made you unhappy and **why you are looking for a job**. The important thing to remember here is to **never go negative** in your answer.

They want to hear that you are **running TO something**, like more responsibility, a chance to use increased skill sets, or just something different than you were doing).

They do not want to hear that you are running FROM something, like a boss you can't get along with or a company that doesn't appreciate you or whatever.

So you must explain this in terms of: "The reason why am here is, in my current role I'm doing fantastic. I'm enjoying the work there but I don't get to use the skill sets that I developed at ABC. I don't get to use the experiences that I had at XYZ. I want an opportunity to do LMNOP."

Or, "I'm here because my former company went through a series of layoffs and cut 30% of the workforce and I got caught in the cuts. I think it turned out to be a stroke of luck for me, though, because although I was enjoyed my work there, I didn't get to use my skill sets in XYZ, and this job would really benefit from them."

Always **talk about what this job has that attracts you**, and **what you could bring to it as a benefit** to the company—and anything you can mention using **numbers, dollars and percentages** of what you been able to do and how you'd like to do more of that, will help.

Job Interview Question 69

What do you do to grow your skills and knowledge of the job/industry?

Employers want to hire people who continuously learn, grow and improve. It means that you are probably a self-starter, and a good communicator. It means that you are invested in your career and striving for success. It also increases your value, because the more you know, the more you can do to make money for the company.

There are any number of ways you could talk about that you use to grow your skills and knowledge:

--Read books, journals or industry newsletters

--Take classes / get certifications

--Attend workshops, conferences or seminars

--Watch online videos

--Participate in LinkedIn group discussions

--Volunteer doing something that relates to your job

--Whatever you choose to mention, be prepared to **give an example** of something you learned there that helped you be more successful in your job or how it will help you be successful in this one.

Job Interview Question 70

What do you expect from this job?

What they really want to know is, why do you want to work *here?* What's in it for you? What aspects of this job appeal to you and why?

You must have done your research in order to answer this question, because you need to be able to explain why THIS job, with this company, is the one for you.

With every answer you give, you should give them another reason to want to hire you, so part of what you say you want or expect from this job should always be **a chance to benefit this company**:

"I expect that in this job, I'll utilize my XYZ skill set to help you accomplish A, B, and C."

Or you could say:

"I expect that because I can utilize my ABC skill set in this role, and be successful and help move you forward, that I will be extremely happy and productive here."

Along with pointing out your **skills match**, point out **what it is that you like** about this particular company:

"I expect to be excited to get up and come to work every day because I will be working at a job that is a great fit for me because of X, Y, and Z, at a great company I've read so many good things about."

Maybe this company:

--Does work you're especially excited about

--Provides a product or service you love

--Fosters a sense of community you can't wait to be a part of

Whatever it is, say it with sincerity.

Here is your chance to **express your genuine enthusiasm** for the job and sum up why you're a great fit for it.

Job Interview Question 71

What gets you up in the morning?

For many people, what really gets them up in the morning and motivates them to get on with the day is a personal thing—maybe it's your kids, or your love of life, or your goal of early retirement. In a social setting, these are acceptable and even noble answers. In an interview setting, they are not your best choices. (The worst answer of all is money.)

In an interview, you always want to **keep the focus on your fit for the job**, even with personal questions like these. Good things to mention are **why you like your work**, why this job in particular is a **good match** for you and why you would **enjoy** it. Show your enthusiasm for the job here—it makes you more likeable.

So a good answer might sound like:

"I am one of the lucky few people in the world who gets to get up and do work I love to do. I know that I am good at my job, and I love the feeling of overcoming challenges and being successful. That gives me a sense of accomplishment that makes me excited to get up in the morning and happy when I go to bed at night."

You might mention that you are motivated by:

--Meeting goals (like when you met the goal for X last year and were recognized for it)

--**Being recognized** for doing a great job (like when you won 'Most Valuable Employee')

--**Making difficult sales** (like when you landed the customer that everyone said you couldn't)

--**A positive and supportive work environment** (like the one that this company is known for)

--**Competition** (which is why you enjoyed being named #1 out of 135 sales reps in your company)

--**The chance to come up with creative solutions to complex problems** (like you did when you got to be on the team tasked with X in your company and you created Y solution)

--**Knowing that the work you do makes a positive difference in someone's life** (like when you help someone be healthier, save money, reach a goal, etc.)

Talk about something that truly motivates you that is a major factor in this job so you can demonstrate that you are a good fit for it. Back up what you say with an example or an accomplishment that adds credibility and sincerity to your statement.

Job Interview Question 72

What have you learned from all the different roles you've had?

This question is just as open-ended as "Tell me about yourself" and just as easy to make a mistake with. When they ask you this, they do not want you to talk about a greater truth you learned or a lesson that changed your life, and they really don't want a long random list of everything you picked up here and there.

Now is the time for you to talk about **when and how you acquired the skill sets and experience that make you a perfect fit for *this* job**.

How have you developed professionally into someone they would be interested in hiring now for this job?

It's important that you **be strategic** and think about **the best answer to this question for YOU**.

Think about what in your **background, experience, or skill sets** is most interesting to this employer:

--What are the key **requirements** or **competencies** of this job?

--What are the **problems** they need to have **addressed** and **solved**?

--What are their **goals**?

Use your knowledge of what this employer is interested in to choose things in your own background to highlight.

For instance, when interviewing for a **sales job**, you might say,

"In my first job, my manager gave me the book SPIN Selling by Neil Rackham and reading it changed my life. I went from mediocre sales numbers to ranking among the highest in the company as a practically brand-new hire.

In my next job, I went into selling a much more technical product, which meant I had to fill in gaps in my background to be able to know my product and discuss it intelligently with my customers.

But what I learned from that is that I can train myself—I don't need my employer to do it for me, and learning those new things boosted my confidence level, too.

In my current job, I worked with someone who happened to be a tremendous time manager and watching her, I learned a lot about how to prioritize tasks and organize my day so that my productivity has gone up I would estimate about 30%."

So what you've told this interviewer in your answer is that:

You are a great sales rep who achieved a **significant ranking** early on; you can **train yourself** on the product even if it is an unfamiliar one; and you are **organized and efficient with your time.**

Maybe what you need to point out is that you:

--**Learned a new software** that this company uses

--**Developed customer service techniques** that help you retain customers at a 20% higher level than before (and this job description puts a high value on customer retention)

--**Created market trials** that helped you hone your skill at matching products to customer need

--**Learned a particular procedure** that helped you increase X

Whatever it is, make sure that **what you learned is something that this employer could use as a reason to hire you.**

Job Interview Question 73

What historical figure do you admire and why?

There are a lot of historical figures that I admire. In an interview, I would choose one that helps me demonstrate a **desirable work quality or fit for the job**.

A historical figure I admire is Joseph Juran, the Italian economist who developed the Pareto Principle, known as the 80/20 Rule. I use the 80/20 Rule daily to **prioritize tasks for maximum results**. It helps me accomplish more in a shorter amount of time and achieve greater success.

For instance, when I was in sales, I used the 80/20 Rule to identify which customers generated the most revenue, and which actions generated the most sales. Then I made sure that I spent most of my time on the things that produced the most results.

So not only have I chosen an admirable historical figure, I have **tied my choice to a positive trait in my work** and another selling point for me. You could also choose **a leader in your field,** someone who's personal life is an example of an **admirable character trait,** or someone who exemplifies great **leadership.**

Try to keep your choice as **uncontroversial** as possible—**no religious or political figures**. Even if you truly admire whoever it is, it's better in this situation to **play it safe.**

80/20 Rule

A long, LONG time ago, an Italian economist named Pareto noticed that 80% of the wealth in Italy was held by 20% of the people. Joseph Juran took Pareto's Principle and successfully applied it to quality management--and the 80/20 Rule was born.

The 80/20 Rule says (among other things) that 80% of sales come from 20% of customers, or that **80% of your results come from 20% of your effort.**

It's about productivity and identifying the significant tasks/actions that contribute most to it. Prioritize the most important tasks, and you become super-efficient and effective. You will spend time on the things that matter.

Job Interview Question 74

What if you worked for someone who managed to take credit for all your great ideas? How would you handle it?

Hopefully, by asking this question, the interviewer is only trying to get a sense of how you deal with conflict and not warning you that they are about to take credit for all your great ideas.

With conflict questions in general, the interviewer wants to know several things:

--How do you see your role at work?

--What is your communication style?

--Do you remain calm?

--Do you confront issues head on?

--Do you try to keep the peace at all costs?

--Do you take things to HR, or handle them yourself?

--How do you approach the situation and how do you come up with solutions?

I probably would try to inject a little humor into this answer:

"Well, part of my job is certainly to make my boss look good, and my great ideas are part of that. I certainly want my boss to be recognized and rewarded for having the good sense to hire me!"

Or, you could just cut to the bottom line:

"Well, part of my job is to provide great ideas that make my boss look good. If I were being rewarded by my boss with raises and promotions, I would be happy."

(And then I would probably go home and get on LinkedIn or Facebook and try to find people who have worked for this person before and see if they would ever work for them again!)

Job Interview Question 75

What is one thing you'd like to do better? What is your plan for accomplishing that?

This question is virtually the same as, "What is your greatest weakness?" With all weakness questions, be sincere (no obviously 'fake,' clichéd answers) but focus your answer on something that is a **minor part** of your job you are **already improving** on, a **personal weakness** but a **professional strength or** something that would be a **benefit to you later in your career** but that you don't necessarily need now

(**All 'strength' questions should be directly tied to key parts of your job.**)

You can't say that there's nothing you'd like to do better—that reveals you as someone who thinks they're already perfect and has no room to grow.

You can't say that you have a major flaw that would directly affect your job—like that you are uncomfortable meeting new people even though you're in sales, or that you struggle with time management and prioritization if you are a project manager, or that you need to pay more attention to details if you are an accountant.

So what should you say? Maybe something like:

"I always want to improve my **communication skills**, because that's the bottom-line key skill everything else depends on. It doesn't matter how good you are technically if you can't communicate effectively with the people you work with and for. So, I regularly read books and articles about improving communication skills, and I put what I learn into practice every day."

****

"I would like to **handle stress better**. I've been making great progress with that personally by making sure I eat right and work out every day and professionally by reading books on time management and prioritization that have taught me a lot about planning and strategizing so that I am always in control of the situation, which is a tremendous stress-reliever."

****

"I'd like to be a **better public speaker**, because that's a skill everyone should have, and it would make me stronger running meetings and giving presentations at work. I frequently watch YouTube videos as tutorials and I watch great public speakers as examples of what to do. I also joined Toastmasters so I can practice."

Job Interview Question 76

What is the last book you read for fun? (Or, what is your favorite book?)

Interviewers frequently want to know:

--**If** you read, because someone who reads is generally seen as **intelligent, curious, and interested in personal growth**

--**What kinds of things** you spend your time reading, because that says a lot about you, your character, and your priorities

This particular question is a personal one, because it's asking what you read for fun. The interviewer is looking at your personality and whether you would be a **good cultural fit** within the organization.

It's OK to answer this question with titles you really enjoy—within reason. Don't talk about any book that might raise an eyebrow. **Keep it mainstream and socially acceptable**.

Maybe the book you mention is **the fiction one the latest blockbuster movie is based on** (so you show that you are socially current), **a non-fiction one on the best-seller lists** that everyone is talking about, or **a book that is important for your field** and you read it for fun because you really like your work

Briefly mention the title and why you enjoy the book—maybe it's got a lot of **humor** (because you have a sense of humor) or it's filled **with plot-twisting suspense** (because it keeps your very intelligent mind engaged) or it's introduced some **new ideas** to you (because you like learning new ways to think about things).

Be prepared to talk about the book you mention. I once interviewed someone who mentioned a book I had just read, so I asked him about something in it. It became crystal clear right then that he did not know what I was talking about and had **lied to me** about reading the book. Right then, I was **DONE** with that candidate.

I always like to use humor in job interviews if I can, but it's probably not a good idea to say, "The last book I read is a book on how to answer interview questions!" It's funny, but it isn't helpful. The books I have recommended to you throughout this book, however, are great things for you to pick up and read quickly before your interview!

Job Interview Question 77

What is the most courageous action or unpopular stand that you have ever taken?

This question could apply to you whether you are a manager or an individual contributor. Managers often have to make tough decisions, and as an individual contributor you might face a situation where someone asks you to cut corners or otherwise slide around the rules rather than stick to them.

This really is a question to measure your **integrity, courage, and leadership**, and you need to show that you are not afraid to make difficult decisions when they are in the best interests of your job or the well-being of the company.

Use the **STAR format** to tell this story:

Situation or Task –

Set the scene. What was going on? What was the **conflict**? Why were you faced with this problem? What **factors** affected the situation? What **risks** did you face?

This situation could be anything…maybe you needed to lay off a certain percentage of your workforce, maybe you needed to set a new policy you knew would make some employees unhappy, or maybe you were leading a team where one member wasn't pulling their weight. Maybe your boss asked you to do something you weren't comfortable with. Maybe this was your decision to leave the company and start your own business.

Action –

What did you do to address the situation? How did you think about it? Did you ask for help or input from co-workers, counterparts, your boss, or mentors? How did you come to the decision you did and what did you do to execute on that decision?

Maybe you had a private conversation with the person causing the problem, maybe you weighed the pros and cons, maybe you gathered data to evaluate to inform your decision, or maybe you more clearly explained the positives that would come from this decision. Walk them through the process.

Result –

What happened as a result of your decision? Was it the right decision? Did the situation get better?

Ideally, this is where you explain the **triumphant happy ending** to your story where everybody came around to your way of thinking, and maybe you even were recognized for your action. Or, maybe this is where you got fired, and this is your chance to tell the story.

Job Interview Question 78

What is the most important thing you're looking for in a company/job besides salary?

The very best answer to this question of what you're looking for is a list of things that this position offers. You'd say it like this:

"What I'm looking for is actually a very good match for this position...that's why I was so excited about interviewing with you."

Then, you can **move into specifics** about why this job and this company is such a good match. You need the **job description** for this, but it will also help you if you have done your **research on the company** before the interview.

For example:

"What this job (or company) offers that others don't is A, B, and C. I believe it's a unique opportunity to utilize my skills in X, Y, and Z, and that's why I'm particularly excited about it."

Pointing out specific things about this job and this company that genuinely appeal to you will give you the **biggest impact** in your answer.

If you wanted to keep this answer **more generalized**, you could say,

"I want to work for a company where I can enjoy going to work each day, because I can make an impact and be recognized and rewarded for it."

Job Interview Question 79

What is your biggest weakness that's really a weakness and not a secret strength?

The first thing you learn in Answering Interview Questions 101 is "don't tell them anything negative about yourself." And now here is this hiring manager asking you to go against everything you've learned about selling yourself for the job and tell him something truly negative about you. Why? Because hiring you is a risk for this person, and trying to find the dirt about you before you're hired is risk-assessment and evaluation. Are you worth the risk?

This question also tells you that this interviewer has heard "I'm a perfectionist" and "I work too hard" a few too many times. So they're looking for a real weakness, and you have to say something because everyone has at least one—what can you say?

Whatever you do, **don't give a weakness that would have a direct negative impact on your job performance.**

For instance, no project manager should say their weakness is organization or delegation, no accountant should say that their weakness is attention to detail, and no customer service rep should say that they have anger issues.

One of the **best strategies** for this question is to give **a real weakness that causes you problems in other areas of your life but doesn't affect your performance on the job**.

For instance, I always gave 'impatience' as my weakness. I am impatient, and it has caused me significant problems in my personal life with my family and friends. However, that same impatience made me super successful in my role as a sales rep because I could not stand waiting around for the sale. I pushed for it every time (and I usually got it).

You could give a weakness that you **actually have**, but that you have a solid, working way to **overcome**: "I get so involved in my work that I lose track of what time it is. I'm so thankful for cell phone alarms or I'd never make a meeting on time!"

'Fear of public speaking' is a real weakness that is also a very **common** one that the hiring manager can probably relate to. Unless your job involves giving presentations on a daily or weekly basis, you can safely get by with this one.

Job Interview Question 80

What is your favorite website?

Do not say:

--Amazon (although, who doesn't love Amazon??)-- because they'll think you online shop all day

--ESPN -- same thing—are you working or checking scores on last night's game?

--Facebook (statistics say people spend 3 hours a day on Facebook—this is a real worry for supervisors)

--Any website that trumpets your political views

--Pinterest (you could get lost in that maze forever...)

Unless you are in a field that relies heavily on social media or other internet-based activity, this question is a general one similar to 'What's your favorite book?' It's just trying to uncover a bit more about you, your personality, and your preferences.

Choose a **useful, practical website** that contributes to your professional success. This would be the website you wouldn't rush to close if your boss walked up to your computer. You could choose:

--a **specialty website** that concentrates in **your career** arena (like AdAge for media and advertising news and trends, or Inc. for sales and marketing tips and tricks)

--a **trend-watcher website** that helps you forecast and make marketing decisions

--**Lifehacker.com** for tips and shortcuts to get things done smarter and more efficiently

--any **mainstream news** site

--**Forbes.com** for business and professional development

--**YouTube** or **Ted.com** for instructional videos

I would answer this question very briefly—naming the website with a quick mention of what it is, if it isn't an extremely common one.

A nice way to end this answer is to say something like, "Do you know of a new one I should know about?" or "What's yours?" that **tosses the conversational ball back to them**. Maybe you'll learn about a great new website!

Job Interview Question 81

What qualities in your co-workers bother you most? What do you appreciate most?

On the surface, this sounds like it's a personality question or a cultural fit question. In reality, it's a **measure of your attitude** and **your ability to get along with others**. For this reason, you want to answer both of these questions very **positively**.

However, I do not think that you have to do the obviously fake, "I can't think of anything that bothers me about my co-workers." I believe that answer is the same kind of bad answer as "My greatest weakness is that I just work too darn hard." It just sounds false.

Everyone can think of things that others do that bother them. The trick is balance. Never tell a story about how one person irritated you—make it about a **general quality**. Tell them something that bothers you, but limit it to one thing and make that one thing **something that would bother anyone**.

For instance, I would say, "I don't particularly appreciate **negative attitudes** because they're not helpful to anyone—the person who's complaining or the person listening to it. I believe that instead of complaining about a problem, you should focus on how to fix it."

Then move right into the **positive**: "I've been very lucky to have worked with some great people in my career who have demonstrated qualities I appreciate a lot, like working hard, being knowledgeable, and having a positive attitude."

Keep both answers general and add a few more attributes on the things you appreciate than the things you don't.

The words you say and the things you focus on say more about you than about whatever you're talking about—so make sure that you present yourself in a positive, professional way.

Job Interview Question 82

What tools or techniques do you use to stay organized and increase your productivity?

Organization is key to true productivity…just ask anyone who can't find something they need to time how long it takes them to look for it, or anyone who missed a deadline because they forgot about it.

Anyone can say they are organized and productive, but not everyone is. This question asks for **evidence**. It's a simple question with a simple answer.

If you have a **great system for staying organized**, tell them about it.

--Are you a Franklin Planner kind of person, a traditional "To Do" list maker or an app user?

--Do you use Google Apps, Outlook, or Remember the Milk?

--Do you use a CRM (Customer Relationship Management) system such as Zoho, Help Desk, or Salesforce.com?

--Do you use a project management system such as Team Support or Basecamp?

--Do you mainly use your computer or your smart phone?

Using an **online scheduling software** or some other **online gadget** to stay organized can make you seem up-to-date and computer savvy, but **what really counts is that it works** (and that you show that it works). What keeps you organized? How do you **manage your workload?**

You might also quickly mention how you **prioritize tasks**, how you make sure you **meet deadlines**, and how you don't let anything slip through the cracks with a **reminder system**.

A nice addition to the end of your answer here is an example of **how many** projects/things/people you are able to keep track of with your system. Keep it short but descriptive. Remember, **quantification is powerful**.

Job Interview Question 83

What will your job references say about you?

You absolutely need to **know what your references will say about you** before you give their names to a potential employer.

If you've ever thought you had the job in the bag—then all of a sudden they stopped communicating with you, it may be that your references brought you down.

How to make sure your references help you get the job

Choose good quality references (people you have worked for or reported to are the best ones).

Ask them if they are comfortable giving you a reference, what they might say about you, if they are going to be available, and what is the best way to contact them.

Prep them before they are called by telling them what to focus on ("Hey, I'm interviewing for X job doing ABC...can you mention the work I did on X, and that I'm amazing?").

But this employer won't expect that you can read the minds of your references, so what they are really asking for is a **list of your strengths**.

This is easy to match up with what your references will talk about if you coach them before they are called.

If you know that one will mention your high-level creativity as demonstrated on a certain project, then you can say, "My references will say that I am extremely creative."

If you know another will be able to speak to your overall skill set, you can say, "My reference will say that this job fits me well because of X, Y, and Z."

If you know another reference would hire you if they could, that is a wonderful thing to report: "My reference would say that they would hire me again in a minute if they could." This is the strongest recommendation of all.

Make sure that you are communicating well with your references so that you do know what they will say about you. The last thing you want is to say something that your references will contradict.

Here's a hint: Go back though your performance appraisals and look for descriptive words. An even better idea is to pick a few trusted people (mentors, previous bosses, past or current co-workers) and ask them what impression you give to others. What 3 words would they choose to describe you? You have to be a little bit brave with this one. It can be difficult to ask. But the answers you get will help you both answer this question and help you make sure you are projecting the image you want to project in this job search.

Job Interview Question 84

What would the person who likes you least in the world say about you?

The person who asks this question really wants to know your **weaknesses**. They might as well say, "What irritating quality are you hiding that's going to show up after you're here for a week?"

As with any weakness question, choose something that is a **real weakness**, most likely in your **personal life**, but provides a **benefit to you in your work life**.

I've always chosen **impatience**, because it's caused me some friction with my family and friends who don't appreciate it, but served me very well as a top sales rep because I couldn't wait to get the sale. Impatience might also be a good quality in someone who needs to drive a team to get something done on deadline.

Another negative quality might be **stubbornness**, which would irritate someone who might have to live with you, but might really be appreciated by a boss who knows you'll stick to the job until it's finished—no matter what.

You might be someone who **isn't particularly good with details**, which drives your spouse crazy, but if you're applying for a job as a manager, you might be needed more for big-picture, strategic thinking and can hire someone to handle details for you. Or you compensate for that by using a killer software program that organizes your life.

Maybe you're **extremely competitive** which has caused you some tense conversations at family gatherings, but makes you an extremely valuable asset in sales and marketing.

Maybe you're a **pessimist**, but that quality of finding flaws and faults has saved your company hundreds of thousands of dollars through avoiding mistakes.

Maybe you've been accused of being **too blunt or direct**, but your direct honesty makes you someone who always tells the truth, even if it is difficult.

You want to be seen as someone who knows you have flaws and doesn't try to act like you don't, but you also want to try and **spin it** so that they can see that **even your flaws can benefit their company**.

Job Interview Question 85

What would you do if management made a decision you didn't agree with?

Why would they ask this question? They ask it to see **how you would react in a very difficult situation**. Would you make a fuss? Would you confront your boss? Would you organize a union and overthrow the company?

Here's an answer that shows you are **a *team player* who respects the chain of command**:

"If asked my opinion beforehand, I certainly give it, because it's in my best interests to always apply my best analytical and strategic thinking skills to my company and spot issues before they become problems. If the decision has already been made, there's nothing else to do but live with it. I would assume they made that decision for a reason and I respect that."

Job Interview Question 86

What would you do if you found out the company you worked for was doing something illegal?

I might be nervous about a company asking this question, because I'd wonder what can of worms I'd open up by taking this job! Most likely, this is simply a behavioral interview question designed to get at your **values, ethics, and loyalty**.

They don't want you to say that you'd call CNN and become the loudest whistleblower the country has ever seen—what if you were wrong and you irreparably damaged the company's reputation?

A calmer, more reasoned response they would be comfortable with would sound like, "I would report it to my immediate supervisor, or if necessary, the Director or VP, and move up the chain from there. I would want to know if this was an isolated incident involving just a few people, or one person, and not a cultural mindset of the entire organization, and I would follow up with it to see if it gets resolved."

This answer shows that you are an ethical person who wouldn't let something illegal and damaging slide, but that you are also a loyal person who would take a calm approach that assumes it's the fault of only a few and can be corrected.

Job Interview Question 87

What would you do if you got behind schedule with your part of a project?

While this is a Behavioral Interview Question that is normally answered using the STAR format, I don't think that I would start telling the interviewer all about a time I got behind schedule. Instead, I would address this problem as a **theoretical possibility** and walk them through a **decision-making process**, taking into account different factors and considering a variety of solutions.

So, for instance, I might say:

"Well, I hate the thought of being the bottleneck in a project, so I try very hard to make sure that never happens.

If it did, the first thing I would do is determine **why** I was behind, because you can't identify a good solution without knowing the problem you need to solve.

I would look to see if I got behind because the work was more complicated than anticipated or because I got sidetracked by a more urgent matter, or whatever the issue was.

Next, I would consider how far along I was in the project and how far behind I was. I would **consider a variety of options**, including working **overtime** to get caught up, **delegating** some of my tasks so the work could get done faster, looking for ways to be more **efficient** with my process, or maybe even **reprioritizing** what had to be done by the deadline and what could be added later.

When you're behind, the most critical thing to do is **communicate and control expectations**, so I would notify my boss of the problem, the solution I had come up with for it, and any new projected end dates to see if she approved or if she had any additional solutions.

Assuming all was a go, then I would execute and work as hard as I could to bring my part of the project to a successful conclusion as fast as possible."

Answering the question this way gives the interviewer a lot of information about how you **manage your time, prioritize tasks,** and **critically think through options**.

Job Interview Question 88

What would you do if you made an important business decision and a co-worker challenged it?

This question gets to **how you deal with criticism.**

Give the interviewer the idea that you are confident enough to be open to criticism or challenges without getting stopped in your tracks with anger or indecision.

In this case, I would say, "I would take this person aside and ask why they felt the way they did, because I'm always interested in hearing the pros and cons of a decision so that I can make the best one. I never like the idea of making a mistake, but if I do, I want to correct it. If what they told me made no difference to my decision or it was something I'd already considered, I'd thank them for their input, let it go, and move on."

You want to show that you are **thoughtful, coachable, and professional** even in the face of criticism of your decisions, as well as confident enough to stick by a good one.

Job Interview Question 89

What would you look to accomplish in the first 30 days/60 days/90 days on the job?

Congratulations, this is your lead-in for your **30-60-90-Day Plan**!

Having a 90-day plan written out for the interview, that you can look at with the hiring manager and discuss, is **THE best interview tool you could ever use**. It shows that you are someone with **drive, ambition, initiative, enthusiasm, good strategic thinking skills, good prioritization skills, and good problem-solving skills** who can **set goals** and know what steps will **achieve** them.

With this question, they are looking to visualize you in this role, and your plan will help them do that.

You say, "I'm so glad you asked that. I've actually created an outline of what I think my action steps and goals should be for the first 30, 60, and 90 days of this job and I'd like to go over it with you and get your feedback."

You'll start with what you need to do in the **first 30 days** to familiarize yourself with the company:

--Training

--Meeting co-workers, team or other departments

--Learning systems, procedures, or software

--Getting your feet wet with your first projects or customers

After you discuss this for a few minutes, you'll move on to the next 30 days (the **60-day** section):

--Get up to speed with your job

--Get feedback on your progress

--Start going off more on your own

--Then, you'll begin discussing the last 30 days (the **90-day** part):

--Start bigger projects

--Set longer-term goals

--Establish new procedures

--Make improvements

As much as you can, add details that are specific to this company (such as the name of the person you'd report to or the name of their training program). Think about what would make you successful from Day 1 in this job.

Key to a Great Interview!

A 30-60-90-day plan helps make it an easy decision to hire you!

Find out more in the resources at the back of the book!

Job Interview Question 90

What would your direct reports say about you?

This question explores your **leadership qualities**. What is your leadership style? What do you do that makes you a good leader?

Great things to mention that they might say are that you **set clear expectations**, you are **fair**, you're a good **communicator** and a willing **teacher**, you give balanced **feedback**, and that you are extremely **knowledgeable** about your industry.

Choose **2 or 3 things that accurately describe you** and say, "My direct reports would say that I am X and Y."

If you happen to have any **evidence** that supports this, offer it. Possibly this could be a direct report who is serving as a **reference**, or a **performance review** discussing your leadership qualities, or an **assessment of your group or team's performance** compared to others in the company (the idea being that if your team was especially successful as a whole, you must be doing something right).

Job Interview Question 91

What, as an organization, can we offer that is better than your current employer?

Your interviewer wants to know that you are genuinely interested in and enthusiastic about working for their company. They don't really want you to compare and contrast the two companies—and besides, if you get into doing that you can veer off track very quickly into badmouthing your current company which is always a no-no.

They want to know **what attracts you to this job**, based on your research and your own opinion—so answer that question.

Your answer should be, "I am especially interested in this job at this company because…" and then give **at least 3 very sincere, positive reasons why you are excited about this job**.

One reason should address the fact that **this job is a good fit for you professionally and culturally**. You are interested in that, after all. So, talk about how your skills will make you successful there:

"…this organization is a perfect fit for me. You need X, Y, and Z, and I have all of those plus ABC. That's going to make me very effective working here, and I am excited about the opportunity. I've been reading about the company and it seems like a great fit for my personality, values, and work style."

Then move into a reason that addresses a **particular professional aspect** they offer that others don't. This is where your **research** is going to come in particularly handy, because the more specific you can be, the better. This could be any number of things:

--They work with a **particular customer**, slice of the **market**, **procedure**, or **software**.

--They are expanding into a **new market**.

--They are **leaders** in their field.

--They are just **starting up** so they have all kinds of room to grow quickly.

--They have a great **reputation.**

--They create **cutting-edge products**.

--They are known for having the **highest-quality** X, and you want to be a part of that.

End your answer with a more personal reason that this job appeals to you, which could also be any number of things:

--They emphasize **employee development** and you are always interested in learning new things and growing professionally.

--They are known for being a great place to work in terms of **community**, and you think of work as an extended family.

--You **personally use their products** and are jazzed about the idea of contributing to their creation, distribution or sale.

--You'll have considerably **more autonomy and responsibility** with this job which will make your work life more rewarding.

--It's **closer to your house**, which will make your commute very short and add to your quality of life.

--It requires **less travel**, because you are ready to be in your own bed more often.

Do you research, be specific, be positive, and show your sincere enthusiasm for working in this role, for this organization.

Job Interview Question 92

What's your favorite dish, and how would you convince someone who hated an ingredient in it to try it?

I think the 'favorite dish' part of this question is a throwaway part. They don't really care what your favorite dish is (mine is pizza). What they care about is **your ability to construct a compelling argument in the face of strong resistance.** This could be a good question for sales jobs, management jobs where they're trying to change the culture, or any other jobs where persuasion would be required.

To convince someone of something, it often works to use the 'feel-felt-found' argument. (I know how you feel…I felt the same way…this is what I found.)

In my case, I would use sweet potatoes:

"I didn't like sweet potatoes either, until I was 30 years old. I thought they were gross and disgusting, like you do—but the ones that you tried aren't like what I want you to try. Those were in a can and disgusting and you are right. But these are fresh sweet potatoes that have been baked with honey and butter and brown sugar all over them and they are incredible.

Sometimes when you find an ingredient that you don't like, in another situation you may very well like it. And sweet potatoes are so incredibly good for you and have so much Vitamin A that they are worth another shot. You need to always try different things and have different foods to eat."

So, I've **established common ground**, I've **engaged their emotions and senses**, I've used **logic** as well as a **good nutrition** argument.

Job Interview Question 93

When would you be available to start?

This question requires a straightforward, factual response.

If you can start as soon as they're ready for you to start, then say that.

If you need to give notice to your employer, then let them know how much notice you are required to give—usually this is two weeks.

However, **don't box yourself into a corner** by giving them a firm date, because you don't know exactly when you'll have a firm offer in your hand, and you don't want to cut yourself too short and burn bridges at your current company.

So say, "I would be able to give two weeks' notice as soon as I have a firm offer, so it would be two weeks after that."

If it's longer than two weeks, you need to have a very good reason for that. It could be that your **contract** requires a longer time frame, so say so. If you are in the **middle of a big project** and think it's only fair to finish it first, you could give that reason—but you run a risk. Either they'll think you are exceptionally **loyal** and dedicated, or they'll think you're **not serious** about wanting to work for them. They will definitely think you're not serious about wanting to work there if you give them an extended time frame. It may make them think you are **shopping around**, and will only take their offer if you don't get something better.

If there is a question of when you could start, or you think they might be in a particular **hurry** to hire someone, answer the question with a question: "When do you need someone to start?" Their answer might change your answer, depending on how badly you want this job.

Job Interview Question 94

Who are our competitors?

An interviewer who asks this wants to see:
- if you have done your homework and **researched their company** before the interview
- if you are really **as familiar with this arena/product/service** as you should be
- what else you mention on this topic that tells them more about **what you can offer them in terms of organizational advantage**

This is a big question in any **sales job**, but it can easily come up in other fields. Not only should you know the **competitors' names**, you should know **a few of the most important facts** about them in relation to this company and the market.

You can get this information through your own research using **Google** and **LinkedIn**, as well as by talking to others in your personal network or LinkedIn groups. The more **specific** you can be, the better.

If you have worked for their competitors, be careful about disclosing anything that would violate a confidentiality or non-compete agreement.

What would be useful to mention along with the names of the competitors?

--**Differences** and **similarities**

--**Recent sales comparisons**

--**Market share/ tactics**

--A specific **struggle in a certain market** or with a certain product

--**Reviews, news stories**

--This company's place in **popular rankings or lists**

--This company's efforts to **gain an advantage over their competitors**

--Why this company is (in your opinion) **better than the others**

If you can, you should **consider offering a general suggestion** for an activity or strategy that would help this company in the fight against their competition, such as marketing opportunities, threats, or current trends.

The biggest point of all this is to show that you have done your research on the company and the industry and that you can have an informed, intelligent discussion about it.

Key to a Great Interview
SWOT Analysis

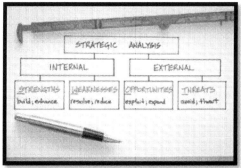

SWOT is a strategic planning tool that stands for:

Strengths (attributes helpful to achieving the objective)

Weaknesses (attributes harmful to achieving the objective)

Opportunities (external conditions that will be helpful to achieving the objective)

Threats (external obstacles or conditions that will harm the process)

Doing a **SWOT** analysis on the company demonstrates your drive, commitment, and skills, along with helping you create a better 30/60/90-day plan.

Job Interview Question 95

Who are the influencers in your life?

The people who influence you in your life obviously have a direct impact on your **character**, your **values**, and your **behavior**.

Who you choose to mention as an influencer tells the interviewer a lot about you personally—what you value, and what you aspire to.

What you need to do here is **give an example of one or two influencers** and say **why** they are an influence in your life.

For instance, I would say, "My influencers would be my parents, who taught me how to work hard, to challenge myself, and to make smart decisions, and my mentors, who I have chosen myself to be my teachers and coaches in different areas of my professional life. I value those relationships and make the time to maintain them so that I can always be learning and growing, and I try to return the favor and help them out as much as I can with information and insights of my own."

Now, I've had many, many people that I've learned from in my life and career—too many to list. The ones I choose tell an employer that I'm **smart**, **ambitious**, I **work hard**, and I am always **striving to improve myself**.

You may have had many influencers or those that you admire, too. What have you learned from them? What parts of that make you better at your job? This could be so many things:

--Dedication

--Drive

--Ethics

--Loyalty
--Integrity
--Hard work
--Service
--Leadership
--Positive Attitude
--Confidence
--Communication Skills
--Courage

What do you want this employer to know and remember about you and your character?

Whatever you want this employer to know about you as a person, that's what you should highlight in your answer by choosing which influencers to mention and what specifically you learned from them.

Job Interview Question 96

Who do you follow on Twitter and why?

First, are you on Twitter? Do you Tweet? This question uncovers how much you participate in **social media** in general, how **computer- and internet-savvy** you are, and who you think is important enough to spend your valuable time on, finding out what they think.

Who you follow on Twitter says a lot about you and what is a **priority** in your life. Are you only following celebrities (I hope not) or looking for relevant and helpful information? Do you follow those who contribute to your personal or professional development? Are you following the **major players** and **influencers in your field**?

Here is a drop in the bucket of interesting people/organizations to follow on Twitter:

Brian Tracy – world-renowned speaker and coach for positive change in business and life

TED Talks – mini lessons by experts in a variety of fields

Brian Solis – digital analyst, sociologist and futurist focuses on business-consumer relationship and social media strategy

Steve Randy Waldman – Private investor with insights on economics and finance

Mark Hunter – The Sales Hunter who tweets motivational insights on sales, leadership, and more

DARPA (Defense Advanced Research Projects Agency) – develops new technology for the military

Neil deGrasse Tyson – astrophysicist who tweets about science and makes great jokes

You can browse interests through a variety of topics to see any names you might recognize.

If you aren't on Twitter, it's worth it to get an account now and start exploring. You really can pick up a lot of useful news and information.

If you aren't on Twitter and aren't going to be, it's OK to say that but then mention other social media you may participate in and how that is beneficial for you.

Job Interview Question 97

Why did you get into this line of work? (choose this as a career)

This is not just a friendly, ice-breaking kind of question (any more than any other interview question is). It's true that they are asking about your motivations, interests and values:

Why do you do what you do?

What **influenced** your decision?

Do you have any particular **talents** that made this an easy choice?

Is this related to a life-long **interest** or **hobby** for you?

Think this question through just a little bit further, with the knowledge that the job search and interview is a sales process, the hiring manager is the 'customer' and you are the 'product,' and you'll realize that what they really want to know is:

Are you interested in and enthusiastic about what you do? If so, you will be a better employee who is more successful and produces more success for the company.

Why and how does this apply to your fit for the job? You need to connect the dots for them…if you have a particular ability or talent

415

that encouraged you to pursue this career, give an example of how you have been successful using that talent.

For instance, here's my answer:

"When I first started out, I entered the field of medical sales. I loved the medical field but didn't want to be a doctor. I enjoy meeting new people and I loved the challenge of persuading someone to buy my product.

When I began recruiting for the medical field, I was looking to reduce my travel because I had a young son. I had been a high-level sales manager in the medical arena and knew how difficult it could be to identify and evaluate good candidates to hire. I knew that I could do that very well because of my particular experience. This way, I kept my hand in the field, I still got to speak with people all over the world, I still got to persuade and influence, but this time it was my clients and candidates.

I started my own company and became a career coach, because I knew that I had a passion for helping others and wanted to expand it outside of just the medical sales arena. I show job seekers how to get hired. Now I get to persuade and influence on a global scale through helping tens of thousands of job seekers in over 90 countries. I get a lot of satisfaction out of knowing I've helped them get hired and receiving their phone calls and emails that thank me for my help."

****

Try to show that **you chose this career on purpose** instead of a random accident—but if you did just happen to stumble into this line of work at least talk about what a **happy accident** it was and how you've made **deliberate steps to grow and learn** more since then.

Job Interview Question 98

Why don't you want to give me your salary requirements?

Salary is one of the most difficult and delicate topics of the entire job search and interview process. I always recommend to my candidates that they try to **completely avoid any discussion of salary** until after the company has decided they want to hire you. Why? Because you want them to fall in love with you and have to have you before you tell them how much it's going to cost. This puts you in a much better bargaining position when it's time to talk dollars.

Whether you are interviewing with HR or a hiring manager, they are going to ask about your salary requirements, both to see if they can afford you and to see how little they can get you for. Your job is to **deflect** as much as possible.

By the time they get to this question, you have deflected many times and they are pushing for an answer. You have several good options:

--Say, "I'm **uncomfortable giving you a salary requirement until I know all the factors.** I'm not sure if we've covered all the responsibilities and goals for this position yet, or what the other elements in your compensation package are. Can you tell me what the entire package would be?" Whatever you might have earned in another position isn't really relevant to what is fair for this job. Even similar jobs will have different responsibilities and goals in different companies. Other factors in a compensation package (healthcare, profit sharing, bonuses, perks, etc.) can make up for a less-than-desired salary.

417

Key to a Great Interview
Negotiating the Best Salary

Find out everything you need to know about navigating salary questions and negotiating the best compensation and benefits: <u>Negotiating Your Salary: How to Make $1000 a Minute by Jack Chapman</u>

--Go ahead and tell them something. Do your **research on salary ranges** for this role, in this size company, in this industry, in this area of the country. Good research sites include Salary.com, Glassdoor.com and Payscale.com.

Tell them that you found out that the range for this job is between X and Y. "Y" should be the top of the range and "X" should be in the middle. This way, you are **setting a bias** that is skewed toward a higher end number. It's an 'anchor' that pulls the entire direction of the negotiation towards it.

--Say, "My **salary requirements aren't relevant** unless we have decided that I am a good fit for this role. If you have decided that you'd like to hire me, I'd love to talk compensation and benefits with you. If you need to know more about my skills and qualifications first, then let's talk more about that. What else would you like to know?"

--**Keep refusing** and say, "I know that you must have a range budgeted for this position. I am sure that **the range you have set will be fair** and commensurate with the responsibilities of this job. **Can you tell me what that range is,** and then I can confirm that I can be comfortable with that range. What is the range?"

Job Interview Question 99

Will you be out to take my job?

In larger companies, managers always need to be looking for the one who can take their place so that they can move up. If this is where you are, they might just be checking out your level of ambition. In this situation, I might answer it with humor: "I'm sure by the time that happens, you'll be running the whole company."

In smaller companies, there might be nowhere for this person to go—so if you want an in-house promotion, it will mean kicking them out the door. In this situation, you need to reassure them that you are there to learn and contribute. So say something like:

"Of course not. I'm sure that I'm going to learn a lot from you and that we are going to develop a great working relationship. As long as I keep getting to learn new things and contribute in a meaningful way and being rewarded for that, I'm going to feel great about coming to work here with you every day."

Job Interview Question 100

Would you rather be liked or feared?

The best answer is, "Neither. I'd rather be **respected**." Some interviewers won't accept this and press for a choice.

If I were pressed to choose only one, I would say, "I would rather be liked, because I believe that people go out of their way to help those they like, and feel more invested in our collective success. I think fear is too negative an emotion and wouldn't produce an environment that is creative, innovative, or motivating to do a great job."

However, the interviewer may accept your "respect" answer and follow up with a question about **how you would inspire respect** in your team or employees. One of the best ways to **earn respect** is to ask great questions, to understand the situation before you make decisions. Many managers do more harm than good by jumping to conclusions and make mistakes that hurt individuals and group morale. A manager who makes decisions based on a complete gathering of evidence makes stronger decisions.

Job Interview Question 101

You are changing careers. Why should I let you 'experiment' with me and basically pay you to learn on the job?

The very best answer to this question is to say, "That is a good question. I created a 30-60-90-day plan to show you how I can practically flatten my learning curve. It's an outline of what I see as the main action steps and goals that would make me wildly successful in this job."

With this, the hiring manager is probably going to be very curious about what you have come up with, and be willing to look at your plan with you.

When you talk about your first 30 days, you're going to want to emphasize how you will **train yourself** to learn what you need to know. It **won't be a problem for this hiring manager** to worry about, and it **won't slow you down**. If you are changing careers, you will need to do a lot of **research** in order to determine what **books** you should read, what **people** you need to talk to, or even what **courses** you need to take to get up to speed.

Key to a Great Interview!
A 30-60-90-day plan helps make it an easy decision to hire you!
Find out more in the resources at the back of the book!

When you talk about your next 30 days (the 60-day part), you're going to want to show how your **transferrable skills** will come into play, along with your own self-training to make you a strong performer in this role.

Think about **what your skills are going to bring** to this role that maybe someone from this field already might not have—like maybe you are an especially creative problem-solver. Think about **what** you would need to do next and **HOW** you would do it.

When you talk about your next 30 days (the 90-day part), show this hiring manager **how you will be moving on your own to benefit the company and succeed in your role.** What will you be doing? (Base this on what you have learned from the **job description.**)

The more **research** you can do for your plan, the more you will be able to show that you are very **capable of doing this job even if you have little to no experience.**

As a bonus, creating a plan shows that you are an **incredibly motivated** and **energetic worker** with **strategic thinking skills, prioritization skills,** and **plenty of initiative** and **will to succeed.**

If for some reason after walking them through your plan, they still are pushing you on the experience factor, say:

"Well, everyone has to start somewhere. No one starts every job with all the experience they need. Did you have any experience in your first job? And yet you are very successful. I would say that even though I don't have experience yet, my plan shows you that I am tremendously motivated and I believe that the skill sets I'm bringing from my previous jobs will make me a versatile asset in this role."

Key to a Great Interview
Job Shadowing

If you are new to a career, a job shadowing experience gives you more "meat" to talk about during the interview. You're going to have more understanding of a typical day on the job and what the challenges and issues will be. That helps you speak more intelligently about what you can bring to the table, and why it's going to be a good idea to hire you. It's also going to help tremendously in creating your 30/60/90-day plan--which is vital to your interview success when transitioning careers.

Bonus:
How to Handle Illegal Interview Questions

Because of the United States' strong anti-discrimination laws, many job interview questions are actually illegal—this includes questions about your **gender, children or future children, marital status, nationality, religion, disability, and age**.

However, this doesn't stop all employers from asking them. Not all of them ask with bad intent—some are just trying to make conversation with you and maybe find common ground—but the question is inappropriate just the same and you do not have to answer it.

You don't want to come right out and tell them that what they are asking is an illegal question they have no right to know the answer to. That tends to increase the tension and create an antagonistic conversation you might not be able to turn around, and your job interview will be ruined—even if the employer actually had a high level of interest in you as a candidate.

If you can, try to tactfully dodge the question without actually answering it. Here are a few illegal interview questions with ideas for how to address them.

My Advice...

If the employer asks you one or two interview questions and allows you to successfully dodge them, then you can probably safely assume it was just a mistake on their part and let it go. If they ask many of these questions, or insist on answers they are not legally allowed, you may not want to work for that company.

Questions About Gender

Usually these questions center around something like, "Do you really think you can run a team of all men?"

A good answer would just slide right past that and say:

"I am very comfortable in a management role. In my last position, my team achieved X."

Questions About Children

These are usually tied to gender, asked only of female candidates. They might say, "Do you have good childcare?" meaning, "Are you going to call in sick when you have to take care of your kids?"

You should say:

"I am absolutely committed to my professional obligations and to the people here who would depend on me."

If they say, "Are you planning on having children?" or "Are you planning on having more children?" Unless you are pregnant right at that moment, I would just say, "No." First of all, you never know what the future holds, and second of all, it's none of their business.

Questions About Marital or Family Status

Any questions about plans to marry, to stay home after you have children, or your spouse's occupation or salary are all illegal.

Employers might ask these questions to get a read on how long you'll plan to stay at the company—but if that's their question, that should be what they ask.

In response to any future marriage or family plans, smile and say, "You know, I'm not making those kinds of plans yet. I am focused on my career, and I'm interested in growth opportunities in this company. Can you tell me more about that?"

If you're asked about your spouse's occupation, it may be in a relocation situation where they're trying to see if your spouse will be OK with moving with you. I would be OK answering that question. If your spouse is in an impressive career, their follow up question may be, "Wow, then what are you doing looking for a job?" Just smile and say, "I work for many reasons other than money. I am very talented and skilled at X, Y, and Z and I enjoy the work as well as achieving goals, like I did last year in my job where I _____." Fill in the blank with whatever outstanding and impressive thing you did.

Questions About Nationality

Sometimes this is a simple, "Where are you from?" and they don't mean any harm by it. Just smile and say, "Texas. How about you?"

Many companies are sensitive to whether or not you are legally allowed to work in the U.S., and that is a question they can ask. They can't ask "What race are you?" or "Were you born in the United States?" They can only say, "Are you legally allowed to work in the U.S.?"

If you have an accent and the interviewer says, "Oh, are you from X?" it is probably an innocent question. Your best bet is to smile and say, "Yes, I moved here X years ago and I am legally allowed to work in the U.S." If this is not your first job in the States, say, "In fact, I've been very successful working as an X for ABC Corporation."

They might say, "Is English your first language?" Feel free to say, "I speak both English and Spanish fluently." (Or whatever language you speak, of course.)

Questions About Religion

Employers are not allowed to ask about your religion, whether you're going to be asking off work for religious holidays or if you go to church on Sundays. They *can* ask if you are available to work on Sundays, or if you will be able to work normal work hours.

Just say, "I'm certain I will be able to work the schedule that is required for this position. Is there anything unusual about the schedule that I should know about?"

(I always like the tactic of asking a follow up question for clarification.)

Questions About Disability

Employers are not allowed to ask direct questions about your disability, but they can ask if you are able to perform specific job duties. If they ask anything you are not comfortable answering, you can just say, "That isn't something that will interfere with my ability to do this job."

Questions About Age

Generally, questions about age are going to be a problem (and a legal issue) for those who are over 40.

If you are asked blatantly, "How old are you?" "When did you graduate?" or "When were you born?" and you truly think they will hold it against you, say:

"My age isn't relevant as to whether or not I can do this job, but my experience is, and I have experience in X, Y, and Z. In fact, I won the award last year in my company for X." Mention some notable achievement that illustrates that you are successful and good at your job.

****

Remember, most illegal interview questions are not asked with malicious intent. Usually, they are innocent questions asked by

426

inexperienced interviewers in an attempt to spark conversation and get to know you.

In most cases, you can tactfully dodge the question with a smile and a sentence that directs the conversation back to your fit for the job, maybe even answering the question they should have asked, but didn't.

If you genuinely feel that this question was inappropriate, and can't dodge it, you can ask how this applies to your ability to do the job.

***Note: *This section on illegal interview questions is not intended to be a comprehensive list of illegal interview questions, and does not substitute for legal advice.*

Asking Questions in the Job Interview:

The Top 2 Questions to Ask That Boost Your Chances of Getting the Offer

Peggy McKee

Introduction

As a recruiter and a career coach for 15+ years, I've had a front-row seat to both sides of the interview table. From my experience of working directly with hiring managers and job candidates, I can tell you that the key to a great interview is communication. The more clearly and effectively you communicate with the hiring manager, the better your chances are at getting the job.

Learn and practice asking the interview questions in this book, and ask them in your interview. They will allow you to communicate in the most effective way with the hiring manager and even get a peek into what they're really thinking in the interview—which is priceless information for you.

I hope you enjoy this quick read and put what you learn into practice in your very next interview. In the back of the book, you'll find a link to the page where you can give a review of the book (I would appreciate you letting me know if this book helps you). You'll also find additional links to more books, information and tools that will help you get the job you want.

Best of luck in your next interview!

Peggy McKee

Why Ask Questions in a Job Interview?

What happens when you ask questions in a job interview? Asking questions about the job and the company shows the hiring manager your interest and enthusiasm for the job, as well as your intelligence and level of preparedness. It turns the entire interview into a much better experience for both of you. In general, asking questions builds rapport, ensures a nicer conversation, and gives the impression that you are a confident, strategic thinker.

As helpful as it is to ask questions about the job, there are two questions you can ask that will actually help you get the offer—by as much as 40%-50%. How? These two questions help you get inside the hiring manager's head so you can find out what they want and what they are thinking about you.

The Most Important Question to Ask in the Beginning of Your Interview

The first question you should ask gives you a peek inside the hiring manager's mind to discover what it is that he or she is hoping to hear from you in this interview: ***"What are you looking for in a perfect candidate for the job?"*** It's important that you ask this question near the beginning of your conversation.

Other Ways to Ask:

--Tell me a little bit about what you are looking for in your candidate or new hire.

--Tell me a little about what qualities or background you are especially hoping for in the person you want to hire for this role.

--What would an ideal candidate for this job look like?

Does the thought of asking for their wish list for the perfect candidate make you a little nervous because you know you aren't perfect and you won't be able to stack up well against the idea? Don't worry. They know they won't get perfection—nobody's perfect.

What this question does for you is important because it helps you be much more effective and powerful in answering their questions throughout the interview. Their answer gives you your first peek into what really matters to this particular person.

Even if you have the job description memorized, it may not tell the whole story. This hiring manager will have hopes and expectations for this role, whether you ask about them or not. All of these things on a hiring manager's ideal wish list will play an influential part in the decision of whether or not to hire you, so it's smart to know what those are. When you know, you will be able to tailor your answers specifically for this person. It will be much easier to communicate what this person needs to know in order to hire you.

For instance, if the answer you hear sounds like they really want someone with technical knowledge, then you know to play up those points about yourself in the stories you tell and the answers you give. If his or her answer mentions customer service, you now know to include a few stories about your great customer service skills.

All of your answers can be chosen to "tilt" the interview in your favor—especially any stories you tell as answers to behavioral interview questions. The stories can highlight your skills that you now know are especially important to that hiring manager. With your new knowledge, every answer you give can have maximum impact for that person.

Alternative Versions
--What do you see as my strengths and weaknesses as a candidate?
--Among the candidates for this position, how do I rank? Why?

These may seem like risky questions to ask because you don't want them thinking about your weaknesses or about how other candidates may be stronger than you—but trust me, they already are. With the insights you'll have from the answer, you can talk up your strengths and shore up any weak spots while you're answering their questions. You can correct anything they may be misinformed about, or show that your weaknesses can easily be fixed.

Asking these questions signal that you are confident but willing to learn. You will stand out from the rest of the crowd.

What If They Won't Answer Your Question?

What happens if they don't want to answer direct questions, or don't give you a complete answer about their ideal candidate? You can uncover clues that help you fill in information you need about their ideal by asking other, more subtle questions.

Why is this position open?

This is a basic question that sets the stage for the follow up question that really uncovers some great information for you.

If they say that the person who was in this position was promoted, follow up by asking what it was that helped them be so successful. With the knowledge of what it takes to be successful in that role, you can then point out instances of where you have found success in similar ways.

If they say that the person is no longer with the company, you can ask, "What was it that you think held that person back from being successful?" When they tell you, you can talk about how you have overcome similar issues, how you have successfully addressed similar obstacles in the past, or how you have avoided such problems.

What are the tasks in this job that are really going to define success for someone in this role?

Look at just about any job description and you'll see that some tasks are far more critical than others for the successful execution of that job. Not only that, but every company faces different challenges at different times. There may be subtle changes in what would define success for someone in this role vs. when the job description was written.

Find out what this hiring manager believes about what someone in this role really needs. Then you can talk about how you have been successful at similar tasks, or talk about how you would approach the essential tasks that drive success in this role.

What would sink an employee in this position?

If you got a vague answer about what would define success for someone in that role, you could turn it around and come at it from a different angle by asking about what would sink someone in this position, or cause them to fail.

When you hear what the failures were, you may be able to speak about how you have successfully addressed those issues in the past. This will catch their interest and help sell the idea of hiring you for the job.

All of these types of questions where you're digging for information or clues should be asked in the first portion of the interview (at least the first half). You need these clues to help you really tailor your interview answers to what this hiring manager is most interested in. This process will ensure that you are maximizing your time with this person and effectively selling yourself for the job.

The Most Important Question to Ask Toward the End of Your Interview

Toward the end of the interview, when it's winding down but before you leave the room, you have to ask the next most important question for any job seeker: "Do you see any reason why you would not consider me for this position?"

This question is basically asking for the job. This is a technique from sales called closing. The reason it also works in a job search and interview process is because both of these are psychologically the same (in terms of evaluating and decision-making) as a sales process.

In a job interview, you are following the same steps as a sales rep. You are talking about your product (that's you), you are answering questions about yourself and you are asking questions to find out what they really want and need. Most job seekers leave it at that, which leaves the hiring manager wondering if they really want the job.

When you close like a sales rep, you ask for the job. Basically, you say, "Hey, can I have the job?" "Are you ready to hire me?" Or at the very least, "Are you ready to move to the next step with me?"

Job seekers who close for the job boost their chances of actually getting it by 30%-40%. It causes the hiring manager to make a decision about you while you are in their line of sight, and while your positive qualities are fresh in their mind. This is why it's worth it to learn to close for the job.

There are several ways to ask this question. Here are two examples:

Is there any reason I won't move forward in this process?

If they say, "No, I can't see any reason to not move you forward," then you know you've done what you needed to do in the interview, and you may very well get the offer. You can respond with something like, "Great!" and ask about next steps. If they point out a couple of reasons, or issues they have, you know that those are points where you may need to clarify or talk a bit more on, in order to overcome those objections and make the decision to hire you. Sometimes, this is a simple misunderstanding. Without clearing it up, you won't get the job.

Are you confident I am someone who can meet the challenges of this position?

This is a more positive way of asking this question. Some people prefer this phrasing. Either way, the result is the same. If they agree that you are someone who can meet the challenges of the position, they will be an advocate for hiring you after you leave. If they say, "No," you should ask why not, discuss their answer, and hopefully change their mind about you.

What you're doing by asking this kind of question is uncovering any doubts the hiring manager might have about you so that you can address them while you still have the chance.

This is one of the most difficult questions for candidates to ask, because it feels pushy, like you're pressuring him for an answer right now. You are, but it's OK. You will never have a better chance than right now of getting this job. If there's any doubt in that hiring manager's mind that you are the right person for the job, it will be there after you leave. You must try to remove that doubt now.

If you leave the interview with those doubts in the hiring manager's mind, he or she will almost certainly not move forward with you. Those doubts will grow, and then the next candidate who takes any doubts away is the one who'll get hired.

Now, when you ask a question like this, you may uncover a doubt that you just can't do anything about, (although if I were you I'd still want to know what it was). However, their doubt or objection might be over something incredibly simple and correctable—for instance, maybe he's worried because he thinks you won't want to move and he can't afford to relocate you. If you can reassure him that you're fine with handling your own moving expenses, he may offer you the job. Or, maybe he thinks that you don't have any experience with something, and you didn't know it was that important, so you didn't bring it up. Now that you know, you can address it and make him much more comfortable with hiring you.

I've had many, many candidates tell me, "I didn't want to ask it because I was so uncomfortable with it, but I heard your voice in my head telling me to do it, and I just jumped in and asked. It turned out great, and I got the job!"

Assuming you get a positive answer to any closing question, no matter how you ask it, your immediate follow up should be, "What's the next step?" or, "When can I expect to hear from you with an offer?" Not only does this follow up move them even further along the path of offering you the job, it allows for crystal clear communication with no room for misunderstandings.

Even if you fail to uncover objections with a closing question, you have no excuse for not asking about next steps, or a timeline for making a decision. The hiring manager expects you to ask about when you'll hear from them, or when a decision will be made. If you don't ask, he will assume that you don't want the job.

Not only will asking about the next step give you information you need about their timeline, it will also give you an idea of when to follow up if you don't hear from them. If their expectation is that they'll make a decision by next Friday, but you call asking about it on the Tuesday before, that will annoy them. If they say they'll make a decision by next Friday and you don't hear from them, it's perfectly acceptable for you to call the Monday after to see what's up—but you won't know unless you ask.

These questions may seem out of the ordinary, but they've been proven to work over and over again by thousands of successful candidates. Try them in your next interview. Best of luck!

How to Ace Your

Phone Interview

By Peggy McKee

Letter from the Author

Phone interviews…as a recruiter (14 years), I call these phone *screens*. Why? Because, when I call a candidate on the phone to ask those first few questions, I'm looking to make a decision: Yes or no, good or bad, move forward or stop right here.

In a phone screen, moving to the next step should be your goal but most folks don't take this very important career conversation seriously enough. For anything to be a great experience, we have to plan, prepare and execute. Then, of course, there is the follow up!

I applaud you for reading this book, because you're taking more action than most. In order to get the job offers you want and go to the places you want in your career and life, you need to do more, and be better than others. This book will help you achieve that.

Enjoy this book filled with my best phone interview tips from 14 years of conversations with thousands of candidates. Read it carefully, and use it to prepare for your next phone interview.

Best of luck (the harder you work, the luckier you get),

Peggy McKee
Career and Interview Coach
CEO Career Confidential
https://CareerConfidential.com

"All our dreams can come true, if we have the courage to pursue them."
—Walt Disney

Phone Interview Tips #1

Understand the Importance of This Call

How Important Telephone Interviews Really Are

A phone interview is never "just" a phone interview. It's the first step in the hiring process. You will never get to the second step (the face-to-face interview) if you don't do a great job here.

Phone interviews are the gating process companies use to whittle down their list of candidates. That's why they are also called phone screens. Companies use these quick, inexpensive interviews to look for reasons to weed you out. You will not get a second chance.

This is the make-it-or-break-it moment that decides whether or not you can be in the running for the job.

Why Companies Do Phone Interviews

Hiring managers (that's the person who would be your boss) don't have time to face-to-face interview all the people applying for the position. So they run you through this conversational test to see if you're worth spending an hour with in a regular interview. This way, they can meet with more people in less time.

They get some bonuses out of it, too. In a phone interview, it's much easier for them to cut the call short because they've decided against you in the first few minutes. No commitment, no expense, no muss, no fuss.

Why People Succeed or Fail in Phone Interviews

Job seekers fail in the phone interview for two major reasons: they don't take it seriously enough, and they don't successfully meet its unique challenges.

All interviews are really about communication, which can be difficult enough. However, the vast majority of communication between two people is visual. In a phone interview, neither of you can see all of the micro-expressions and gestures that give your words clarity and convey meaning. So you are at a disadvantage.

However…if you take the phone interview as seriously as a face-to-face interview, and you learn to work with the unique circumstances of a phone interview, you can easily succeed.

Why This Book?

Each tip in this book will give you another "lesson" in phone interviews that will make sure you succeed in your goal, which is to get invited to interview in person. You'll discover how to prepare, what to say, how to follow up, and much more.

Phone Interview Tips #2

Check Your Voicemail Greeting, Ring backs, and Message-Takers

This is really a *pre*-phone interview tip. Often, the company or recruiter will call you to set up the phone interview (and sometimes, they'll call a few minutes early for a scheduled interview in order to catch you off guard and see how you react). If you can't answer the phone, their first impression of you is whatever is on your recorded greeting—or whoever answers your phone.

For a professional, friendly greeting:
- Keep your message to 30 seconds or less (no music)
- Eliminate any background noise
- Possibly offer an alternative way to contact you, such as your email address

What is the best voicemail message? Short and sweet:
- "Hi, this is Joe Smith. Please leave a message and I'll get back to you as soon as possible."
- "You've reached the Burtons. Please leave a message."
- "You've reached 555-555-1212. Please leave a message." (If you are not comfortable leaving your name.)

A very nice touch is to show some enthusiasm and thank the person for calling: "Hi, this is Jane Smith. I appreciate your call, but I am not available right now. Please leave a message and I will call you back soon."

After you get the job, you can change your voicemail back to anything you want.

Worst Voicemail Greetings I've Ever Heard

The one that made me listen to the person's favorite song before I could leave my message (it wasn't MY favorite song). The one that was recorded by charming (I'm sure) but difficult-to-understand 3-year-old. The one that tried to be funny but wasn't: "How do you leave an idiot in suspense? Leave a message and I'll get back to you." (…leaves you feeling all warm and fuzzy, doesn't it?)

Ring Tones

If you have changed the standard ringing sound that callers hear to your favorite song or some other custom sound, change it back—at least while you're in the job search.

Message-Takers

If roommates or family members will be answering your phone, either train them to answer it professionally (which means being ready to take a message complete with name and telephone number—and making sure that you actually get the message), or insist that no one answer the phone and instead let it go to your very professional voicemail greeting.

If your cell is your primary number…

Be cognizant of where you are and what you're doing when you answer the phone. If you're going to answer the call of a recruiter or hiring manager, don't be in a very noisy store or out of breath from running. If you're not already in a quiet spot, it is better to let it go to voicemail so you can get to somewhere appropriate to call back.

"You never get a second chance to make a good first impression."
- Will Rogers

Phone Interview Tips #3

Control the Time of Your Call

You have the power to control the day and time of your phone interview—and it is in your best interests to use it. Why?

You need enough time to prepare. This phone interview is a very big deal. If you blow it here, you don't get another chance, so you want enough time to prepare and research for this interview very well.

You'll have a better interview because you're always going to come across stronger and more effectively if you schedule the interview for a time when you're calm, alert, and focused. (Personally, I would never, ever schedule a phone interview first thing in the morning. I need a little while to warm up first. On the other hand, I have a friend who is at her most chipper in the wee hours. So for her, earlier is better.)

You can leave yourself a time cushion in case the interview goes longer than expected (a great sign!). I've seen phone interviews go over the allotted time by 5, 10, or even 30 minutes. (If they don't tell you how long they expect the call to take, ask.)

Setting a time for a phone interview is just like setting any other appointment. It shows good time management. Most hiring managers won't have a problem with it at all, and in fact expect to schedule the interview with you.

There's always an exception to the rule, of course…so what happens if they call you out of the blue and want to talk about the job right then?

444

You can choose not to answer it and let it go to your voicemail (but return the call as soon as possible). If you do answer it, it is perfectly acceptable to say, "I'm so glad you called. I would love to talk to you now, but I'm really not going to be able to give this the attention it deserves right at this moment. Can we talk tomorrow morning?" (Or whenever a good time for you is.)

> *"The definition of insanity is doing the same thing*
> *over and over and expecting different results."*
> *–Benjamin Franklin*

A Tip for Scheduling Phone Interviews
If You Are Employed

Please do not schedule your phone interviews during your normal work time—unless you have taken time off. If the interviewer realizes you are using company time to conduct your job search, they will question your ethics and might decide not to move forward with you on that basis alone.

I am curious....Do you ask outright in your phone interviews if they will move you forward to the face-to-face? Let me know if you do or don't in your comments on the book. (We'll be talking about this later—Tip #35.)

Phone Interview Tips #4

Control the Location of Your Call

Bad locations for any phone interview:
- Restaurants or coffee houses (too noisy and unpredictable)
- Bookstores or libraries (you'll be the one who's too noisy)
- Your current office (too risky)
- Your car (especially if you're driving!)

The only good spot for any phone interview: **your home.** At home, you have control over your environment and can keep it quiet. That being said, you have to exercise that control—which means no pets, no kids, and no significant others, either.

Make sure that all creatures big and small in your house are occupied elsewhere, and that the two-legged varieties (big and small) understand that if they interrupt you, there had better be gushing blood involved. An emergency involving an ambulance is the only truly acceptable reason for your call to be interrupted.

What do you do if something interrupts your call?

No matter how hard you try, things of the non-emergency variety still sometimes happen. The dog barks. FedEx shows up at the door. You can get interrupted for a lot of reasons. Hiring managers understand that, but at the same time, they will be looking to see how you deal with the unexpected. What do you do?

First, keep your cool. If the distraction isn't going away, say, "Excuse me, please," deal with the issue, apologize for the interruption, and steer the conversation back to where you were in the interview.

Maintain your professionalism and your control. If you do, you will provide that hiring manager with a very clear picture of how you deal with interruptions or difficult situations on the job, which can be very impressive.

Phone Interview Tips #5

Use the Phone That Never Fails

The best phone for your interview is always a good old- fashioned landline. (A cordless phone works, as long as you are *certain* it's charged.) Why a landline? The sound quality is better, there's no risk of dropping the call, and you never have to ask, "Can you hear me now?"

If you don't have a landline, and will use a cell phone no matter what I tell you, follow these **cell phone rules**:

Make sure your cell phone has a good signal. Call a friend before your interview starts to make sure all the signals are connecting like they're supposed to. Bad reception will ruin your call.

Make sure your phone is charged. You can prepare to an extreme degree, with every single detail taken care of...but if your phone dies during the call, the interviewer will think you are unorganized, unprepared, and not worth talking to again.

Phone Interview Tips #6

Know Who You're Interviewing with— HR or the Hiring Manager?

In a larger company, your first phone interview is likely to be with Human Resources, rather than the actual hiring manager (the person who will be your boss). In a smaller company, you might speak with the actual hiring manager first. However, usually doesn't mean always, so be sure to ask.

When the interview is scheduled (through email or a phone call), ask who you'll be interviewing with. They will usually tell you "Jane Smith, from HR" or "Sue Jones, the Accounting Director." If they just give you a name and you don't recognize it, ask for clarification: "And this person is...?" You want name and title.

Why should you care about knowing the difference? HR and Hiring Managers are coming to this interview from different places, so they are looking for different things. (Plus, HR interviews tend to be shorter than hiring manager ones, so you can plan accordingly.)

HR's function in the hiring process is to be a gatekeeper. Their job is to present qualified candidates with no red flags for the hiring manager to choose from. So their focus is "Do you have the basic qualifications and is there anything wrong with you?" They are (more than anyone else) looking for someone safe that won't make them look bad if they present you to the hiring manager. Be aware that you are playing defense here.

Hiring managers are looking less critically at your potential problems, and more intensely at your fit for the job: What have you done? What can you do? What can you bring to the team? Do you have the potential for fitting into the company well, and can they get along with you? In this interview, you're switching from defense to offense. Tell them why you would be an asset to them.

Remember that the job search is a sales process and you have to communicate in the language of your customer. Tell them what matters to THEM as they consider you for this job.

Hint... Ask How Much Time to Allow For This Call

When they schedule your call, ask how much time they think it will take. If they tell you 10-15 minutes, it's probably a simple screening call with HR. If they tell you more than 30 minutes, you'll probably be speaking in greater depth with the actual hiring manager.

"You were born to win, but to be a winner, you must plan to win, prepare to win, and expect to win."
–Zig Ziglar

Phone Interview Tips #7

Research the Company

"What do you know about our company?"

This is a reasonable question you are likely to be asked. Hit a home run with your answer by doing your research on the company.

Start with the **corporate website** to see what the company does and how large it is. See how technologically-savvy they are based on how well the website is done. You'll get a sense of corporate values from their mission statement.

Then go to **Google** for news about the company. Are they growing? Have they started any projects? Have they been hit with lawsuits? What are others saying about this company?

Check them out on **LinkedIn**. Corporate pages on LinkedIn give you additional information you can't get from the website. Also, check out the profiles of **employees** who work at the company. What's their background? How long have they been there? Those are big clues for you.

Look at the company's **Facebook** page, if they have one, for less formal information. It gives you a different perspective.

Find them on **Twitter**. You might or might not be able to find company tweets. But you might easily find employee tweets, which can be pretty valuable for you.

Ask your **network**. Just ask around among your friends and colleagues what they know about the company. Your recruiter is a good resource, too.

Everything you find out from this process will help you be so much better in the phone interview. You'll be more comfortable, you'll be more confident, you'll answer all their questions better, and you'll make it much more likely to move forward to the face-to-face.

"The key to success is to focus our conscious minds on things we desire, not things we fear."
–Brian Tracy

Phone Interview Tips #8

Research the Interviewer

Why research the interviewer before your **phone interview**? Because the job interview is a sales process in which you are both the product and the sales rep. One of the first rules of sales is "Know Your Customer." You will sell more effectively if you know a little something about the person buying the product.

What Should You Search For?

You need some basic background on this person, such as: Where are they from? How did they come up in the business? Is their background similar or different than yours? What companies have they worked for? What hobbies do they have?

Finding these answers will help you with two important things:

Establishing rapport

Maybe you're from the same part of the country, or maybe you share a hobby. Or maybe you definitely don't—if you find out that your interviewer is a member of PETA, you won't want to talk about your love of hunting.

Tailoring your interview answers

The interviewer's career background might provide some clues as to what he or she values. If you can talk about things in your own background you know they'll value, that will give you an advantage in the process.

Use LinkedIn to Research the Interviewer

LinkedIn profiles are invaluable sources of information. What jobs have they had? What groups are they in? What things to they talk about in their status updates? All these things can give you important clues that will help you in your conversation.

Use Facebook to Research the Interviewer

Since Facebook is more of a social site than LinkedIn, you're going to be able to get another, more personal perspective on your interviewer. What do they post? What do they think is funny? Do they hold strong political views?

This research will make you feel more comfortable speaking with this person because you won't be going in cold. Being more comfortable means also being more confident.

Why Phone Interviews Are Like Coffee Dates

A phone interview is a little like setting up a date though an online dating service. You like the profile, but the safe thing to do is meet for coffee to see if your date is normal or bat-crap crazy. Dinner is too much of a commitment yet. Interviews follow the same logic. Phone interviews are the coffee date, face-to-face interviews are dinner.

Phone Interview Tips #9

Know What They'll See When They Research You

Recruiters and hiring managers will look for you online as a part of their research into you as a candidate. They will make judgments on what they find and they may ask you about it in your phone interview. Will anything especially impressive (or questionable) show up about you? To know what they will see when they search your name, search your own name first.

Use Google. Put quotes around it, like "John Smith" or "Jane Jones". Using the quotes means that your search results will be more focused and relevant for you.

Know what's there, and be prepared to discuss it.

Phone Interview Tips #10

Prepare Answers to Common Phone Interview Questions

It's simple: The more prepared you are for your phone interview (or any interview), the better impression you'll make.

Have great answers ready for these common phone interview questions, and boost your chances of moving forward.

Tell me about yourself.

This question really means, "Tell me something that will matter to me as I consider you for this job." So, always focus on your key professional "selling points."

Briefly mention your degree or any relevant classes you've taken, and then go into your background: promotions, awards, or key accomplishments that matter to your future success at this job.

You can say something along the lines of, "I have a degree in X, and over the last couple of years I've added classes in Y to round out my knowledge base. I started out at ABC Corporation, and moved to the Acme Company, where I achieved XYZ, and was promoted 3 times and received an award for X." Or whatever you can say that sums up your education, background, and significant accomplishments.

You don't need to talk longer than a minute or so—just deliver a targeted message that says: "I am skilled, I have accomplished some great things, and I can bring that to work here for you."

Why are you interested in this job?

Your company research should help you answer this question. Tell them why your skills are a good fit, and then give about 3 reasons why you'd like working at this company. How will it benefit you personally and professionally?

Always keep this answer **positive**. Talk about how great this company is and what makes you enthusiastic about working there. Focus on why you're looking forward to this opportunity and using your skills in X, Y, and Z to succeed in this job.

Here's an example:

"Based on the research I've done, I was very impressed with your track record in X and your plans for Y. This company is a place where my background in ABC and my strengths in XYZ can be put to great use. I can make the kind of contributions you need to achieve the company's goals, and that's exciting for me."

See? You're not talking about how the company can help you develop or get further in your career. That's what **you're** going to get out of it, and they don't care. Tell them what **they're** going to get out of this deal—someone whose skills can help them reach **their** goals. Tell them the benefits of hiring you.

Why are you leaving your current job?

This can be a difficult question, because you never want to be negative in any job interview answer—however, most people don't leave a job that's a positive situation. Never, ever say anything like, "Because I can't stand it there anymore."

Try to answer this question by focusing on why *this* job appeals to you, rather than why your last one doesn't anymore. If you must give a reason, try to choose one that was a factor in your old job that won't be in this one (location, commute, or something else that's a "neutral" answer).

For instance, if this job requires no travel, say, "There's a lot of travel in the old job and I'm ready to be in my own bed more often."

Or if you're moving from a small company to a big one: "I've loved my time at XYZ company and learned many things, but there's just not as much room for growth as I'd like."

Be as brief as you can. Mostly what you want to do here is focus on how it's not that you're running **from** that job, it's that you're running **to** this job. This job is such a great fit, and offers so many things you're looking for, and so on…

"Believe in yourself! Have faith in your abilities! Without a humble but reasonable confidence in your own powers you cannot be successful or happy."
–Norman Vincent Peale

One Caution About Preparing Answers Ahead of Time...
Even though you have these great prepared answers, be careful not to just read them out loud. Some people cannot do this naturally and sound like they're reading something out loud, which is bad. Either practice ahead of time so you sound smooth and natural, or just jot down a few notes and phrases to incorporate into your on-the-spot answer.

Phone Interview Tips #11

Prepare Answers to Tricky Phone Interview Questions

Here's a secret…every job interview answer can trip you up, but I often see candidates make mistakes with these:

What are your weaknesses?

As in all job interview answers, YOU have the power to mold and shape this answer into one that serves you best (while sticking to the truth, of course).

There are several approaches you can take, but this is the one I think will help you most:

Choose a real weakness that might cause you a problem in other areas of your life but actually helps you achieve in this job. (Just don't choose perfectionism, because it's too much of a cliché.)

For instance, I always used impatience as my weakness. No one can argue that impatience isn't a real weakness—it is, and it's caused me problems. Impatience is also something that's driven me to succeed faster than other people.

Someone else could answer that they get frustrated with people who don't work as quickly as they do—which says that you work fast and are dedicated.

Thinking about the greatest weakness question this way requires a little more creativity and thoughtfulness on your part, but the strategic advantages you'll gain from it in your interview will be worth it.

What are your strengths?

To answer this question, think about the things this hiring manager is looking for: skill sets, relationships, background, character traits…everything that is necessary to be successful in this role, and include these things (as they pertain to you) in your answer.

Maybe this job is going to be an incredible amount of work—so point out your work ethic. Maybe it's going to require tremendous communication skills—give an example of yours. Maybe it requires a quick learning curve—so say why you're going to be able to get up to speed quickly. Maybe it requires a particular background, and you have that.

Know how your skill set equals the skill set required for this position, and then deliver a concise but detailed statement that explains that. Show them that you fit. And provide a few examples of how you have done that in the past (which means that you can do it again for them). What have you achieved or accomplished that make you a great fit for this role?

Always tie your answer to your fit for the job.

When could you start?

The best answer to this is "I can start right away" or "I have to give my current company two weeks' notice, so I could start as soon as two weeks after I accept a written offer."

If you don't answer this directly, you could look like you're not serious about this job, and get knocked out of the running for it.

Are you willing to relocate?

If your answer is "Yes," you have no issue. If you're not sure, the knee-jerk answer many people give ("I'd consider it for the right opportunity") is not your best answer because it puts your motivation for wanting the job more into the 'money' category rather than the 'fulfilling work / great fit' category. It's a subtle but important distinction that will take the shine off your candidacy if you say it. What can you say?

If you're a 'No'…

If your answer is unequivocally 'no', you have to say so. It's only going to cause you problems if they do end up offering you the job and you won't move. (Although, let me just say that life can turn on a dime. What looks like "never" right now might not look like that in a few months or a year.) If you really want this job, and you can't move immediately, say so. But consider saying something like, "I'd rather not move right now, but you never know what tomorrow will bring. And I'm very interested in this position and this company."

If you're a 'Maybe'...

You'd rather not commit to packing up your entire life just yet, but you don't want this job to slip away because of it. Try something like, "I'm interested in growing my career, and if relocating for the job is a necessary part of that, of course I'd consider it." That doesn't commit you to moving. It just confirms that your career (and this job) is important—and it's tactful.

These answers don't commit you to anything, but they do help you appear to be more sincere, flexible, tactful, and reasonable than "I'd consider it for the right opportunity." They keep the conversation going in a positive direction, which is a big plus for any job interview.

Where do you see yourself in 5 years?

In other words, are you going to bail on them in a few months for another job, or are you going to stick around and make their training and investment in you pay off? Is this a stepping stone on your career path, or is this a job to pay the bills until you can do what you really want to do?

Many, many people believe that the best answer is some version of: "I see myself in your job!" or, "I want to be in management" because they think it shows ambition. That is not always the best answer.

If you are interviewing with a very large company, it might be just fine to talk about your desire to be promoted and to grow within the company, because they have room for you to do that.

If you are interviewing with a small company, an answer like that might be considered a threat to this person's job. If they don't have anywhere to go, they're certainly not going to let you push them out.

A much better answer in both situations is to say something more along the lines of "I want to grow and develop my skills," or "I want to be all I can be." Talk about how you look forward to greater responsibility as you learn more about the company, and that you hope to be ready to do more things.

Then you can say, "if you are looking at me for a management position at that time, I would be interested in it, but that's not necessarily my end goal. What I really want out of this is to learn, to grow, and to contribute in a meaningful way."

There is no hiring manager who won't be impressed by a strategic job interview answer like that.

461

Advice for the Over 50 Candidate
If you're an "over 50" candidate, don't say that you'll be thinking about retirement. You want to give the impression that you are still looking forward to learning and growing and working, not looking forward to golf.

Phone Interview Tips #12

Have Stories Ready for Behavioral Interview Questions

Hiring managers love **behavioral interview questions**, because they dig deeper into what kind of employee you really are. Answers to behavioral interview questions must be in the form of stories, or examples, from your career.

To answer behavioral interview questions well, come up with real life examples of how you have excelled in your work. Develop these stories for your behavioral interview.

A great way to organize your stories is with the STAR technique.

Begin with S, the "Situation", or T, "Task".

Give a little background into the problem you faced and set up the scenario. Provide some details about when and where it took place and some general context as to why it occurred. Explain what the situation required from you and what you did to resolve the issue.

Then comes A for "Action".

Tell what your options were and which one you chose, and explain to the interviewer what role you played in the outcome.

The last letter stands for "Results".

Emphasize the measurable results that wrapped up the situation in your favor. Be very specific about the results you personally achieved, what you learned and how your organization benefited from your part in the resolution.

With this structure, walk them through your thought process to show that you are strategic, thoughtful, knowledgeable, and can communicate well. How did you think about/approach that situation? Why did you choose that particular plan of action? How did you implement it? What happened? Did you have to adjust your approach? What did you learn from it? If you had to do it again, would you do it differently, and why?

Here are 3 examples for how to answer behavioral interview questions:

What do you consider to be your most significant accomplishment?

Don't just answer this by talking about the end result of your effort, as in "I ranked #1 among sales reps for 5 years in a row" or "I saved my company $5 million dollars last year." That's fantastic, but if you limit your answer like that, you're missing out on some prime selling time here.

Tell how you approached the problem or the goal and how you used the resources you had available. Talk about what obstacles you came up against and how you overcame them.

An Interviewer's Thoughts

Always focus your answer on work-related accomplishments. I have interviewed too many well-meaning but clueless candidates who answered this question with, "My kids are my greatest accomplishment," or some other personal-life answer. That's a truly lovely sentiment, but it will not get you hired. This answer should ALWAYS be a work-related accomplishment—especially, a work-related accomplishment that is relevant to the job you are currently applying for.

Have you ever had difficulty working with a supervisor or manager?

Be very careful when answering this question. Even if you had legitimate complaints about your old boss (and lots of bosses earn every one of those complaints), it's never a good idea to badmouth your former boss.

If possible, avoid it: *"I can't say that I've ever had trouble working with anyone. I appreciate the personality differences I've seen in my various supervisors and found that I learned something from working with each of those styles."*

If you can't avoid it, tell the story along with your thought process. But keep in mind that any story you tell should be the Disney version—positive, with a happy ending.

For example, you could say something like: *"I did get off to a bad start with my manager in my very first job because we had different expectations and at the time, I didn't know enough to ask about those before I started work. But I got some very good advice to go talk with him about it, and we cleared the air. It turned out to be a great experience for me, and it was a good lesson to take forward in my career. Good communication is essential to a productive working relationship."*

See? You haven't said anything negative about yourself or about your manager. It was the *situation* that was difficult. You took proactive steps to resolve it in a mature fashion, and the end result was a productive relationship.

How do you deal with stressful situations?

Every job has stress. Show that you can handle yours in a professional manner, possibly taking them through your thought process:

"If a situation seems overwhelming, I mentally break it up into smaller steps, or doable goals, and focus on reaching each one on the way to accomplishing the larger task. In fact, that's what I did with XYZ project. We had a major issue with X problem, but I broke it down into 'what needs to happen first,' and concentrated on one step at a time. I was able to see more solutions to the larger problem, and in fact, we got the entire project done in record time."

Or, *"I find it best do concentrate on remaining calm, maybe taking a few deep breaths. When I run into a customer who's upset, it helps them to calm down if I'm calm and we can work together to resolve the situation."*

Above all, choose an answer that shows that you can meet a stressful situation head-on in a productive, positive manner and let nothing stop you from accomplishing your goals.

Hint: *If you ever hear silence after you've finished an answer, or you get the feeling that you didn't quite hit the nail on the head, ask the interviewer: "Did that answer your question?" or "Was that what you were looking for?" or "Would you like more information?"*

465

Phone Interview Tips #13

How to Avoid the Salary Question

"What salary are you looking for?"

Some interviewers will ask you this. They are trying to find out if they can afford you (maybe because you're overqualified). Try to avoid answering. You never want to talk about money until they make you an offer. Depending on your personality and your individual situation, you've got a couple of good avoidance tactics.

Be straightforward and say, "I'm really interested in finding out more about the job and telling you more about me so that we can see if we're a good fit before we start talking about the money."

Put them off. Say, "I'm looking for a great opportunity, and I'm sure you'll offer a salary that's commensurate with the responsibility of this job." This is a good, diplomatic answer.

If they push for a more specific answer, say something like,

"I'm sure that you're offering an appropriate range for this position, and it won't be a problem. What range have you budgeted for it?" (Turning the question back to them is one of my favorite tactics.)

Why is it so important to avoid answering this question?

Because you don't want to price yourself out of the job by naming something too high, and you don't want to shortchange yourself by naming something too low. Be sure to do salary research before your interview so you at least have a ballpark of what's appropriate for your experience level, in your area of the country.

Your ideal goal is to get them to want to hire you first—and *then* you talk about the money. If they don't want to hire you, the money doesn't matter anyway.

Be Positive!

When answering all job interview questions, keep your answers focused on the positive. Talk up your strengths as much as you can so that you sell yourself for the job.

Phone Interview Tips #14

Practice Your Phone Interview

How do athletes win championships? Practice.

How do you get better at interviews so you win the job? Practice.

Interviewing well is not a talent—it is a **skill**. To get better at a skill, you have to practice.

Here's how to practice a phone interview:

Prepare answers for questions you'll probably be asked.

Several questions always get asked, like "Why are you interested in this job?" or "Tell me about yourself." They will want to talk about your basic skill sets, they'll want to go over your resume with you, and they want to know why they should be interested in talking more with you. Having answers ready that you can deliver smoothly is very helpful.

But phone interviews are also where employers are looking for any knockout factors, or red flags. Anticipate questions about difficult situations in your past and come up with good answers to give. For instance:

If you've got an employment gap on your resume...

Put yourself in the shoes of this hiring manager. Think about what their greatest fears are with this—that you were fired for cause, or there's something wrong with you and that's why you haven't already been hired. Then think about what will make them feel better.

If you were laid off, it will help a lot if you can tell them that you were part of a mass layoff, and that it wasn't just you—and that you've been taking your time to find the right job.

If you can truthfully say that you took time off to deal with a family emergency, or to take care of your children, or to go back to school, all those things make sense, too.

If you can provide strong references from people you have worked for, that is a big help. It reassures them that you were a good choice for someone else, and you will be for them, too.

Come up with an explanation that makes sense to them, and be confident when you explain it. Confidence covers a multitude of sins. If you're OK with it, it makes it easier for them to be OK with it. If you're nervous or apologetic, it makes them wonder what it is that you have to be guilty about. Be confident and make sure that your explanation addresses those fears of the hiring manager.

If you've been a job hopper, give a brief but reasonable explanation, and point out why this job would allow you to settle down for a while.

Rehearse your answers and explanations.

This is where the true practicing happens that will help you win the game. Rehearse your explanations and your answers either by recording yourself to see how you sound, or getting someone to role-play the interview with you and be your "interviewer." Through role-playing, you can get valuable feedback about not just the quality of your answers, but how you come across over the phone. Is your voice strong? Do you sound confident and enthusiastic? A friend can do this for you, or a career coach.

It takes time to practice your answers, but the results will be worth it. You will be more confident in the phone interview, which will come across to the interviewer as competence, professionalism, and enthusiasm…all good things to help move you to the face-to-face.

"I'm a great believer in luck, and I find
the harder I work, the more I have of it."
–Thomas Jefferson

Phone Interview Tips #15

Build Your Confidence

The more confident you are, the more relaxed you'll be and the better interview you will have.

Use these **3 tips** to **build your confidence** so you can have a great phone interview:

1) Dress in a Killer Outfit

The clothes we put on have a major impact on how we behave. (I have a friend who's noticed that the days she wears her boots, she's got a little more strut in her step than if she's kicking around in her sneakers.) It is a proven fact that the clothes you wear affect your behavior.

Put on a suit that makes you feel not just professional, but fantastic. If you feel it, you will act it. It will come across even over the phone.

2) Be Prepared

Do all your pre-interview research, list out the questions you want to ask, and write down some key points you want to make. The more you do, the more prepared you will be and the more confident you will feel.

3) Be Organized.

Go old-school and lay out all your papers on your desk in front of you—your resume, your question list, your notes, everything. Don't just keep it on your computer screen so you have to click to find it—paper is the way to go. It's faster and more reliable. What if your computer freezes up? You can certainly have the company's website up, and maybe another site or two in other tabs, but for the most part, play it safe and keep your most important documents safely in front of you on your desk.

> *"One important key to success is self-confidence. An important key to self-confidence is preparation."*
> *–Arthur Ashe*

Phone Interview Tips #16

Get Your Cheat Sheets Ready

Cheat sheets are just what they sound like: notes that help you do better on the test, which in this case is the phone interview. Phone interviews don't have many advantages for you, but this is a big one. Make the most of it with these cheat sheet ideas:

Your Resume

Always have your resume in front of you. In a phone interview, they will ask you questions about your resume. Highlight a few especially relevant lines on your resume so you can find them faster.

The Job Description

Print out the job description to keep in front of you, with notes for yourself of examples/stories of when you have done the things in the description.

A List of Questions to Ask

Asking questions is a powerful interview strategy. You'd be surprised at how many candidates just answer questions and don't take the initiative to ask any—and they're hurting themselves. Asking questions shows enthusiasm and asking the right ones will give you a lot of helpful information you wouldn't otherwise get.

A few good questions to ask:

Why is this job open?

How long was the last person in this position?

When do you expect to have someone hired?

What are the biggest challenges of this position?

How do you plan to deal with X? (X is whatever is appropriate for your field—do your research.)

When can I expect to hear from you about next steps?

Key Points You Want To Make About Yourself

You should have a few key 'selling' points that make you a great fit for this job, and you need to make sure that you mention them. Write them down so you won't forget.

Also, write down the terms you want to use to describe yourself. If you have a certain phrase or wording that describes you in a powerful way, write it down so you will remember to say it that way.

Written-Out Answers To Interview Questions

You can always anticipate a few interview questions:

Tell me about yourself.

Why are you interested in this job?

Why are you leaving your current job?

Jot down some good answers to these standard questions so you're ready. Just don't read it word for word. It should sound natural.

Keep A Pen And Paper So You Can Take Notes

Take notes throughout your conversation. It will help you write a more intelligent and customized thank you note, and it will help you better prepare for your face-to-face interview. And, if they ask you to write down a website or a phone number, you will be able to do that quickly.

"Opportunities don't often come along.
So, when they do, you have to grab them."
–Audrey Hepburn

Cheat Sheet Hint:

You want to print out hard copies of your cheat sheets just in case your internet fails….plus, it's quieter to look at papers (if you're not shuffling) than to type or click around finding things on your computer.

Phone Interview Tips #17

Prepare to Be 'Screened'--But Not Screened Out

Phone interviews are really phone *screens*. They're screening candidates to narrow down the list of who to invite for a face-to-face interview. Your job is to keep them from eliminating you. How?

Follow good phone interview practices:

- Make sure you've got a quiet room with no distractions.
- Research the company.
- Practice answering typical phone interview questions.
- Communicate enthusiasm.
- Be positive all the way through your conversation.

Help them see that it would be feasible to hire you. Are you in the right **location**? If so, great. If not, mention any plans you might have for moving to that location. If you don't need relocation help, that can be a big plus. How fast will you be **available**? That's totally up to your own situation, but generally, sooner is better. Do you **understand the job**? Are you very clear on what the job will entail?

Be ready to talk about your resume. **Be prepared to give more detail** about your bullet points, and don't say anything that contradicts your resume. **Are there any worrisome parts of your resume?** Are you currently out of work? Do you have a big employment gap? Have you had too many jobs over the years? Be ready to explain all your jobs and transitions—and keep it positive. If something was a problem before (family issues, health problems, etc.), point out that it is resolved and you are ready to devote your time and effort to this job.

Throughout the call, they're going to be listening to what you say and how you say it, looking for a reason not to like you. Don't give them one. Be aware of any red flags of yours that might catch their attention, like less experience or employment gaps or job hopping, and come up with a positive answer before they ask you about it. Be upbeat, answer all their questions concisely but completely, show interest, ask questions, and be polite.

"Whenever you are asked if you can do a job, tell 'em, 'Certainly I can!' Then get busy and find out how to do it."
–Theodore Roosevelt

Phone Interview Tips #18

Biggest Phone Interview Mistakes

For such a short conversation, phone interviews are a surprisingly wide-open opportunity for screw-ups. Here are 9 ways to make a fatal phone interview mistake:

Failing to Prepare

If it isn't clear that you found out something about the company and the job before this call, they will assume that you are not very interested in it.

A Noisy Environment

This is an important meeting, and you should treat it as such. Be respectful of the interviewer and yourself by making the effort to set aside time and a quiet place for this call. Don't let any distractions keep you from being your best.

Talking on a Cell Phone with Poor Reception

If you can, always use a landline. If you must use a cell phone, be certain you have crystal-clear reception *before* your call—call a friend to make sure.

Drinking Water with Ice (Or Anything with Ice)

While it's good to have a glass of water nearby to keep your voice from getting scratchy, it's a bad idea to put ice in it. Over the phone, clinking ice is distracting and tends to make your listener think you're drinking alcohol. I don't know why, but that is the image that will show up in their mind's eye, and it will hurt you.

Keeping a Poker Face

If you don't smile when you speak during your conversation, it comes across to your interviewer as disinterest in the job, or even downright unfriendliness. Even if it's not a completely genuine emotion on your part, a smile will still communicate confidence, enthusiasm, and likeability.

Chewing Gum

Smacking in your interviewer's ear is a great way to get them to delete your name from the list. It's distracting, and it's rude. (Plus, what if you accidentally inhale it? That coughing fit won't really add to your professional image…) Spit out the gum.

Smoking

Listen to someone smoking a cigarette sometime….those long pauses with each drag, the hard exhales blowing out the smoke, the occasional coughs…and you'll understand why you don't want that in your conversation. For some interviewers, the fact that you smoke might be enough to knock you off the list—and you'll never know.

Driving

Never interview while driving. That tells them that you aren't taking this opportunity seriously enough to devote time to it, and you will be seriously distracted. Not only will you not have a good phone interview, you increase your chances of having an accident.

Using Your Speakerphone Function

Even if your intentions are good—like, you only want to put them on speakerphone so you can take notes—the result of putting them on speakerphone is bad. The sound quality of your call goes way, way down. They will hear any little background noise, and it will be distracting. When they realize you have them on speakerphone, their immediate reaction will be a negative one: "this person is not professional," "this person is not focusing their full attention on this call," "this person doesn't care about this job opportunity."

Bringing Up Any Concerns You Have About This Job

Even if you have valid concerns about commute time, health benefits, or the company itself, this is not the time to bring it up. Any negativity puts a damper on the whole conversation. Even if it turns out that there's no problem and it will be wonderful, they will feel differently about you if you bring up concerns this early in the process. Just wait.

Pay attention to the details in your phone interview. The smallest actions can make the biggest impact on your call. It all affects whether or not you get to the face-to-face interview.

"Fall seven times, stand up eight."
–Japanese proverb

Phone Interview Tips #19

Phone Interview Etiquette

In any job interview, it's important to use your best manners—and telephone interviews are no exception. Besides your resume, this is their first impression of you. Make it a great one by being super-polite and professional. Here's how:

Answer the Phone with Your Name

Don't just say "Hello." Say, "Hello, this is John Smith." Answering the phone with your name helps the interviewer feel immediately comfortable that they have the right person on the line.

Address the Interviewer by Name

Make sure you know the name of your interviewer before you speak to them, even if you have to call and find out from someone else. It's much nicer to be able to say, "Hi, Mr. Smith" if you can.

Address the Interviewer Formally

Always address the interviewer as "Mr." or "Ms." So-and-So until you are told otherwise. Until they specifically say, "Please call me John," you may not address them by their first name.

Don't Interrupt

No matter how excited you are about the job, it's rude to interrupt while they are speaking. Wait for them to finish their question.

Don't Put Them On Speakerphone

Speakerphones convey the impression that you have something more important you need to be doing right now, and you're going to do it while you talk.

Turn Off Phone Features That Might Interrupt You

Call waiting, or anything else that might beep, buzz, or cause a blip in the conversation should be disabled for this call.

Respect Their Time

An important way to show that you respect the time of the person you're speaking with is to be very prepared for this interview. Research the company. Have questions prepared to ask. Know how you're going to answer at least the most typical interview questions so you can answer them fairly quickly. (Taking a few seconds to think about your answer is fine on some questions, but not all.) Have your resume, as well as all your notes, right in front of you so you can see them easily. You don't want to shuffle papers, looking for something while you're on the call. While you're at it, make sure you have a pen and paper to take notes on during the call. You will need the notes for later, and you'll be ready just in case they want you to write something down.

Ask About the Next Step

Express your interest in the job by asking about what the next step will be. When will you speak in person about this opportunity? Don't wait for them to bring it up. They might not…maybe they're waiting for you to do it to see if you want it, or maybe they have a few doubts about you that you need to clear up. **Do not end the call without knowing what happens next.**

Send a Thank You Note

Follow up after your phone interview by emailing a thank you note to the person you spoke to. Thank you notes are always the polite thing to do, and they make you stand out from the other candidates. Why email? Because it's faster. A fast response time is a positive thing.

"Manners are a sensitive awareness of the feelings of others. If you have that awareness, you have good manners, no matter what fork you use." - Emily Post

Phone Interview Tips #20

Tips to Help You Relax

One of the easiest ways to make a good impression in your phone interview is to be calm, cool, and collected all the way through. Here are 4 tips that will help you relax and have a great phone interview.

Be Over-Prepared

Nothing calms nerves like being ready for anything. That means, don't just go to the company's website…read it carefully. Go to the company's LinkedIn page and Facebook page, if they have it. Google them for the latest news. Look at their competitors. The more you can learn ahead of time, the better off you'll be. Knowledge is power.

Arrive Early

Be ready to start your call at least 5 minutes before it's supposed to start. Be sitting in your quiet room with the door closed, your glass of water on the desk, all your cheat sheets spread out, doing some deep, relaxing breathing. When it's time for the interview, you will sound calm, cool, and collected. And if they try the tactic that some interviewers do of calling early to catch you off guard, you'll be ready for them. It will impress them.

Keep Your Cheat Sheets Handy

Cheat sheets are anything that will help you do better in the interview—your resume, your list of questions to ask, references, key points to make, and a few phrases you want to use to describe yourself. Spread them out in front of you so they are easy to find. You will feel comfortable knowing if you forget anything, it's right there for you.

481

Practice Relaxation Breathing

Take a deep breath, hold it for a few seconds, and let it out slowly. Do this a few times before your call. Relaxation techniques like this do wonders for slowing down your heart rate and giving you a feeling of calm and control. If you need to do it during the call, go ahead—but don't breathe hard into the phone. That could sound a little awkward!

"The future belongs to those who believe in the beauty of their dreams."
–Eleanor Roosevelt

Phone Interview Tips #21

Tips to Help You Focus

To be successful in your phone interview, you need to be on your toes and focused on the call. It's easy to get distracted when you don't have eye contact with the person you're speaking with. They can tell if your attention is wandering (which is bad), and you can easily miss a word in a question and answer it wrong.

Here are tips to help you focus:

--Set up in a **quiet room with no distractions—no TV, music, or other people.**

--**Eat before your interview.** Food is fuel, and hunger pangs or blood sugar dips are a distraction.

--**Go to the bathroom.** You can't do your best thinking when all you can concentrate on is how bad you've 'gotta go'.

--**Wear comfortable clothing.** Dress professionally to put yourself in the right frame of mind, but be comfortable so you're not fidgeting with scratchy or too-tight clothing.

--**Keep your notes in front of you.** Keep your resume, your list of questions to ask, your notes on the company, and the important points you want to make about yourself laid out right in front of you. You don't want to be shuffling papers, trying desperately to find something in the middle of your call.

--Breathe. Just before your call, take a few minutes to do a few deep, relaxing breaths. You want to calm your nerves so you don't sound jumpy or jittery. Relax and you'll be able to focus.

The key to success is to focus our conscious mind on things we desire, not things we fear."
–Brian Tracy

Phone Interview Tips #22

Expect a Positive Outcome

Expect your phone interview to go well. Visualize having a great conversation and getting invited for the face-to-face. Feel the happiness and enthusiasm you'll get from this success.

Visualization is a great tool. It can be extremely helpful in calming your nerves and putting to rest any self-doubt before the interview. If you expect a positive outcome, you will behave differently than if you don't. Your breathing will relax, your words will change, you'll project energy, your voice will sound more upbeat, you will project confidence, and so then your actual outcome will change.

"A positive attitude causes a chain reaction of positive thoughts, events and outcomes. It is a catalyst and it sparks extraordinary results."
–Wade Boggs

Phone Interview Tips #23

Make Your Voice Phone Interview-Ready

Interviewers concentrate very hard on your voice in a phone interview: Do you sound alert? Confident? Enthusiastic? Are there any red flags they need to worry about?

They don't have much to judge you on when you're on the phone, so they focus on what they can—the words you say, how you say them, and the sound of your voice.

Warm Up Your Voice Before the Interview

An hour or so before your interview, talk to someone else to warm up your voice. It's sort of like warming up before you work out. You want to hit your speaking stride for that conversation, not sound scratchy or worse—sleepy—when you talk. If necessary, drink some hot tea with honey to smooth out your voice before the call.

A Fun Voice Warm-Up Tip

If you like to sing, warm up your voice with a song. Choose one that pumps you up and makes you feel fantastic so it not only warms up your voice, but ramps up your energy level before the call.

Get a Glass of Water

Set a glass of water close by during your interview. Every so often, take a quick drink to keep your voice smooth. (But remember—no ice.)

Convey Enthusiasm with Your Tone

Aim for **positive, upbeat, energetic, and enthusiastic.** You don't have to be Perky Pamela if that's not your natural personality, but remember that this interview could be the beginning of a beautiful new job. That's a good thing, and you should act like it.

Speak Smoothly

Don't get flustered and tongue-tied. Practice your answers before the interview so that you are comfortable delivering them, and if necessary, slow down your speech so you don't trip yourself up.

The Deadliest Phone Interview Speech Sin

Please make sure you don't use irritating speech fillers like "um" and "uh." Taking a second or two to pause before your answer is much better than filling it with those.

"Big jobs usually go to the men who prove their ability to outgrow small ones."
–Ralph Waldo Emerson

Phone Interview Tips #24

Establish Rapport

People hire people they like, and that they connect with. For hiring managers to feel as though they like you and connect with you (and hire you), you need to establish rapport. How?

Greet them by name

People like to hear the sound of their own names. When you answer the phone (with, "Hello, this is Jane Smith"), and they say, "This is Susan Jones of Acme Company," you say, with warmth in your voice: "Hi Ms. Jones! I'm so glad to speak with you today!" or something similar that includes their name and expresses your enthusiasm.

Match the interviewer's energy and style of conversation

As the interviewer begins speaking, listen to how they sound: Are they warm and friendly? Matter of fact? Calm and low-key? Whatever it is, try to match it in your own voice. Don't mimic them and don't put on a 'fake' personality; just coordinate with them.

If you don't, you'll sound "off." If the interviewer is cheerleader bouncy, and you're matter of fact, you'll seem to that person as if you are uninterested in the job. Project some enthusiasm. If the interviewer is snappy and to-the-point, and you're so warm and friendly that you elaborate too long on your answers, the interviewer won't take you seriously for the job. Find out what 'page' they're on, and get on it with them.

Mention things you have in common

If you and the interviewer graduated from the same school, know the same people, or have read the same book lately (all of which you should know from researching the interviewer), mention it.

Deliver a sincere compliment

It's human nature to be attracted to people who compliment you, but an obviously fake, 'suck up' kind of compliment is worse than no compliment at all. If you find something in your research about this person or the company that truly impresses you, mention it.

Participate in the conversation

Do more than just answer the questions you're asked. Listen to what they're saying so you can ask intelligent, insightful follow up questions. Ask questions about the job, the company, and how they see your role or primary tasks.

Look at a photo of your interviewer (maybe)

It might help you to look at the smiling face of your interviewer that you find on their LinkedIn profile or company website so that you feel more connected and comfortable.

Phone Interview Tips #25

Speak Positive Body Language
(Yes, Even On the Phone)

Even though your interviewer can't see you, using the right body language in your phone interview will give you a better outcome.

Smile

It's amazing what smiling does to the sound of your voice. You sound friendlier and more confident.

Stand Up

You will project more energy if you stand up while you talk than if you sit, and you will actually feel more powerful and confident.

Walk Around (Maybe)

If you have a headset, walking around while you talk is a great way to make yourself more comfortable in a phone interview. Your feet spend some of the nervous energy that might come out through your voice—but don't walk around so much that you end up out of breath. That won't sound good on the other end of the line at all.

Follow Your Mother's Advice and Sit Up Straight

If you are more comfortable sitting for your interview, make sure you sit up straight with good posture and don't slump in your seat. Slumping will make you sound tired and uninterested in the job. Sitting up straight ensures that you sound attentive and interested. You'll breathe better, which will make you sound better.

Practice Relaxed Body Language

What you do physically while you're on the phone will show up in your voice. If you're sitting there all tensed up, you'll sound tense. If your arms are crossed, you'll sound just a little less friendly. Sit (or stand) with a relaxed, comfortable posture and it will help you sound like you are relaxed and comfortable with the interviewer.

Don't Fidget

Movement is good; fidgeting is not. Nervous habits will not help you feel more relaxed in the interview, and may even be distracting to the interviewer. Tapping your pen on the desk, tapping your foot, drumming your nails on the table…these are all attention-diverters. They will give away your nervousness and make the interviewer think you're not confident in your ability to do the job.

Phone Interview Tips #26

Make Them Like You—
Project Interest in and Enthusiasm for the Job

What hiring manager doesn't want to choose someone who is sincerely enthusiastic and excited about the job? They all do. If you're excited about the job, you'll try harder and do better than someone who isn't. Plus, your genuine enthusiasm will make them like you more. If they like you, they'll be more likely to hire you.

Here are **6 tips for projecting enthusiasm** in phone interviews:

Smile

Always smile while talking. Even though they can't see your smile, it will show up in your voice. You will sound warmer, friendlier, and more enthusiastic.

If you need reminders, sometimes it helps to keep a **mirror in front of you to remind yourself to smile. If that's what it takes, do it.

Be Animated

If you talk with your hands normally, then talk with your hands (even though they can't see you). If you want to walk around while you talk, do it. In fact, standing while you talk can lend you power and confidence.

Ask Questions

Ask about the process, the job, and the company. All your questions should be based on your research—not questions that could be answered in the job description or by Google.

Thank the Interviewer for Speaking With You

Always thank the person for taking the time to speak with you while you're on the call. After the call, send your thank you note.

Tell Them You're Interested

Don't assume the hiring manager knows you're interested in the job. It should be obvious (because why else would you be bothering with this interview?), but it really isn't. They might think you're on the fence about it...so going forward with you might be a waste of time. So tell them how much you're interested in the job.

Phone Interview Tips #27

Don't Talk Too Much

What happens if you talk too much or reveal too much information? Both show poor communication skills that could keep you from getting invited to the face-to-face.

Knowing how much to talk really depends on your interviewer. If they're talking a lot, it's OK to listen and see what you can learn. If they ask a lot of questions, you talk. As long as it feels like a back-and-forth conversation and not a monologue, you're probably good.

Don't spend too much time on an answer. A minute or two should be plenty. Practice your answers ahead of time to make sure they are succinct and focused.

While you're watching how much you talk, also watch what you say. Here are a few ways to avoid offering Too Much Information:

Keep your answers job-focused.

Many job seekers offer up personal information out of nervousness, an attempt to bond with the interviewer, or because they don't understand how to answer interview questions. For instance, when they hear "Tell me a little about yourself," they say things like, "I have two

494

kids," or "I'm a Facebook junkie." Don't say those things. Your answer should always be, "I have a degree in X," "I have experience in Y," or something that relates to the job.

Don't be negative.

Negativity of all kinds is "too much information." Don't talk trash about your last job or boss. Don't talk about any personal problems (that's a double-whammy….personal AND negative). Don't even talk about things you don't like. Keep it positive.

Don't reveal your concerns about this job.

If you are worried about the salary or the hours or the travel requirements, DO NOT bring it up at this point. Even if there's no problem, expressing your concern will make you seem like a negative person, and it will be a mark against you.

"Be interesting, be enthusiastic…and don't talk too much."
-Norman Vincent Peale

Phone Interview Tips #28

Listen Well

The art of conversation requires that you not only express yourself well, but also that you listen well. Good listeners are valued. Being a good listener means that you're going to have a more productive, higher-quality conversation than you would otherwise.

How can you be a good listener in a phone interview?

Create a quiet space for your interview. You can't listen well if you can't hear what they are saying to you. This conversation is a priority, so treat it like one.

Pay attention. Don't let yourself get distracted by ANYTHING. Don't try to conduct it in a restaurant, while driving, or anywhere near a child or a pet. And try not to be thinking about what you're going to say while they are talking. You could easily miss something important.

Don't interrupt. Assertiveness is fine in an interview; rudeness is not. Don't interrupt your interviewer, ever. If they mention something that confuses you or raises a question for you, write it down to ask when it's your turn.

Take notes. As your interviewer talks, take notes on what he or she is saying. This will help you when you're asking questions, it will help you write a better thank you note, and it will help you prepare for the face-to-face interview. They might even ask you to write down a phone number or website. If you've been taking notes, you can do it without missing a beat.

Ask follow up questions. Asking relevant follow up questions is a powerful way to show that you are listening and you are interested.

Clarify for understanding. If the interviewer asks you a question and you're not sure what they want to know, ask. Blindly launching into an answer that turns out to be wrong is much worse than saying, "Do you mean X, or Y?"

Phone Interview Tips #29

Watch Your Language

Pop quiz: When you answer questions in a phone interview, which answer would hurt you the most?

(A) "Um…I'm not sure…"
(B) "I hated to leave that job. My boss was my BFF."
(C) "That customer was a pain in the @$$, but I won him over."
(D) All of the above.

The correct answer is (D).

In job interviews, the language you use can make or break your chances—and that's even more true in a telephone interview, where your voice is all they have to focus on. Your conversation must be professional. That means:

No using "um", "uh," or other speech fillers. If you need to stop and think before you answer, then stop and think. A pause is fine. Nervously filling that pause with "umm…." Is not. It's distracting and chips away the professional image you're trying to project. Most people use speech fillers like "um," "uh," "you know" and "like" more than they realize—especially in high-pressure situations like interviews. Record yourself answering interview questions so you can determine if you need to work on eliminating those very annoying speech fillers.

No weak language. Weak words and phrases will kill your offer because they cast doubt on your ability to do the job. I coach candidates all the time to avoid saying things like, "I think," "I hope," "with luck," or "if it goes well." Some people qualify their statements with phrases like these because they don't want to seem cocky. But what they're really doing is making themselves seem weak and not up to the job. Practice saying, "I can," "I will," and "I do." That shows confidence. Confidence is appealing.

No slang. Avoid using slang words or expressions. It doesn't make you look young or hip; it just makes you look unprofessional. You should be putting your best foot forward in the interview, and that includes your language.

No questionable language. Never, ever use swear words in an interview, even mild ones. I once had a candidate (because she was nervous) say "crap" 3 times in her interview—and she lost the job. Use your best manners.

No sarcasm. Avoid sarcasm and jokes in phone interviews. Even if you feel you must break the ice, don't do it with a joke. They can't see your facial expression or body language, so you can't be sure that what you mean is what they hear. Play it safe.

It can be more difficult than you think to watch your language in an interview. A lot of these things just roll right off our tongues without us even thinking about it. And when we're in a high-pressure situation like an interview, it happens even more.

Your best bet to avoid these issues is to practice answering interview questions, or role-play your interview with a friend or an interview coach. The practice will help you be more aware of what you do so you can fix it, and it will help you be more comfortable so you don't slip up.

"Never say anything about yourself you do not want to come true."
–Brian Tracy

Phone Interview Tips #30

Watch Your Tone

To speak confidently in any business situation, but especially on the phone, pay attention to the tone you use.

One of the worst tone offenders is the person who always ends a statement on a higher note, so that it sounds like a question. This is a sure-fire way to undermine your own authority and credibility. End your sentences on a lower note. You will sound more confident, so then you can inspire their confidence in you.

Overall, strive for polite, warm, and friendly—try to imagine that you're speaking with someone you already know and like.

Phone Interview Tips #31

Take Advantage of the Fact That They Can't See You

Even though phone interviews present challenges, they also present a few advantages that you can work with to make the most of it. Besides keeping all your notes (cheat sheets) out in front of you, here are **4 secret tricks** you can use to take advantage of your phone interview situation and overcome some common obstacles:

Look at a picture of your interviewer during the call.

Establishing rapport can be difficult because you can't see the interviewer's face. So, you might try setting up a photo of the interviewer to look at while you talk to feel more at ease. You can probably find their photo on their LinkedIn profile.

Look in the mirror —or not.

I've seen two competing schools of thought on the mirror issue:

One says, "Keep a mirror in front of you so you remember to smile while you talk"—and it is important to smile and stay relaxed, because that comes through in your voice. A mirror is a visual reminder, so you can easily see if you start to frown or tense up.

The other says, "Never look in a mirror while you talk because it will make you self-conscious and you'll sound stiff."

I think you should try it both ways in practice conversations and see which one works for you.

Stand up.

In a regular interview, you're sitting across from the interviewer. In a phone interview, you obviously have the choice about whether to stand or sit. In my opinion, you should stand. People tend to sound more energetic when they stand up, and their voices are stronger because they aren't slumped over in a chair. So, show your energy and enthusiasm by standing up!

Have the internet open and ready to use.

Just in case, keep the company's website open on your computer, and set another window open to Google (or the search engine you use). If you run across something you need to know right now, you can find it—but never, ever let them hear you typing.

In a phone interview, you actually have a lot of leeway to do what is going to make you feel more comfortable and confident. Use every advantage you can think of to do well in the phone interview and get to the face-to-face.

Phone Interview Tips #32

Questions You Should Ask

In every interview (phone or face-to-face), it is critically important to ask questions. Why?

1) It makes you seem **engaged and interested** in the job.
2) It makes you seem more **intelligent**—IF you ask good questions. (Don't ask questions you could easily find the answers to on Google.)
3) It gives you a **strategic advantage**—ask good questions, and you find out what the interviewer really cares about.

What questions should you ask?

Why is this position open?

This answer can give you all kinds of information you can't get anywhere else. Maybe the last employer was a poor performer. Why? Maybe they were promoted. Is that a typical career path in this company?

How long was the last person in this position?

Their answer to this tells you about the turnover rate for the job. If they name a very short term, your follow-up question should be, "Why? Is that typical?" You want to know if there was a performance issue, a fit issue, or some other issue that might rear up to bite you when you're on the job.

What are the biggest challenges of this position?

If you know their biggest problems, you can talk about how you can solve them.

How would you describe a typical day on the job?

First, their answer will give you tremendous insight into whether or not you want to work there. Second, what they say will give you big clues to what they see as the most important tasks for that job, and what they're looking for you to do. These clues will help you tailor the rest of what you say to most effectively sell yourself for that job.

These questions uncover information, show your professionalism and interest in the job, and move you forward another step in the process. Ask these kinds of questions and you'll have a great phone interview.

Phone Interview Tips #33

Questions You Should NEVER, EVER Ask

It's important to ask questions in your phone interview—but here are 9 questions you should never, ever ask.

"What does your company do?"

The only time this might ever be acceptable is if you are surprised by a telephone interview sneak attack—in other words, they call you up out of the blue and want to conduct your interview right there, right then. Otherwise, you've got time to prepare. Use it to research the company and find out what they do. Then you can focus your conversation on how you would be a great addition to their organization.

"Can you hang on while I take this call?"

This phone call is THE most important conversation you could possibly be having right now. Never allow other callers to interrupt. In fact, turn off call waiting, text alerts, or anything else that might beep and distract you during this call.

"I'm worried about...."

Even if you're very concerned about some factor in this new job (the commute, the transition, the hours, whatever), never, ever bring it up in the phone interview. It's just too soon. Bringing up something negative too early just makes *you* look negative. I've seen firsthand how fast job seekers get knocked out of consideration by bringing up problems before they should.

505

"What's the salary range for this position?"

Never, ever bring up money at any point in the interview process—not until you have an offer in your hand.

"How much vacation time would I get?"

Nothing more clearly says, "What's in it for me?" than asking about benefits and perks. That's always a bad move. The job interview is a sales process—you are the product and the sales rep. That interviewer is your customer—which means your focus must be on what's in it for *them*. Once you've convinced them that you are the right person to hire, then you can talk about what you're getting out of it—and you can decide if you're interested or not at that point.

"How much overtime is required?"

You don't even have the job yet, and you're complaining about the hours? No one wants to be chained to their job, but asking about hours this soon makes it seem like you'll work as little as you can get away with.

"Do I have to pass a drug test or background check?"

Nothing says "I do illegal drugs" like "Do I have to take a drug test?" Ditto for the background check—they will suspect you have something to hide.

"What kind of health insurance do you offer?"

Not that this isn't an important question, but there's a time and a place, and this isn't it. This question plants the seed that you have some medical issues (chronic illness, pregnancy plans) that will cause you to miss work.

"Will I be able to work from home?"

When they hear this question, they won't picture you actually working from home....they'll picture you *saying* you're working while you're at the racetrack, getting your nails done, watching TV, whatever...a nightmare waiting to happen.

Phone Interview Tips #34

The One Question You Absolutely Must Ask, No Matter What

One question will improve your interview performance more than any other. What's the question? It's: **What does your ideal candidate look like?**

What's on their ultimate wish list of skills and qualifications of someone in this role? If a person with those qualities walked through the door, they'd hire them on the spot.

You might say, "Why should I ask about their perfect candidate? I'm not perfect. Won't it make me look bad?" No, it won't. In fact it will help you.

Odds are very good that their ideal candidate is not going to show up—because it's an ideal. So what's the point of asking about it?

Their answer tells you what they really care about. It's like asking (without saying directly), *"What would you really like to hear from me in this interview? What can I say to you that will get me this job?"* That is POWERFUL information. With this knowledge, every interview answer you give for the rest of the interview can be geared to what will appeal to them most.

When should you ask this question? Ask it fairly early in the interview, before you start to get too deep in talking about yourself.

Does it have to be those exact words? No. Use whatever words are comfortable for you:

- *Tell me about your ideal candidate.*
- *If you had a checklist for a perfect candidate, what would be on it?*
- *What are the qualities of someone who would be perfect in this role?*

507

It should feel like a natural part of your conversation, so ask it however it works for you.

Do you really have to ask this? Yes.

Can't you just go by what the job description says? No. It's possible that someone besides the person interviewing you wrote the description—so maybe it's not completely accurate. It's too much of a gamble for this important conversation.

What do you do with this information? You use it to help **tailor your answers** to their interview questions.

If they ask about your proudest accomplishment, choose one that speaks to their wish list. You don't want to talk about something that they won't care about hearing.

If they ask why you think you'd be a good fit, then you can talk about the skills that match up with what they told you.

Every time they ask you a question, say something that answers that wish list as much as you can.

Delivering these types of super-targeted answers help you CRUSH the interview. It's being strategic and smart in how you approach the entire process. It will help push you along to getting the face-to-face interview.

"Do one thing every day that scares you."
–Eleanor Roosevelt

Phone Interview Tips #35

Before You End the Call...Make Sure You've Hit Your Target Goal

The entire goal of your phone interview is to get to the face-to-face. The best way to get to that next step is to ask for it. So before you end this call, ask for a time to meet face-to-face to discuss this opportunity in more detail.

You could be direct and say,

"I am very excited about this opportunity. When can we get together to talk about this in greater detail?"

Or, "I'd really like to visit with you in person to show you what I can do for you. When can you meet with me?"

Or, "Based on what we've talked about, this sounds like a great fit for me and I am very interested in meeting with you to discuss it further. When can we schedule it?"

Or, "Thank you so much for speaking with me today. I am excited about this opportunity and think I would be a great fit. My skills in A, B, and C line up with what you said you were looking for. I would love to come in and talk with you in person about it. When can we schedule that?"

This is where the rubber meets the road. Many candidates will wait and hope to be invited because they don't want to seem too bold or desperate. That's a weak position to be in and won't help you. A few braver candidates will say, "When do you expect to make a decision?" That's a lot better, but not the best. **The bravest candidates who see the most success at getting to the next step** say something like, "I am really interested in this position. It sounds like a great fit. When can we meet to discuss this further?"

Asking "When can we meet?" is a great move because it either secures your interview, or it forces them to tell you they're not planning to bring you in. If that's the case, you can probably find out why they have doubts. Sometimes it's a real issue that you can't say anything to fix—but sometimes, it's a simple miscommunication that you can clear up right then. Once you clear it up, they feel comfortable with asking you to come in and interview. This simple question can be what gets you to the face-to-face interview.

If that's too much for you, at least ask about next steps, or the timeline:

"I am very interested in this job, and I would love to move forward. What are the next steps?" The best answer would be, "I want to set you up to come in." If they say, "I have more people to interview," ask "What is your timeline for beginning face-to-face interviews?" At least this way you'll know when you can to expect to hear something, and you won't have to worry about it.

You need to know, before you hang up, what their expectations are for the next steps, what their timeline is, and what their process for getting all this done will be. They expect you to ask, and you deserve to know so you don't have to sit and wonder (and worry).

Also before you hang up, make sure you have the interviewer's contact information so you can send a thank you note. Aim for at least getting his or her email address.

If they invite you for the face-to-face interview during this call, thank them for the opportunity, and get all the details:

- When and where is the interview?
- Who will you interview with—what is their contact information?
- When do they expect to have a final decision made?

Bottom line: Before you end this call, know what is happening next.

"It is never too late to be what you might have been." –George Eliot

Phone Interview Tips #36

Clarify, Clarify, Clarify

Job interviews are all about communication. You will only get the job if you can successfully communicate that you *understand* the job, that you *can* do the job, that you *will* do the job, and that you *pose no risk* to this person's continued employment. (That's why 30-60-90-day plans are such great job interview tools.) This requires good, clear communication.

The phone interview is the first step in this communication process—but there's a problem. Phone interviews mean that you can't see the person you're talking to. When you can't see them, your communication suffers. You have no handy facial expressions or gestures to read, so that cuts a big source of information. They can't see you, so your charming personality and winning smile is muffled. You can't show them your 30-60-90-day plan or your brag book. You only have your words and your voice.

This is why it is so important to clarify for understanding all the way through the interview:

Before the interview

Set yourself up for clear communications by controlling the time, place, and quality of your call. Find out everything you can know before you start the interview.

During the interview

If you don't understand the question, don't answer it. Ask what they mean. You can put your foot in your mouth really quickly by plowing ahead and answering something you don't understand because you think they have to. If there's any doubt at all, ask. Say something like, "Do you mean X?" or "Are you referring to Y?" or "Are you asking about ABC?" You can't communicate well if you're not answering the question they asked.

Ending the interview

Do not hang up from this call without being clear about what happens next.

- Say, "I've really enjoyed talking to you. From what we've discussed so far, it sounds like a good fit to me. Do you agree?"
- Say, "Have I given you enough information so that you feel comfortable moving me forward in this process?"

You can say any number of things that make it clear that you want to move forward and ask if they agree with you.

If they're thinking of crossing you off the list, you need to find out BEFORE they hang up. *That's* your chance to change their mind. Sometimes, it's a misunderstanding, an assumption they've made, or even just because you forgot to tell them something. If you can correct whatever it is, you've just saved your face-to-face interview.

Most job seekers would never dream of asking for this next step. Instead, they keep answering questions until the interviewer says something like: "Well, it was great talking to you. We've got a few more people to talk to. I'll be in touch." Know what that tells you? Nothing. You hang up not knowing if they liked you, if they're calling you back, if you're moving forward, nothing. Then you're stuck waiting, and waiting, and waiting. If the call doesn't come, that's when you find out they've screened you out. By then, it's too late to do anything about it. The time to act is during the interview.

Clarify, clarify, clarify. You deserve to know.

"Success doesn't come to you, you go to it."
–Marva Collins

512

Phone Interview Tips #37

Write a Thank You Note

How do you follow up after a phone interview? You follow up the exact same way you would after a face-to-face interview: send a well-thought-out, comprehensive, and timely **thank you note.**

Your thank you note should actually be a **thank you email.** Why an email? Because it's faster.

It's in your best interests to get your thank you note in their hands **within 24 hours** of your interview. Why? Because they will make decisions quickly about who to ask in for a face-to-face interview.

A good thank you note can easily tip the scales in your favor, and get you that invitation.

A good thank you note is a substantial one. Say much more than, "Thanks for interviewing me. I hope we can talk again."

Say (for example, depending on your conversation):

"Thank you for speaking with me today. I am very excited about this job and think I'd be a great fit. I really see how my skills and experience in X, Y, and Z can help you meet your ABC goals. My skills in D, E, and F would be an additional advantage. I am looking forward to meeting with you to talk more about it. I will call you on Wednesday to set it up.

Sincerely…"

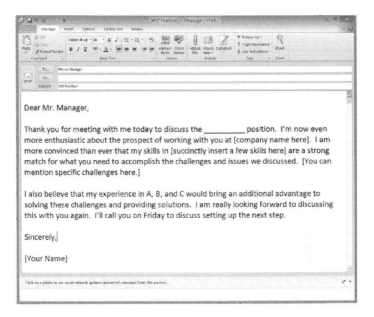

That kind of note does a lot of things for you. It shows your good manners, because you've thanked them for taking the time to talk to you. It shows your professionalism, because you're talking about how you can help them reach their goals. It reinforces the idea of you being a good fit by highlighting your skills. And it shows that you want the job because you're going to call to make sure you get a chance to discuss it. All good things.

Who should you send your email to? **Everyone you speak with deserves a thank you email.** If a recruiter set this up for you, send the recruiter a note, too. If the hiring manager arranged for you to speak with someone else, send that person a note AND send the hiring manager a note saying, "I spoke with so-and-so and it went well."

Even if your interview didn't go well, you should send an email. It's a chance for you to do some damage control. Address whatever you think the problem was and try to rectify it. Mention things you forgot to say that would be helpful to your cause. Correct any misconceptions. It might not work, but it could work and you should try.

514

"None of us got to where we are alone. Whether the assistance we received was obvious or subtle, acknowledging someone's help is a big part of understanding the importance of saying thank you."
- Harvey Mackay

Send a thank you note even if you know you are not moving forward.

Why? It lays the foundation for a potential positive outcome to be determined in the future. Maybe they'll have another position that's a better fit later on, maybe they'll recommend you to someone else....you never know.

BONUS

Phone Interview Checklist

Want to be organized for your phone interview? Leave nothing to chance? Give yourself the best possible outcome? Then create a phone interview checklist like this one so you won't forget any vital detail.

Pick a good time and place – The first thing you have to do when setting up a phone interview is to choose a good time for you, when you will be at your best (most alert), and then choose where to have this very important conversation. It must be somewhere quiet, where you will not be distracted. No pets, kids, or chatty people at the next table. Quiet.

Research the company – Phone interviews aren't 'get-to-know-you' sessions—they're the first step toward getting an offer. Get to know them before your interview in your pre-interview research. Learning what you can about the company ahead of time signals that you are a professional, and that you are taking this opportunity seriously. It also allows you to come up with better interview answers as well as higher-quality questions of your own.

Research the interviewer – What does the person who's interviewing you do at this company? Is it going to be your potential boss? Is it someone in HR? What is their background? What do they care about? Remember that the job interview is a sales process. This person is the customer, or the buyer. This is the one who's going to say 'yes' or 'no' to moving you to the next step. Find out what you can about your customer before you get there.

Prepare answers to common interview questions (and practice saying them) – It's always a good idea to practice answering interview questions before any interview. Interviews are stressful. Take away some of the stress by knowing you have fantastic answers to "Tell me about yourself," "Why do you want to work here?" and other common questions.

Create a list of questions to ask – Candidates are often asked, "Do you have any questions for me?" toward the end of the interview. It's a bad idea to say, "No." Come up with some intelligent, thoughtful questions to ask then and during the course of your conversation.

Get your 'cheat sheets' ready – The best thing about phone interviews is that you can cheat. By 'cheat,' I mean that since they can't see you, you are free to keep all your notes in front of you. Keep a copy of your resume, your list of questions to ask, some key points you want to make about why they should hire you, your list of references, and anything else that will ensure you have a great telephone interview.

Find a landline to use – If you have access to a landline, use it rather than your cell phone. With a cell phone, there's always a chance (even a small one) of bad reception, dropped calls, and "Hello? Can you hear me?" kinds of issues. Make sure you have a smooth, worry-free experience with a very stable landline.

Think about your voice – The person on the other end of the line only has your voice to judge you on. Do you sound friendly? Professional? Competent? Confident? Think about projecting those qualities with your voice.

Watch what you say – You don't want to be giving only 'yes' or 'no' answers, but you also don't want to be delivering a speech with every answer. Keep your answers under a minute or two, and limit yourself to answering the question—don't joke, don't ramble, and don't give them too much information. (And don't ask about salary, vacation, or benefits.)

Smile – Remember to smile when you speak. All by itself, smiling helps you sound friendlier, more enthusiastic, and more confident. If you have to keep a mirror up in front of you to remember to smile, do it.

Ask for the next step – Don't get off the phone without asking when you can meet in person to discuss this opportunity in greater detail. They might not even realize how much you want this job unless you express your enthusiasm and ask for it.

"Nothing in the world can take the place of persistence. Talent will not; nothing is more common than unsuccessful men with talent. Genius will not; unrewarded genius is almost a proverb. Education will not; the world is full of educated derelicts. Persistence and determination alone are omnipotent. The slogan "press on" has solved and will always solve the problems of the human race."

–Calvin Coolidge

PS. *I would not go into my face-to-face interview without a 30-60-90-Day Plan. You can learn more about how to create a plan on my blog:* <u>*30-60-90-Day Plan – How To Create and Use It to Knock Their Socks Off in the Job Interview*</u>

Must-Have Resources

Free Training Webinars on CareerConfidential.com

Free Articles on the Career Confidential Blog

Career Confidential Job Search Tools and Courses

Check out all the tools, courses, and my proven templates for 30-60-90-Day Plans on my website: https://CareerConfidential.com

Other Peggy McKee Books Available on Amazon

Personal 1:1 Job Search and Interview Coaching with Peggy McKee

Find out more at https://careerconfidential.com/

If You Liked This Book, Please Give It 5 Stars!

Reader reviews are so important...both for the success of this book and for me, so I know that I have given you what you need to be wildly successful.

If you put the tips and principles of this book into practice and it results in an amazing interview for you, let me know!

Review this book on Amazon

Made in the USA
Las Vegas, NV
13 December 2024

14013936R00286